Ta[illegible] Dec. 1995

To my [illegible] —

May your
dreams become
a reality.

love
Suzanne

THE HEROES
OF
AMERICAN INVENTION

THE HEROES
OF
AMERICAN INVENTION

L. SPRAGUE DE CAMP

BARNES
&NOBLE
BOOKS
NEW YORK

To my sons Lyman and Gerard,
who share with countless other young Americans
a love of tinkering and invention.

ACKNOWLEDGMENTS

For answering queries and helping me out with this book in one way or another, I am grateful to Robert Abels, Marie M. de Forest, Bern Dibner, George C. Frank, Melvin Kranzberg, Morris B. Lore, Hiram Hamilton Maxim, P. Schuyler Miller, C. Hall Thompson, Ruth M. White, Ernest W. Williams, Jr., and "Pat," who prefers not to be named. My wife has as usual ably edited the manuscript.

The sections on Armstrong, Fessenden, Langley, and the Maxims have appeared in slightly different form as articles in *Science Digest;* copyright © 1957, 1958 by Science Digest, Inc., and copyright © 1959, 1960 by Popular Mechanics Co. Permission to use these articles herein is gratefully acknowledged.

CONTENTS

I

INVENTION
COMES TO AMERICA

In 1641, the Massachusetts General Court granted to one Samuel Winslow a patent for a novel method of making salt. In 1646, the same court granted to Joseph Jenkes[1] the first American patent on machinery, namely, on a mill for making scythes. So, with simple salt and humble harvest tools, began the stirring story of invention in America.

In the colonies from which the United States of America sprang, there were no general patent laws, covering the entire area. Each patent had to be obtained by special petition from the governing body of the colony in which the inventor sought his monopoly.

Furthermore, the colonies, and later the thirteen original states, did not always mean what we mean by "patent." The term included many licenses that we should call franchises, such as the exclusive right to run boats of a certain kind on a particular river.

Life in the days of George Washington was certainly different in many ways from life in present-day America. Farms were many and isolated; towns were small and unsanitary; travel was slow and painful over endless waterways or rutted dirt roads. Nearly all work was done by muscle power. Life for most people meant a hard twelve-hour working day; plagues were common and were fought by embattled superstition. If we glance back across fifty centuries, life had everywhere been much the same.

During the scant two hundred years since the men of George Washington's time transformed the thirteen colonies into states, another far-reaching revolution has taken place, silently, without proclamation, but increasing in pace as the years passed by. It started in England about 1765 and is still changing people's lives all over the world.

The basis of the Industrial Revolution was a series of inventions. Of these inventions, the first and most important was the steam engine. The steam engine and the other inventions that followed it brought about modern transportation, the mass-production factory system, mechanized farming, enormous cities, leisure for the masses, and a whole new way of life for everybody. Today the food we eat, the clothes we wear, the vehicles we travel in, the tools we work with, the amusements we enjoy, the books we read, and the light we read by are all the product, in one way or another, of inventions made since colonial times.

To be sure, there have also been many other changes during that time. Scientific knowledge has grown; religious beliefs and moral convictions have changed; political organization has evolved. But none of these changes affects every moment of our lives so intimately as the inventions of the past two centuries.

In the Industrial Revolution, American inventions have played a major part. It is significant that the United States Patent Office has issued about three million patents for inventions, a number roughly equal to the total issued by the patent offices of Great Britain, France, and Germany combined.

However, the early settlers in the colonies were not, in general, especially inventive. American inventiveness came later. The first settlers, largely farmers, were conservative in the manner of farmers everywhere at all times. Messrs. Winslow and Jenkes were among the few exceptions.

The early settlers did adopt some of the inventions of the American Indians, when they could do so without disturbing their accustomed routine of life. They took over the tobacco pipe, the canoe, and native domestic vegetables like maize, squash, potatoes, and lima beans. Otherwise, they tended to cling to their ancestral European beliefs and techniques until forced by overwhelming pressure to change.

People have been inventing things ever since our apelike ancestors learned to chip a flint and feed a fire. But the way in which inventions were made, and the frequency of inventions, and the effect of inventions on the lives of men have all changed drastically over the centuries.

Among primitive men, inventions occur only at rare intervals. For one thing, tribes are small; their numbers are few. Since only a tiny fraction of mankind ever has inventive ideas anyway, such ideas occur within a tribe of a few hundred persons only once in many years.

For another thing, tribal society is ultraconservative. Everybody knows everybody else and keeps tabs on everybody else. Young people learn to obey the tribal moral code because it is almost impossible to get away with violating it. This code is likely to lay down in detail exactly how everything should be done, on pain of the gods' displeasure. Hence, original thinking is quickly smothered.

Anthropologists do find tribes using special techniques, sometimes very ingenious techniques, which must have been invented by somebody, some time. But the tribesmen insist that it was a god who taught the tribe the art of making harpoons or planting greens or carving great stone faces. Was this god a former man, with greater vision than his fellows, promoted by legend to godhood? Perhaps he was. At least, the true inventor was more than a common mortal.

Even in historic times, thousands of years pass before we begin to learn the names of inventors. We know that some ingenious Anatolian discovered how to smelt iron about 1500 B.C., and that some Chinese invented gunpowder around 1200 A.D.; but we do not know their names.

Some classical writers credit inventions to demigods and other mythical persons. Thus Pliny the Elder says that carpentry was invented by Daedalus and the flute by Pan. But the real inventors of even such revolutionary inventions as the stirrup, the water wheel, and the magnetic compass remain unknown.

In the three centuries before Christ, however, a startling eruption of scientific research and invention took place in the eastern Mediterranean region. The Hellenistic Age burst into bloom with the conquests of Alexander the Great and continued to flower down to the time of the early Roman emperors.

In this far-flung, Greek-speaking, international community, scientists and engineers traveled, studied in libraries, exchanged ideas, and tried out new ideas and devices, just as they did eighteen hundred years later when our modern scientific revolution began.

Ktesibios of Alexandria, in the third century B.C., invented the pipe organ, the water clock, the force pump, and catapults worked by metal springs and compressed-air pistons. In the next century, Archimedes of Syracuse invented the compound pulley, the worm gear, and a complex clockwork device for showing the positions of the heavenly bodies. In the last century B.C., central indirect heating was invented by Sergius Orata, a Roman businessman who devised the system to warm the tanks in which he raised fish and oysters to sell throughout the year. In the first century of the Christian era, Heron of Alexandria invented a steam engine, a slot machine, and many other gadgets.

Along with this flood of inventions went many advances in pure science, especially in Alexandria under the Ptolemies. For a while it certainly seemed as though the scientific age were about to be born.

But it was only a false dawn. The scientific revolution aborted. In Roman imperial times the pace of invention slowed, while the advance of pure science came almost to a complete stop.

Historians have advanced almost as many reasons for this retardation of science and invention, under Rome, as they have for the fall of the Roman Empire. They blame the prevalence of slavery, the rigor of Roman rule, the anti-intellectual Roman tradition, and the rise of otherworldly sects like Christianity. But the facts are that slavery declined under the Empire; the early emperors were on the whole no more tyrannical than the Ptolemies had been; the upper-class Romans of the Empire were strongly Hellenized; and Christianity had only local influence through its first three centuries.

One fact may partly explain the failure of Hellenistic science to become the self-perpetuating, ever-growing thing that science is today. This is the separation of pure science from applied science—that is, from engineering and invention. Nowadays, pure science could not advance unless inventors provided it with new tools and instruments, while inventors would soon bog down without new scientific discoveries to apply and exploit.

In ancient times, however, pure science was a matter for upper-class philosophers, while inventions were mostly made by obscure common workmen. Archimedes, deeming himself primarily a pure scientist, apologized for his inventions as beneath the dignity of a gentleman. As a result of this attitude, scientific research was brought to a standstill because nobody had invented the microscope, the telescope, and the wheeled clock to enable scientists to observe phenomena beyond the reach of their unaided senses.

For another thing, people somehow got the idea that all possible inventions had already been made. Thus in the first century A.D., the eminent Roman engineer Julius Frontinus wrote a book on military stratagems. Frontinus said that he would ignore "all considerations of works and engines of war, the invention of which has long since reached its limit, and for the improvement of which I see no further hope in the applied arts."[2]

The advance of applied science was also stultified by the lack of any positive encouragement for inventors, and by the tendency of many societies to confine people to hereditary classes. Not only were there no patent systems to reward inventors, but also the inventors themselves were viewed with suspicion. A tale is told of a man who went to the emperor Tiberius with a scheme for making unbreakable, malleable glass. The emperor had the man's shop demolished (or, in another version, had the man beheaded) lest his glass should somehow lower the value of gold and silver.[3]

We know enough about glass today to be sure that the story as it stands is untrue. But it may have a basis of truth; in other words, somebody, at some time, probably got into trouble with some emperor by putting forward some technical discovery in glassmaking.

As for hereditary classes, young men everywhere tend to follow in their fathers' footsteps. Many societies have made a rule of this tendency, forcing sons to carry on their fathers' occupations willy-nilly. India's caste system is the outstanding example. Ancient Egypt showed a similar tendency; and hereditary occupations became compulsory in the Roman Empire from the reign of Diocletian (284–305 A.D.) on.

Such restrictions are fatal to technical progress. What baker's son will fool around with an idea for a bicycle, when he is constrained to bake bread all his life? And when all occupations are hereditary, how could anybody even imagine an occupation, such as that of a maker of bicycles, if it did not already exist?

Despite these discouragements, invention continued in a desultory way through the Roman and medieval periods. The windmill, the horse collar, the fore-and-aft sail, and the gun came into existence. Windows and saddles, forges and armor improved. The Arabs of the Caliphate revived science and invention from the ninth to the eleventh centuries. But then the Turkish and Mongol invasions, together with a religious revival in Islam, choked off this movement. Technical leadership passed first to China and then to Europe.

In ancient and medieval times it took a man of strong drive to persist in making an invention. Lacking patent protection, he could hardly hope to make money out of his invention, unless it were something like a chemical process that could be kept secret.

Furthermore, people who thought that their trade or business was threatened by a new invention would oppose it with vigor. They might try to get laws passed against the invention. If that did not work, they resorted to direct action.

Thus, charcoal burners destroyed Dudley's coke furnace in the 1620s. When the French physicist Denis Papin undertook in the 1690s to build a boat driven by paddle wheels, a mob of Rhine sailors destroyed the boat and would have lynched Papin if they could have caught him. In the 1820s, Scottish compositors secretly battered the stereotype plates invented by Robert Gad and ruined the inventor.

In the seventeenth and eighteenth centuries, some Englishmen tried to set up water-powered sawmills, such as were known on the Continent since Roman times. Mobs of hand sawyers, fearing that their bulging muscles would become obsolete, destroyed the mills. During the same period, other mobs wrecked Hargreaves' spinning jennies and Thimmonier's sewing machines. Sailing-vessel captains rammed Fulton's steamboats in hope of putting him out of business. Steam-locomotive drivers sabotaged the electric locomotive invented by the Scotsman Robert Davidson in 1838. Charles Welch, an inventor of coal-mining machines in the late nineteenth century, had to stand guard over his machines with a gun to keep the coal miners from wrecking them.

Even more discouraging, because there was no way of fighting it, was the public's stubborn incredulity towards new inventions. A certain amount of public skepticism towards sweeping claims is healthy, as it protects people from charlatans. However, in former times, most people went far beyond a reasonable skepticism. When the inventor demonstrated his invention for all to see, witnesses refused to believe their senses.

Thus when Oliver Evans, in the 1790s, showed off his automated flour mill to the millers of Brandywine, Pennsylvania, one of them exclaimed: "It will not do! It cannot do! It is impossible it should do!"[4]

In time, however, many people came to realize that inventions are advantageous in the long run and so ought to be encouraged. The simplest method of doing this seemed to be to grant the inventor a temporary monopoly called a *patent*, so that he could sell the things he had invented at a higher price than he would obtain under competition.

The granting of patents began in fifteenth-century Italy. The first known patent was given by the Republic of Florence in 1421 to Filippo Brunelleschi for a cargo boat. The Republic of Venice adopted the first formal patent law in 1474 and in 1594 gave the great astronomer Galileo Galilei a patent on a system of raising water, although it is unlikely that Galileo made any money from this patent.

Patent systems grew up with the scientific revolution that began with Copernicus and Galileo. At first, no clear distinction was made between inventions—things that had not existed before—and improvements of other kinds, such as the introduction into a country of methods known elsewhere. In sixteenth-century England, kings and queens handed out many monopolies indiscriminately as an easy way of raising money and doing favors. In 1624 Parliament stopped this tyrannical practice by passing the Statute of Monopolies, which forbade monopolies on anything other than new inventions. This law was the ancestor of all the later British and American patent laws. The first American patent law was passed in South Carolina in 1691.

During the early stages of the scientific revolution, people also began to realize that science and invention are closely connected. Robert Hooke, the cantankerous English physicist, put this fact to use in 1665, when he exploited the scientific law he discovered.

Hooke's law states that, in elastic bodies under stress, the strain or deformation of these bodies, within limits, is proportional to the stressing force. Hooke applied his law to the invention of the carriage spring. Before Hooke's time, vehicles had no springs; the nearest approach had been to hang the body of a carriage from leather straps fixed to the tops of posts at the corners of the chassis. Naturally, passengers were so bounced and battered that most able-bodied ones preferred to ride horseback.

The scientific studies of Hooke and his colleagues, like Boyle, Papin, and Guericke, on valves, pumps, and pistons, led to the invention of the steam engine in the next century, and hence to the world-shaking Industrial Revolution.

In the eighteenth-century American colonies, men began to show that talent for gadgeteering which ever since has been such a conspicuous trait of our national character. Clockmakers made clocks with brass works and fancy dials for the rich, and with wooden gears and plain faces for ordinary folk. Housewives used a battery of wooden gadgets for beating eggs, paring apples, and mincing meat. Swiss and German immigrants developed the Pennsylvania rifle, a long, small-bore firearm of much greater accuracy than earlier guns.

As this Pennsylvania rifle was effective about fifty yards farther than the sightless smoothbore musket of the British Army, rebel snipers so fearfully galled the British troops in the Revolutionary War that British officers demanded their men be given sights, too. But, when sights were finally provided during the Napoleonic Wars, a British officer commanding Irish troops protested that, if his men were given the new guns, there wouldn't be a landlord alive in Ireland in two weeks.

Colonial America would not have appeared so inventive had it not been for one man, a man of such extraordinary genius and versatility as to seem almost like a one-man Renaissance. This was Benjamin Franklin (1706–90). Besides being an abolitionist, athlete, author, civic leader, composer, diplomat, economist, fireman, hoaxer, journalist, landlord, legislator, librarian, linguist, Mason, musician, nudist, paper manufacturer, politician, postmaster, printer, promoter, publisher, scientist, soldier, spelling reformer, statesman, storekeeper, and jolly good fellow, he found time to be the most active American inventor of his day.

This inventive bent appeared early. As a boy in Boston, Franklin invented paddles to be held in the hands to speed swimmers.

In his thirties, Franklin—a massive, moon-faced man with long light hair—made his fortune as a printer, stationer, and publisher. In 1742 he created his first major invention: a stove. The open fireplace, used in England with cheerful effect, allowed four-fifths of the heat to escape up the chimney and hence failed to heat houses adequately in the subarctic Pennsylvanian winters. Iron stoves of the German kind were used in Franklin's Philadelphia, but they heated the same air over and over, until it was barely breathable.

Franklin enlarged the hearth and stood the stove upon it, with a pipe to carry the fumes up the chimney. He called his arrangement a "Pennsylvania fireplace," but posterity has named it the Franklin stove. This stove became the progenitor of all the kitchen stoves in the world. Although the governor of Pennsylvania offered him a patent, Franklin declined because "as we enjoy great advantage from the inventions of others, we should be glad of an opportunity to serve others by any invention of ours; and this we should do freely and generously."[5]

In the later 1740s, Franklin spent several years on researches into electricity. By a series of brilliant experiments, including the famous one with a kite, Franklin proved three things: that a charge of static electricity tends to leak off the charged object at sharp points; that electricity consists of one single "fluid," not two as some had thought; and that lightning is a form of electricity.

His discovery that lightning is nothing but a big electric spark suggested to Franklin that "houses, ships, and even towers and churches may be effectually secured from the strokes of lightning."[6] By 1752 he had worked out plans for his lightning rod. He understood that such a rod had to be grounded. He published an account of the invention in his almanac and sent a letter to England to be read before the Royal Society.

Use of the lightning rod spread swiftly, though some objected to putting it on churches lest such an action be "presuming on God." In the 1770s, a dispute arose as to whether lightning rods should have blunt or pointed ends. Franklin advised sharp ends to draw off as much of the charge as possible, to avert lightning flashes altogether. A blunt rod merely conducts flashes into the ground. The British government, on the advice of Franklin and other members of the Royal Society, mounted pointed rods on its powder magazines.

Later, during the Revolutionary War, the British government asked another committee for advice on lightning rods, and this committee also advocated pointed rods. However, points had become identified in simple minds with Franklin and hence with the American rebellion. George III patriotically ordered knobbed rods installed on his palace and asked the president of the Royal Society to change its recommendation. Sir John Pringle protested:

"Sire, I cannot reverse the laws and operations of nature!"

"You had better resign," growled the mad king.

Pringle did, and Whigs ridiculed the king's action with the verse:

> While you, great George, for knowledge hunt,
> And sharp conductors change for blunt,
>   The nation's out of joint;
>
> Franklin a wiser course pursues,
> And all your thunder useless views,
>   By keeping to the point.[7]

In the 1750s, Franklin built a flexible catheter to relieve a bladder obstruction from which his brother suffered. He designed an improved street lamp for Philadelphia, with four easily replaced flat panes instead of an expensive and fragile imported glass globe.

When Franklin went off to London as agent for several of the colonies, his life became so filled with diplomacy that thereafter he had little leisure time left for science and invention. However, he found time to invent an ingenious but rather impractical clock. In this, minutes and hours were both shown by one hand, the hours being marked on spiral bands.

In 1762, Franklin invented a musical instrument called the "armonica," which consisted of a series of glass bowls of different sizes, mounted in a row on a shaft. The player turned this shaft by a foot treadle while brushing his fingers against the edges of the bowls, bringing out faint, sweet tones. The instrument became so popular that Mozart and Beethoven composed music for it and Marie Antoinette played one in her childhood.

When the Revolutionary War began, the Continental Congress sent Franklin to France as its minister. Though in his seventies and crippled by gout and bladder stone, Franklin continued active in science and invention. He invented another stove and suggested daylight saving. Finding it awkward to change back and forth from reading to walking eyeglasses, he invented bifocals.

His genius burned right to the end. During his last years in the United States, Franklin invented a long-handled grasping device for taking books down from high shelves. A descendant of this device was used in grocery stores for over a century, until the rise of self-service supermarkets made it obsolete.

In fact, the French writer Balzac, not unreasonably, credited Franklin, on the basis of his abortive plan for union of the colonies in 1754, with having invented the United States of America.

In 1787, when the Constitutional Convention was winding up its labors on a proposed Federal Constitution, the delegates sometimes wandered down the streets of Philadelphia to the Delaware River to watch a skiff rigged up as a steam-powered galley. Above the boat rose a gantry frame, to which twelve oars were articulated. As the little engine chuffed, the six forward oars rose while the six after oars dipped. With a rattle of levers and connecting rods and a spurt of steam, the boat moved slowly out from shore like some strange water insect, circled, and came back.

The inventor of this craft was John Fitch (1743–98), after Franklin perhaps the most brilliant inventor of colonial America and certainly the unhappiest. He was a tall, straight, dark man with a square, lined face and the nervously bellicose manner of one whose life is spent under intolerable strain.

Fitch was a native of Connecticut who had been apprenticed to clockmakers. He had run away before his term expired because, he claimed, his masters (as unscrupulous masters often did) refused to teach him their trade while they worked him as a houseboy. He married but deserted his wife because, he said, she nagged.

For a time he made a living as a silversmith in Pennsylvania. When the Revolution broke out he enlisted, deserted in a quarrel over rank, made a small fortune profiteering, and lost it by inflation. He bought land warrants in the Ohio Territory, set out to survey his estate, was caught by Indians, and spent the rest of the war as a prisoner of the British. Repatriated at the end of the war, he made a living by printing and selling a map of the northwestern territories. In 1785 he began to think about steamboats.

He was not the first to do so. In France, one unlucky seventeenth-century Frenchman had been put in the madhouse for insisting that boats could be driven by steam. Nevertheless, by 1783, the Marquis de Jouffroy d'Abbans had built a steamboat of sorts. The engine, a huge mass of brick and iron, towered up from the waist of a 130-foot river boat and drove a paddle wheel at the stern by pawls and ratchets. With a great sighing and clattering, the thing moved slowly along the Saône River for a quarter of an hour. Then everything started to fall apart at once, and Jouffroy had to beach his boat to keep it from sinking. Before the inventor could improve his craft enough to make it practical, the French Revolution drove him into flight.

In America, an adventurer named James Rumsey was also talking steamboats and experimenting with a mechanical canal boat, designed to pole itself upstream by means of power furnished by the current through a paddle wheel.

John Fitch made models of his projected steamboat with various driving mechanisms, such as a pair of endless chains with scoops. Then he went to Philadelphia to find backing and to petition Congress for help. He called on General George Washington, who received him with frosty courtesy but declined to help him because he had already promised aid to Rumsey.

Fitch filed petitions in various states for monopolies on steamboat navigation. Some he was granted. He called on old Franklin, who declined to buy stock in his company but, seeing Fitch in want, offered him money for himself. Fitch, always his own worst enemy, haughtily spurned this "insult."

A voluble German watchmaker, Henry Voight, became Fitch's mechanic. Together they built the steam galley while Fitch engaged in a war of petitions, counterpetitions, and pamphlets with Rumsey, who was also seeking steamboat monopolies.

Fitch's and Rumsey's friends suggested a merger. Although

Rumsey's boat, which sucked water in at the bow and squirted it out astern like a squid, was less effective than Fitch's. Rumsey was a shrewd and reasonable man. He offered Fitch a half-and-half arrangement. But, when Fitch demanded seven-eighths of the profits, negotiations broke down.

Rumsey went to England, failed to get the steam-engine makers Boulton and Watt to go into business with him, juggled his debts, and enjoyed the excitement hugely. In 1792, with his next squid boat nearly finished, he dropped dead while lecturing on steamboats before a learned society.

Meanwhile, Fitch found backers and built a better boat. This vessel was driven by three shovel-shaped paddles, which hung down over the stern and kicked the boat along like a swimming waterfowl. Another duck boat, the *Perseverance*, proved even more successful, making all of eight miles an hour.

During the summer of 1790, Fitch ran the *Perseverance* commercially on the Delaware between Philadelphia and Trenton. Although this boat worked, it lost money. For one thing, it competed with the best road and the fastest coach lines in the United States; for another, it was so full of engine that there was no room for a good payload of passengers.

Next winter, a storm pulled the boat loose and grounded it downstream. Fitch broke up with Voight in a quarrel over the affections of Fitch's landlady. Lacking money to salvage the *Perseverance*, Fitch went to France in hopes of building another boat. There he stumbled into the Reign of Terror and left without accomplishing anything. Back in the United States, he drifted out to Kentucky and tried to drink himself to death. Failing in this as in everything else, he ended his miseries with a handful of opium pills.

Poor Fitch was doomed from the start by his own shortcomings. Though brilliant, he was so touchy, quarrelsome, excitable, and foolish in worldly matters that he could never work for long with anybody. He had what we today call a schizoid personality, so wrapped up in its own ideas and aims as to be utterly unaware of how its words and actions affect others. The type is not uncommon among inventors.

Yet, even had he combined his brilliance with his rival Rumsey's charm and practicality, he probably could not have achieved the fortune he sought. The world in which he lived was not prepared for him. American patent law was in its infancy. Nobody knew how to distinguish one inventor's contributions from those of another. When Fitch, Rumsey, and John Stevens of New Jersey all applied at the same time for steamboat patents, the Federal Patent Commission, unable to decide among their conflicting claims, gave each applicant the patent he asked for and left it to the courts to determine whose claim should prevail.

Moreover, the nation was technically backward. There were no engineering libraries or institutes of technology where an inventor could learn what he needed to know; the first engineering schools had only lately begun operation in France. There were not even machine shops where he could have his parts made accurately. He had to make his own parts and suffer the consequences if he was not handy with tools.

By European standards, eighteenth-century American workmanship was slipshod. Most of the American gunsmiths, clockmakers, and other artisans were part-time technicians only; they were farmers who turned an extra shilling by tinkering in the winter. They were ingenious and versatile but not highly skilled in any specialty.

Even in England, the world's leading industrial nation, Matthew Boulton thought his mechanics were doing well when they bored steam-engine cylinders without an error greater than "the thickness of an old shilling."[8] So you can imagine what American machine work was like.

Nor did American inventors of Fitch's time have any true idea of the inventive process. They did not know what others had done to try to solve the same problem. They did not realize what a long way it is from a brilliant idea to a working specimen. They did not suspect that when the first sample is built, the inventor's troubles have just begun; he still has to get the bugs out of his invention and commercialize it.

They did not know that most invention is a matter of many men's making successive improvements on the prior art. Only a few inventions such as Edison's phonograph, Judson's Zipper, Westinghouse's air brake, and Calthorp's streamlined railroad train have been wholly original.

Not knowing these things, an early American inventor, when he got an idea, thought that his fortune was already made. He fancied that a few weeks of tinkering would suffice to whip the device into shape, that he was the only man ever to have such a wonderful idea, that any competitor was a liar and thief, and that the invention, once perfected, would continue to dominate its field for all time. No wonder they encountered difficulties!

When our nation was young, farsighted men realized that the first step towards encouraging inventors was to offer them reasonable rewards. Therefore, the United States Constitution was written with a provision that:

> The Congress shall have Power . . . to promote the Progress of Science and useful Arts by securing for limited Times to Authors and Inventors the exclusive Right to their respective Writings and Discoveries.[9]

The monopolies of inventors and authors are confined to "limited times" because it was not intended that such a monopoly should last forever, giving the inventor's remote descendants a permanent grip on the nation's economy.

Benjamin Franklin, despite his lofty words about giving one's inventions "freely and generously" to the world, raised no objection to the patent clause in the new Constitution. No doubt he realized that, as a successful businessman, he could afford to be more altruistic in such matters than a starveling like Fitch.

Even Thomas Jefferson, foe of monopolies, wrote that: "Certainly, an inventor ought to be allowed a right to the benefit of his invention for a certain time. Nobody wishes more than I do that ingenuity should receive liberal encouragement."[10]

In 1790, President George Washington signed the first Federal patent act. This law placed the responsibility for granting patents on a board, consisting of the Secretary of State, the Secretary of War, and the Attorney General. The board fixed the term of the patent for any period they thought it deserved, but not exceeding fourteen years. Applicants had to submit a description, a drawing, and when possible a model. They also had to pay a patent fee of four to five dollars.

Thus the new nation acquired a patent system which, it was hoped, would stimulate invention by rewarding inventors. But, like most new things, this patent system contained many hidden defects, which only several decades of struggle and experience would bring to light. By trial and error the system was modified and reformed until at last it became a practical, workable means of fostering the progress of science and the useful arts. Then, and not until then, did the heroic age of American invention begin.

THE HEROIC AGE

BEGINS

The three officials comprising the Patent Board soon discovered that their regular work did not leave them time to consider all the applications for patents. In 1793, therefore, the law was changed, and the duty of granting patents was imposed upon the Secretary of State alone.

The original Patent Board had been required to consider whether the invention claimed in each application was really new. Under the revised law, however, the Secretary of State had to give a patent to anybody who asked for one and leave it to the courts to decide if the patent was valid.

The Secretary of State at this time was the one American best qualified to administer the patent act. He was Thomas Jefferson: former governor of Virginia and Minister to France, later to be Vice-President and President of the United States—a tall, angular, sandy-haired man whose large nose and long bony jaw adorn our nickels.

Jefferson was one of the three Presidents of the United States who can justly be called a scientist. The other two, Theodore Roosevelt and Herbert Hoover, lived a century later. Jefferson did more actual scientific work than either of these, although he protested that he was only a "zealous amateur."

As President, Jefferson sent out the Lewis and Clark expedition, filled the White House with fossils, and kept a pair of young grizzly bears tethered on the lawn. He collected data on the weather, encouraged Jenner's method of vaccination against smallpox, tried to determine the origin of the American Indians by a study of their languages, and found the Biblical myths of Adam and Noah incredible.

Although he never took out a patent himself, Jefferson invented the curved-moldboard plow, the swivel chair, the shooting stick, and a drydock. He improved the polygraph (an apparatus for duplicating writings or drawings), built improved music stands and writing desks, and invented a machine for processing hemp.

In the White House he installed a dumbwaiter, a revolving clothes rack, and a set of revolving shelves pivoted in the wall for passing food from one room to another. He filled his home, Monticello, with gadgets such as a clock with two faces, one indoors and one out, and cannon-ball weights that showed the day of the week by their height. One can still see this clock at Monticello, as well as Jefferson's weather vane, whose shaft passes down through the house to a dial on the ceiling of the main hall.

As Secretary of State, Jefferson tried to establish decimal systems for the coinage and for weights and measures. He succeeded with the coinage but failed to oust the ridiculous English system of weights and measures, which continues in use to this day.

On July 31, 1790, Jefferson issued the first United States patent to Samuel Hopkins for an improvement in "the making of Pot ash and Pearl ash by a new Apparatus and Process." The patent was signed by President George Washington, Attorney General Edmund Randolph, and Thomas Jefferson.

Two more patents were issued that year. One went to Joseph Simpson for the Manufacture of Candles; the other to Oliver Evans for Manufacturing Flour and Meal.

Oliver Evans (1755–1819) was one of the most active inventors of the infant republic. He was a stout, pudgy man, volatile and hot-tempered. As a youth in Delaware, he had invented a machine for making the card teeth used in carding wool and cotton. Lacking the protection of a national patent law, Evans got no profit out of this invention.

Then Evans set himself to improve milling machinery. In so

doing, he took one of the major steps towards the Industrial Revolution: using machinery not merely to process a raw material but also to convey it around the factory. He proposed to carry grain and flour about a mill by means of belt conveyors, screw conveyors, hoppers, and the like, all driven by steam or water power. Most of these devices had been used before in handling liquids, but this was the first time that anybody proposed to use them on solid materials.

Unfortunately, Evans was trying to revolutionize an old, established industry that did not want to be revolutionized. Nobody took out licenses under Evans' patent save a few daring experimenters like George Washington.

Evans also pioneered in steam engineering. When, in the 1780s, he applied for state patents in several states, he included not only his milling machinery but also plans for a wagon driven by a high-pressure steam engine. All the states but Maryland forced Evans to take his steam wagon out of the application, Pennsylvania on the ground that he must be mad to think of such a thing.

In 1792, Evans moved to Philadelphia and set himself up as a millwright and mechanic. His life was one of struggle, many disappointments, and some small success. In 1795 he published the first engineering handbook written in the United States, *The Young Mill-Wright and Miller's Guide.* This book went through fifteen editions, the last in 1860. As you can see, milling technology took over sixty years to catch up with Evans' ideas.

Evans also patented an improvement in the manufacture of millstones in 1796, in stoves and grates in 1800, a screw mill in 1805, a high-pressure steam engine in 1804, and an improvement in sawmills in 1811. He developed the high-pressure steam engine at the same time as the Englishman Richard Trevithick, the inventor of the steam locomotive, and he made and sold at least fifty steam engines. Evans wrote that "The time will come when people will travel in stages moved by steam-engines, from one city to another, almost as fast as birds fly, fifteen or twenty miles an hour."[1]

In 1805, Evans got a contract to make a steam dredge to dig the muck out of the harbor of Philadelphia. He built the dredge in his shop, a mile and a half from the Schuylkill River, and erected the engine and the brick furnace on the deck of the dredge. Then, to the city's astonishment, he sent the contraption chugging down the street on huge iron wheels. For several days it waddled around Center Square.

When an onlooker gibed, the peppery Evans offered to bet the entire price of $3000, which he had just received from the city, that he could make a steam carriage that should outrun a horse. There were no takers.

Then Evans rolled his machine (which he called the *Oruktor Amphibolos,* bad Greek for "double-acting digger") to the river, took off the wheels, hooked up a temporary paddle wheel at the stern, and sailed about for some hours before setting the dredge to do the dirty work for which it was meant.

Evans' machine was not the first vehicle to move on land under steam power. A retired French artillery officer, Nicolas Cugnot, had built an unsuccessful three-wheeled steam carriage to tow cannon in the 1760s. Nor was the *Oruktor* the first steamboat. But it was certainly the world's first powered amphibious vehicle.

When Evans sued an infringer who was making his patented "hopperboy," the judge held that, as a result of an oversight on the part of the Secretary of State, the patent did not dominate this detail. When the Secretary said he was sorry but he had no authority to correct the error, Evans applied to Congress, which granted him a new fourteen-year patent.

However, when Evans tried to collect royalties, he was denounced as a monopolist. The infringers, having begun using hopperboys before the grant of the special patent, saw no reason to stop.

Subsequently, Evans wrote Thomas Jefferson asking for a license fee for the use of one of his inventions, thus making Jefferson the only President of the United States to be accused of patent infringement while in office. Jefferson paid promptly, though in his letter he politely doubted whether Evans was in the legal right. The precise boundaries of a patent owner's rights had not yet been worked out.

For the rest of his life, Evans was embroiled in litigation with infringers of his milling-machinery patents. He appealed judicial decisions, applied to Congress for relief, and abused his opponents in horrible satiric poetry.

In 1809, Evans heard that his old nemesis, Supreme Court Justice Bushrod Washington, had issued an opinion injurious to inventors, holding all patents to be an infringement on the rights of the people. In a fit of temperament, Evans burned all his papers and drawings concerning his inventions. He wanted to spare his family, he said, from the risks of so unprofitable an occupation as inventing.

In 1822, three years after Evans' death, the last of his infringement suits was decided against him. The Supreme Court held the hopperboy patent invalid because it did not clearly distinguish Evans' contribution from the prior art.

This decision led to the requirement in the new patent law of 1836 that each patent have a set of "claims." These are little numbered paragraphs at the end of the specification, setting forth just what the inventor thinks is new about his invention.

In 1794, another of the young nation's leading inventors took out his first patent. This was Whitney's patent on the cotton gin.

Eli Whitney (1765–1825) was a native of Connecticut who had worked his way through Yale, partly by whittling walking sticks. Then he went to Georgia to take a tutoring job that a fellow Yankee, Phineas Miller, had obtained for him. Although the job fell through, Whitney had been in the South only a few days when a great idea struck him.

Two species of cotton grew in the South. One was sea-island or long-staple cotton, with fibers loosely attached to slippery black seeds. The other was short-staple or upland cotton, with fibers of two different lengths, the shorter fibers being tightly affixed to green seeds. Long-staple cotton, which grew only along the coasts, was separated from its seeds by running it through a roller frame like an old-fashioned clothes wringer. The Southerners called this device an "engine," slurred to "gin." But the only way of separating the seeds from short-staple cotton, which could be grown almost anywhere, was by laboriously picking them out by hand.

Whitney invented a machine consisting of a cylinder from which hundreds of bent wires (later changed to saw-toothed disks) projected as in a Victorian music box. These pieces of wire worked in slots wide enough for the cotton but not wide enough for the seeds. As the cylinder turned, the hooks pulled the cotton through the slots. Whitney added a revolving brush to remove the cotton from the cylinder.

Whitney formed a partnership with Miller, went to Washington to apply for a patent, and thence returned to New Haven to build the device.

Although the gin was an instant success, it was not profitable to Whitney and Miller because any smart blacksmith could make it, once he grasped the idea. Even before Whitney's gin came on the market, infringers were selling and using gins. The attitude of the Southern planters was "That they should take, who have the power, And they should keep who can."[2]

Whitney and Miller at first proposed to set up ginning stations about the South and make all planters come to these stations to have their cotton cleaned. In Georgia, the governor denounced "the patent gin monopoly," which, he said, inflicted "a manifest injury to the community and in many respects, a cruel extortion on the gin holders." The South, he cried, had been made "tributary to two persons . . . Monopolies are odious in all countries but more particularly so in a government like ours . . ."[3]

Whitney and Miller spent years of their time and thousands of dollars in suing and lobbying. In Georgia the planters, who were also the jurors, conspired to vote against Whitney in any infringement trials in which they served on juries, regardless of evidence. In one such trial, all the Georgians blandly denied that such a thing as a cotton gin had ever been seen in Georgia, although Whitney could hear three gins rattling away within fifty yards of the courthouse.

At last South Carolina agreed to pay the partners $50,000 for the free use of the gin in that state. North Carolina and Tennessee offered smaller amounts on a similar basis. Miller died in 1803. When Whitney went to South Carolina to protest the legislature's reneging on its promise to pay, he was jailed in a suit by the state to recover the money already paid him.

Whitney got out and all ended well. He was able to cope with the politicians mainly because of his pleasant and dignified personality and the deliberate, patient, systematic, and businesslike way in which he went about converting them to his views. However, most of the $90,000 that he and Miller collected for the gin was spent on lawyers' fees.

During most of the nineteenth century, the United States patent law allowed inventors to apply for renewal or extension of their patents, for an additional term of seven years. This was done either by act of Congress or, later, by a special board. In such a case, the inventor pleaded that he had been unable, in the fourteen years of the original term, to get far enough with exploitation of the invention to repay him for his contribution. Many important patents, such as Kelly's iron-refining process patent, were thus renewed.

The trouble with this system was that, when an inventor applied for renewal, everybody whose interests were affected by the patent began frantically lobbying. Therefore renewal was likely to become a matter of who could bring the most political pressure to bear, the inventor and his backers or the people who wanted to use the invention free.

In Whitney's case, the influence of the South was strong enough to defeat his application for renewal. As a result of these contests, renewals were abolished in 1861. Thereafter, patents were granted for a single term of seventeen years only. In theory, a patent can still be renewed by act of Congress, but today in practice this is impossible.

The gin profoundly affected the future of America. At that time, slavery was declining in America. Many opposed it, including a number of the Founding Fathers. Moreover, the Declaration of Independence and the Constitution contained high-sounding declarations about the natural equality of men and the duty of the Federal government to maintain republican government—meaning one with no aristocracies or hereditary ruling classes—in the states.[4] Such ideals are hardly consistent with slavery, which the more advanced European nations had already abolished.

The gin, however, made the cultivation of upland cotton by Negro slaves immensely profitable. The lust of profit overrode all other considerations, and the South became so heavily committed to slavery that it took the Civil War to end the institution.

As if one revolutionary invention were not enough, Whitney then made another. While still lawing over the gin in 1798, Whitney received a contract from the United States to make 10,000 muskets.

The War Department naturally thought that, if it took Whitney two years to make 10,000 muskets, he would complete 5000 in one year. When no muskets had been made at the end of the first year, the Department got worried, and at the end of the second year it became gravely alarmed.

Whitney went to Washington to persuade the Department to extend his contract and advance him more money. Before a group of skeptical officials, possibly including Jefferson, Whitney took apart a number of musket locks and mixed the parts. Then, taking up parts at random, he assembled a complete lock and showed that it worked. Thus he convinced the officials that he really knew what he was about.

Up to this time, every machine consisted of hand-made parts, individually fitted and assembled. Even when two machines were supposed to be made from the same plans, the corresponding parts in the different machines differed. Therefore their parts were not interchangeable. If a part broke or wore out, another had to be made by hand and fitted by trial and error.

A Frenchman, Le Blanc, had made muskets with interchangeable parts in the 1780s, but his idea died out. Another Frenchman, Brunel, fled the Revolution, practiced engineering in the United States, and went to England. There he and Jeremy Bentham the economist set up a factory for the British government at Portsmouth, to make pulley blocks for the Royal Navy by mass-production methods.

But Whitney applied these methods outside this limited field. His parts were made on machine tools guided, not by mechanics' faltering fingers, but by jigs and templates. These are patterns shaped to match the outline of some part of the final product. Therefore each machine went through exactly the same motions over and over, and hence the parts were truly interchangeable.

It was the devising of these machines that took Whitney so long. With a little more time and money, Whitney gave the government all the muskets it had ordered. (A British inventor, Joseph Bramah, who invented the hydraulic press and the water closet, developed similar methods at this time for making locks.)

Whitney devised many other ingenious manufacturing methods and invented the milling machine, one of the most important machine tools. But his realization of the principle of interchangeable parts stands beside Watt's steam engine among the outstanding contributions to the Industrial Revolution.

We left the story of the steamboat at the point where John Fitch gave up. For several years thereafter no steamboats ran, although several inventors tinkered with them. The man who came nearest to success was the Scottish engineer William Symington. Around 1802, Symington built a couple of stern-wheel steam tugs, but each time his backers let him down before he could perfect his boats to the point of practicality.

Two Americans, M'Keaver and Valcourt, tried to get steamboat service started on the Mississippi in 1803. Oliver Evans built and shipped them an engine, which they mounted on a boat of local construction. But a flood carried the boat far inland and left it stranded. To salvage their investment, the owners used the engine to power a sawmill. The sawmill worked very well until a local mob of hand sawers succeeded in burning it down, together with the watchmen supposed to protect it.

The first man to make a steamboat not only run but also to run profitably was Robert Fulton (1765–1815).

Fulton was not *the* inventor of the steamboat, as he himself sometimes admitted. If anybody merited that title, said he, it was Jouffroy. The steamboat, like most major inventions, was the product of several inventors. Jouffroy, Fitch, Rumsey, Symington, Evans, Stevens, and Fulton all had a hand in it.

Still, Fulton was one of the most fertile and energetic of the early American inventors. If not quite so brilliantly original as Fitch, he was far shrewder in enlisting backers with money and in managing his affairs.

Born in Lancaster County, Pennsylvania, Robert Fulton grew up to be a tall, handsome, versatile youth with artistic ambitions. Encouraged by William Henry of Lancaster, the colonies' leading gunsmith, who had talked steam in England with Watt and in 1763 had tried an unsuccessful steamboat on Conestoga Creek, Fulton went to Philadelphia. There he painted mediocre miniatures, saved some money, and borrowed some more. In 1787 he sailed for England with a letter of recommendation from Benjamin Franklin and an introduction to Benjamin West, an American artist who had become court painter to George III.

In England, Fulton lived on his debts, studied art, and became interested in canals. He took out several British patents on improvements in canals. About 1797 he began talking about abolishing war by two inventions: a system of canals linking all nations and a method of undersea warfare that should destroy all navies. He sold some of his canal-machinery patents and went to France to exploit his naval inventions.

These ideas for submarine warfare were mostly improvements on those of David Bushnell, a Connecticut Yankee who tried to defeat the British in the Revolutionary War by a series of brilliant inventions that did not quite succeed. The first of Bushnell's inventions was a one-man submarine.

Called *Bushnell's Turtle*, the craft resembled some kind of bivalve. Screw propellors turned by cranks from inside moved the submarine horizontally and vertically. The submarine had a depth gage lit by phosphorescent light, a water-ballast system, and even a snorkel valve for ventilation. It was supposed to sneak up to a British warship, fasten a mine to its victim's hull, and depart, leaving the mine to explode by clockwork.

Bushnell made two trials, but the first time his operator could not drive a spike into the copper-sheathed hull of a Britisher in New York Harbor. The second time, the operator missed his quarry in the murk. Still, it was the world's first attempt at submarine warfare.

Bushnell also attacked British ships with mines. Although he did succeed in destroying one small British craft and damaging another, noninvention-minded critics poured ridicule on Bushnell until the man ahead of his time quit America. Later he returned and settled in Georgia, where he opened a village school and practiced medicine under the name of "Bush."[5]

Fulton probably heard about Bushnell's inventions from his host in France, a middle-aged American named Barlow, who had gone to Yale with Bushnell. The French, although they considered Fulton's plans for undersea warfare "atrocious," let him try them out on the British fleet, since France and Great Britain were again at war.

Fulton built a two-man submarine driven by hand cranks. In the summers of 1800 and 1801 he set out from Le Havre in his 20-foot shell to attack the world's greatest navy. But his *Nautilus* was too slow to catch the British ships; while the British, warned by their agents, kept a sharp lookout for sea monsters.

In France, Fulton also met the American minister to France, Robert R. Livingston. Livingston, a leading member of the New

York squirearchy, had been chancellor of New York State and had unsuccessfully tried his hand at inventing a steamboat.

Livingston suggested a steamboat partnership to Fulton. Fulton therefore tested a series of models in France, trying out various shapes of boats and means of propulsion.

When his negotiations with the French government fell through, Fulton, not at all embarrassed by the fact that he had just been waging a private war against Great Britain, slipped over to England to try to sell his inventions there. There was a touch of the adventurer about Fulton. An alert, astute, fearless, suave, and charming man, quick to profit from others' mistakes and fantastically energetic despite chronic tuberculosis, he was one of those who, as the ancients said, praised the good while seeking his own profit. No matter how crassly mercenary his actions, he was always ready with a spirited and eloquent defense of the lofty altruism of his motives.

After two years of indecisive experiments in England, the British government paid off Fulton. The Admiralty was understandably cool towards inventions that promised far more woe than weal to the British realm.

Before leaving England, Fulton bought a 20-horsepower steam engine from Boulton and Watt. Meanwhile Livingston, who had previously returned to America, had obtained from his indulgent legislature a monopoly of steamboat navigation on the Hudson River.

In less than a year, Fulton's boat took shape in New York. It was a very long, very narrow side-wheeler. A guilloutine-like framework rose from the waist to transmit power to the wheel shaft by means of a bell crank.

Some features of Fulton's design, such as his application of the bell crank to paddle wheels, were possibly new. Most of Fulton's advances, however, consisted of the careful choice of proportions for his boat and machinery. Under modern patent law, most of these improvements would not be patentable; but they still made all the difference between commercial success and failure.

Another reason for Fulton's success was that, having been an artist, he drew such beautiful pictures of the parts he wanted that the mechanics who made them got them right the first time. He had also made drawings for Thomas Paine's applications for patents on Paine's iron bridge.

Fulton called his boat by several names, such as the *North River*. He registered it at the customhouse as the *North River Steamboat of Clermont*, after his partner's estate. The public took to calling it the *Clermont*, and so it has remained to most people ever since.

After a preliminary test, Fulton took his boat out on the Hudson on August 18, 1807. He carried a boatload of Livingstons, including a pretty young cousin of the chancellor with whom Fulton had an understanding. The boat had hardly started when it stopped. The well-dressed crowd exchanged looks. One said:

"I told you so; it is a foolish scheme: I wish we were well out of it."[6]

With his well-practised air of lordly but affable poise, Fulton reassured his passengers and repaired his machinery. Off they went. The passengers smiled despite the rain of soot and the splash from the unguarded paddle wheels. Although the newspapers ignored the voyage, a considerable crowd watched Fulton's boat. Some cheered; but one yokel ran to his cabin shouting that the Devil was going upriver to Albany in a sawmill.

The steamboat reached Albany two days later. There the Scottish engineer got drunk and had to be replaced, while the passengers worried about the boiler's blowing up. When the time came to return, only two of them, the French botanist François Michaux and a friend, had the nerve to go back on the *North River*.

As soon as he got back to New York, Fulton improved his boat in the light of experience—for there were many errors in the original design—and put it into regular service. He made money from the start, because he plied a long route between two great cities connected only by abominable roads and by a magnificent river, which lacked towpaths and good winds for sailing, yet was deep and straight, with a gentle current and no rapids.

Then Fulton married his pretty young Harriet Livingston and became rich. He gave his money away liberally, supporting his kin in upstate Pennsylvania and patronizing American artists.

In 1809, Fulton applied for a United States patent. As the Secretary of State no longer had time to go over all patent applications in person, Congress had allowed him in 1802 to set up a separate Patent Office. The head of this office came to be known as the Superintendent of Patents.

The first Superintendent was Dr. William Thornton, a native of the British West Indies. Thornton was a dilettante artist and scientist who had designed the first Capitol building in Washington. He had also been one of John Fitch's backers in the days of the *Perseverance*. Besides money and prestige, Thornton also furnished Fitch with some ideas for condensers, which he insisted on Fitch's trying out although they did not work.

When Fulton applied for his patent, Thornton indignantly protested that Fulton's design did not constitute original invention. As a former associate of Fitch, he, Thornton, ought to know.

However, the law at this time did not give the Patent Office authority to deny a patent on such grounds. The office was supposed to issue a patent when requested to do so in proper form, and leave to the courts such questions as priority and inventiveness. The French Patent Office follows this system to this day.

When Fulton persisted, claiming everything in sight in the art of steamboats, Thornton had to give him his patent. But Thornton took the precaution of issuing a steamboat patent to himself first.

Certainly, Fulton claimed a lot of things to which he was not entitled. On the other hand, he can hardly be blamed for so doing in the primitive state of the patent law. In the long run, he owed his fortune much more to his monopoly on Hudson River steamboating than to the feeble protection of an 1809 United States patent, just as his friend Whitney made his fortune from his acumen as a manufacturer rather than from his patents.

A few years later came the War of 1812. The Americans burned the Canadian capital. In revenge, the British landed an army in Maryland, scattered the American militia, took Washington, and burned the governmental buildings. A detachment appeared in front of the Patent Office. Thornton faced them and asked the officer in command not to "burn what would be useful to all mankind."[7] Just then it began to rain; and the British, for one reason or the other, went away without harming the office.

Meanwhile, Fulton kept improving his product. Paul Revere furnished his boilers. Fulton built twenty-one steamboats, each an advance on the last. They included the world's first double-ended steam ferry and the world's first steam warship. This last was the "floating battery" *Demologos* ("Voice of the People").

This ship had a brilliantly original design. She was a catamaran with the engine and boiler below the waterline, one in each of the twin hulls, and the single paddle wheel turning in the well between the two hulls. Her armament included guns shooting under water, to punch holes in the enemy's bottom at close range, and a nozzle for squirting boiling water on the enemy's deck, as well as the more conventional artillery. Her sides were of oak five feet thick, making her practically an armored vessel.

In the winter of 1815, Fulton caught pneumonia while overseeing the building of the *Demologos* and died at forty-nine. The steam warship was never altogether completed. With the coming of peace she was tied up in Brooklyn until destroyed by an accidental explosion in 1829.

In 1808, the State of New York extended Fulton's steamboat franchise on the Hudson for thirty years. Subsequently a former governor of New Jersey named Ogden contracted with the owners of the franchise to run steamboats between New York and Elizabethtown. Ogden's former partner Gibbons, however, refused to work under a Livingston-Fulton license and started a competing steamboat line of his own. Ogden sued Gibbons for violating his franchise.

The case of Gibbons v. Ogden aroused national attention, because upon its decision turned the rights of the Federal government to regulate interstate commerce. (Another Fulton-Livingston monopoly on the Mississippi had already, in 1819, been overturned by a Federal District Court.) When the case was finally argued before the Supreme Court in 1824, Daniel Webster, as one of the lawyers for Gibbons, made one of the most effective speeches of his career.

The right of the Federal government to regulate interstate commerce, Webster argued, must be deemed an exclusive right.

If every state could set up its own tariffs and other restrictions on commerce across its borders, chaos would ensue. And Chief Justice John Marshall, agreeing completely with Webster, found the New York State franchise unconstitutional.

The patent laws, under which Fitch, Fulton, and other early American inventors struggled, were grossly inadequate to protect their interests. In 1811, quite in the modern spirit, Fulton got together with Oliver Evans, Eli Whitney, and some other inventors to hire a lawyer to lobby in Washington for revision of the patent law.

Nothing came of this effort at the time; although, as the years passed, others such as President Madison made similar proposals. In 1835 a senator from Maine, John Ruggles, who was also an inventor, persuaded the Senate to set up a committee with himself as chairman to study the American patent system. Ruggles reported:

> For more than 40 years the Department of State has issued patents on every application, *without any examination into the merits or novelty of the invention.*
>
> Many patents granted are worthless and void and conflict upon one another, and a great many law suits arise from this condition.
>
> Frauds develop. People copy existing patents, make slight changes, and are granted patents.
>
> Patents become of little value, and the object of the patent laws is in great measure defeated.[8]

As a result of Ruggles' recommendations, Congress in 1836 reformed the patent system. The Patent Office was made a separate bureau under the Department of State, with a Commissioner of Patents at its head.

The "registration" system of granting patents without regard to the prior art was abolished. The "examination" system, which had been in effect for the first three years of the nation's history, was reinstated. Thenceforward, every patent application was scrutinized by an official called an examiner, who compared the application with the prior art to determine its novelty and usefulness.

Applicants were made to set forth the distinctively new features of their inventions in the numbered paragraphs called "claims" at the end of the specification. Patents were for the first time given serial numbers; Senator Ruggles obtained Patent Number 1, for an improvement in locomotives.

At this time, patents were being issued at the rate of six hundred or seven hundred a year. Under the more stringent requirements of the new law, however, the number of grants per year was cut in half.

No sooner had the reformed Patent Office begun to function than disaster struck. The Patent Office, the General Post Office, and the Washington City Post Office were housed in the old Blodgett's Hotel, which the government had bought. On the night of December 14–15, 1836, the building caught fire, probably from stove ashes stored in the cellar, and burned to the ground. People rushed about yelling "Fire!" but doing little to put it out. The nearest fire engine had been allowed to get out of order for lack of money; and besides there was not enough water pressure.

Postmaster General Kendall caused his clerks to save some of the Post Office papers, but the Patent Office was wiped out. Gone were 7000 models, 9000 drawings, and 168 rolls of records. As a result, the early history of the United States patent system is hazy in many details. For some early patents, no copies exist.

For several years the Patent Office occupied itself with restoring its old records as best it could. It replaced some of the lost models and continued to require models of applicants down to 1880. By that time the Patent Office had become so cluttered with models, and the models themselves, with the advance of the mechanical arts, had become so costly that the requirement was dropped. Although the Patent Office is still entitled to ask for models, it now does so only in cases involving perpetual-motion machines and other inventions that seem to violate the laws of nature.

Whereas in 1839 the Commissioner asked Congress to increase his examiners from two to four, the Patent Office now has more than a thousand examiners. It has issued about three million patents and continues to issue them at a rate of over 40,000 a year.

As a result of the reform of 1836 and the court decisions that clarified the rights of inventors, the latter were now in a much better position to know where they stood. The industrial growth of the nation provided them with mechanics and machine shops to make parts for them, and colleges and textbooks made technical information available.

Best of all, every radical invention, like the steamboat and the cotton gin, made things easier for the next inventor. It did this by showing more and more people that inventions could work after all. Thus each new invention helped to erode away the conviction of the masses that what had been always would be.

This belief had taken form during the thousands of years in which progress was so slow as to be imperceptible. But in the nineteenth century, the advance of technology became so swift that a man could see the world around him changing radically in the course of his own lifetime. Before, only a few educated people knew that such changes had taken place, and they knew only because they had read about them, not because they had seen them. Few living people had observed with their own eyes any change other than in styles of dress and coiffure. Now, rather suddenly, everybody was forced to admit that the world *does* move and times *do* change.

In these ways, the ground was laid for the heroic age of American invention. This was the age during which the patent laws were well enough organized, and conditions were favorable enough to inventors, so that those with meritorious inventions had a fair chance of success—provided that they also had a reasonable degree of business and legal sense and a little luck as well.

This was the age that, more than any other in history, inspired and encouraged the individual inventive mind. At this time, the profession of inventing had not become so large and highly organized, nor had it fallen so completely under corporate control, nor had the pace of technological change become so swift, that the individual inventor ceased to count for much and inventing became just another job.

Although these changes were gradual, we may date the heroic age roughly from 1836 to 1917. It began with the reorganization of the Patent Office and ended with the entry of the United States into the First World War.

III

THE STEVENSES
AND RAILROADING

Important though the steamboat was in speeding up travel in the United States, the steam railroad, which followed close upon it, affected the lives of the masses even more. Boats could go only where rivers ran and lakes lay, while railroads could go almost anywhere.

In a few decades the railroad shrank the United States, in terms of travel time, from its original vastness down to the size of New England. The railroad carried millions and employed tens of thousands; it governed the course of the Civil War; it became one of the nation's foremost problems in the days of trusts and early labor union organization.

The British invented the steam railroad. Still, it comes into the story of American invention because one of the nation's leading inventors introduced it into the United States, while other Americans conceived major improvements in railroading.

Running a vehicle on rails is an old idea. As soon as people began to use wheels, in ancient Sumer, they found that cars run more smoothly and carry bigger loads on a smooth, hard surface than on a rough or soft one. If the entire road cannot be paved, good results can be had by paving two narrow strips and providing a groove or flange to keep the wheels of vehicles from slipping off.

In ancient Greece, many roads consisted of a pair of man-made ruts, often lined with cut stone and provided with switches and sidings. Each part of the Hellenic world had its own road gage, so that a Syracusan who brought his chariot to Greece found that his wheels were too far apart to fit the ruts.

As early as the fifteenth century, in Germany, rails were laid in mines for hauling cars of coal or ore. First the rails were of wood or stone; then of wood with strips of iron along the top; and then, about the time of the American Revolution, of solid iron bars.

Sometimes the flange to keep the wheels on the rails was put on the rail and sometimes on the wheel; sometimes it was on the inner side and sometimes on the outer. In 1789, William Jessop in England devised the modern system of putting the flange on the inner side of the wheel. He also standardized the common mine-car gage of four feet, eight and a half inches. It is perhaps not wholly a coincidence that this is just about the gage of Roman chariot wheels, as shown by the ruts at Pompeii and of some earlier vehicles, as far back as ancient Babylonia.

In the early nineteenth century, a few railroads were built as a kind of public toll road, on which people might run horse-drawn wagons and carriages. This did not work out well, because it was hard to control the traffic on a single-track line. Two wagoners, meeting head-on, would settle with whips and fists the question of who should back up to the nearest siding.

The inventor of the steam locomotive was Richard Trevithick, an English engineer who also invented a mining pump, a high-pressure steam engine, a steam carriage, a steam threshing machine, and mining machinery. Trevithick had more success than his contemporary John Fitch but managed to die just as poor.

Trevithick's steam locomotive, a one-cylinder contraption with an enormous flywheel, ran in 1804. It proved something that many had doubted. This was the fact that there is enough friction between the wheels of a locomotive and the rails to provide the needed traction. Therefore it is not necessary, except in certain mountainside railroads, to clinch the engine to the track by a rack and pinion gear.

As Fitch was followed by the shrewder Fulton, so Trevithick

was followed by the more worldly Englishman, George Stephenson, who made railroading profitable. After Trevithick, several British engineers built small locomotives to haul coal cars in collieries. Stephenson, who had worked on a colliery stationary engine as a boy, was one of these. In 1825, the Stockton and Darlington Railway Company laid tracks for a public horse-powered railway. Stephenson persuaded the directors to use one of his locomotives instead.

In 1829 the directors of the Liverpool and Manchester offered a prize of £500 for the best locomotive to be entered in a seven-day contest. Ten locomotives were entered. Five actually started. Stephenson's *Rocket* easily won, pulling thrice its own weight at 12.5 miles an hour and a passenger coach at 24 mph.

Soon, despite opposition from stagecoach and canal-boat interests, more lines were running in Great Britain, and people in other countries began laying tracks and ordering British locomotives to run on them.

The man who did the most to bring the railroad to the United States was John Stevens, Jr. (1749–1838) of a landowning New Jersey family. Stevens graduated from King's College (our Columbia University) and served in the Revolutionary War. He ended as a colonel and the state treasurer of New Jersey and married Rachel Livingston, the sister of his college friend Robert R. Livingston.

After the war, Stevens bought Hoboken, a 564-acre tract across the North River from Manhattan, which the government had confiscated from a Loyalist. On this estate Stevens built a villa, improved the property, begat twelve children, and began tinkering with steamboats. He took out one of the first dozen United States patents, for a fire-tube boiler.

Although a tireless improver, full of brilliant ideas for steam-driven vehicles, Colonel Stevens was not a mechanic. He had to hire mechanics. When this did not work out well, he hit upon a more radical system. One of his sons, Robert Livingston Stevens, showed mechanical aptitude; so the colonel saw to it that the boy was brought up with the most complete knowledge of the mechanical arts that could be had.

Although this was not the usual training for a young gentleman, it worked. Robert became one of the leading engineers of his day, while his equally energetic brothers John Cox Stevens, Edwin Augustus Stevens, and James Alexander Stevens managed the business ends of their joint enterprises.

In 1797, Colonel Stevens entered into partnership with Chancellor Livingston to make a steamboat. Stevens needed his brother-in-law because the latter could get a steamboat monopoly of the Hudson from the New York Legislature.

Unfortunately, the Chancellor also had ideas as to how the boat should be built. Though Livingston was a first-class gentleman farmer, politician, and diplomat, he was not much of an engineer. His designs all failed. In 1801 he went off to France, to negotiate the Louisiana Purchase and to form a new partnership with Robert Fulton.

Meanwhile, Colonel Stevens kept pushing his many enterprises. He built a turnpike, designed the pumps for New York's first municipal water system (promoted by Aaron Burr) and experimented with illuminating gas. For a while he employed a French monarchist refugee, Marc Isambard Brunel. Brunel was a prolific inventor of industrial machinery, who experimented with a primitive internal-combustion engine. In 1799, Brunel left for England, where he invented the tunneling shield and pioneered in mass production methods. His son, Isambard Kingdom Brunel, became equally renowned as an engineer and built the *Great Eastern,* by far the largest and most advanced steamship of her day.

With Livingston abroad, Stevens and his son Robert built a small open steamboat with a high-pressure engine and twin screw propellers. Stevens called her *Little Juliana* after one of his many daughters. The ship's propelling machinery, however, was too far ahead of its time. Although it sometimes held together long enough to cross the North River, whenever Stevens tried to work up the steam pressure he aimed for, the boiler sprang a leak or burst.

Convinced that American workmanship and materials were too crude for his purposes, Colonel Stevens sent his son John Cox Stevens to England to buy a high-pressure steam engine from Boulton & Watt. James Watt, now retired, referred him to his son and Boulton's son, who were running the firm. Young Boulton politely refused the order. They had, he said, experimented with high-pressure engines, but the boilers always blew up, to the peril of people nearby. Many years passed before the art of boilermaking reached the point where high-pressure steam could be safely used.

When Livingston and Fulton came back to the United States and began construction of the *North River*, they offered another partnership to Stevens. The colonel, working on a new steamboat design, declined. Later he reconsidered. For years he, Livingston, and Fulton haggled over proposed agreements, but it proved impossible to get all three to agree on any one plan at any one time. For the most part this chaffering was kept on a friendly basis, though in 1812, just before Chancellor Livingston died, Stevens quarreled with Fulton, and the pair broke off relations with an exchange of angry letters.

Stevens' *Phoenix* used low-pressure steam and side wheels, like those of the *North River*. Her hull, however, was more seaworthy. To avoid Livingston's monopoly, Stevens sent the *Phoenix* by sea to Chesapeake Bay under Robert L. Stevens' command. Although the *Phoenix* had to scuttle for a cove every time the wind rose, this was still the first oceanic voyage under steam. Robert L. Stevens put the ship into service between Philadelphia and Trenton, on which run she served for six years.

Colonel Stevens next proposed a tunnel under the North River and a bridge over it. He tried to get official approval of a pontoon drawbridge, but ferry owners howled ruin and the legislature denied the colonel his charter.

Stevens and his sons also tested explosive artillery shells, which Robert manufactured for the government. These tests convinced the colonel that the days of the square-rigged wooden ship of the line, firing broadsides of solid roundshot, were over. He therefore proposed to build an armored steam warship for the Navy, but horrified naval officers hastily buried the idea.

Colonel Stevens also began, around 1810, to agitate for steam railways. He wrote:

> Concede that there are now no Steam Rail-Ways anywhere in the world. This is not to say that they will not come—and that soon. As civilization progresses, water-carriage will prove too slow and cumbersome to satisfy the demands of humanity . . .[1]

At this time most American roads were frightful. There was a great enthusiasm for building canals. The most ambitious of these projects was the Erie Canal, opened with oratory and cannonades in 1825. Stevens urged railroads upon his brother-in-law, but the Chancellor answered with a long and dismal list of objections.

In 1825, not much slowed by his seventy-six years, Colonel Stevens laid out a circular narrow-gage track on his estate and built a one-ton rail car to run on it. At one end the car had a steam engine with a vertical boiler. The engine drove a cogwheel, which meshed with a rack between the rails. At the other end were seats for passengers.

Then the colonel took part in the chartering of the Pennsylvania Railroad. In 1832, at the age of eighty-one, he put his own railroad, the Camden & Amboy, into operation in New Jersey.

By this time other railroad companies were springing up like weeds, thanks to Stevens' long agitation and the news of the success of Stephenson's *Rocket*. In 1829 the Delaware & Hudson imported the six-ton *Stourbridge Lion* from England. It proved useless, being too high for the bridges and too heavy for the track. The next year Peter Cooper of New York launched his *Tom Thumb;* but, whereas the *Stourbridge Lion* was too heavy, *Tom* was too light to be practical. Effective American-built locomotives, such as the *Best Friend*, built in New York for the South Carolina Railroad Company, soon followed.

Robert Stevens went to England, became friendly with George Stephenson's son Robert Stephenson, and brought back the Stephenson-built *John Bull*. It ran well except for a tendency to leave the rails on curves. To cure this fault, Robert Stevens added an iron frame to the front end of the locomotive. The after end of the frame was bolted to the engine, while the forward end rested upon a pair of small wheels and carried a plow-shaped extension to clear the track of obstacles. Thus Robert Livingston Stevens invented the pilot truck and the pilot or cowcatcher. The *John Bull* served for thirty years.

Colonel Stevens lived to be eighty-nine, writing voluminously on philosophy and economics in his last years. As brilliant an inventor as Fitch or Fulton, he achieved less fame because he was such an active man of affairs, pursuing so many projects at once, that he never followed any one art long enough to identify himself with it.

Robert Livingston Stevens (1788–1856) inherited his father's inventive genius as well as the happy longevity that gave him time to realize his ideas. After his father died, he became the leading American steamboat and railroad engineer. His actual list of inventions is longer than those of either his father or Fulton, although he never bothered to take out patents.

Robert L. Stevens built a number of steamboats after the *Phoenix*. He added such features as the anthracite-fired boiler, the skeleton walking beam,[2] and balanced poppet valves. When he built the *New Philadelphia* in 1826, he invented the false bow, thus giving the ship finer lines without weakening her structure. By these and other improvements he raised the speed of steamboats, which Fulton once thought would never exceed nine knots, to fifteen.

When he sailed for England in 1830 to buy the *John Bull*, Robert L. Stevens passed the time by whittling cross-sections of railroad rails. At that time, several shapes were in use in England, with various L-shaped and I-shaped cross sections. The leading British rail was a symmetrical I-shaped rail, held in place by a series of iron clamps called "chairs."

Stevens designed a new rail, called the T-rail. This had a broad, flat bottom, a narrow vertical web, and a moderate bulge at the top. This rail could be spiked directly to the crossties, doing away with the chairs and lowering the cost while giving a quieter ride.

At that time most railroad builders mounted their rails on blocks of stone. In building the Camden & Amboy, Robert Stevens ran out of stone and went ahead with wooden crossties only, imbedded in gravel. He was delighted to find that his new track was not only cheaper to build but, thanks to the shock-absorbing qualities of wood, was also more durable and gave a smoother ride than a masonry roadbed. Track of the Stevens type came into use all over the world.

In 1841, the Stevens brothers Robert, Edwin, and John performed experiments of firing cannon against iron plates. As a result, they got a contract from the Navy to build an armored steam warship. This ship, called the Stevens Battery, was a long, low, narrow craft that looked a little like a submarine on the surface. Its deck bore seven cannon in a row along the centerline, and its bow was tipped by a ram. Although it lacked protection for the gunners, it was in most other respects as advanced as the first armored warships used in the Civil War.

However, one Secretary of the Navy after another held up money for the project, demanding changes and detailed plans. This went on for so long that the ship was still unfinished at the time of the Civil War, and a naval board refused to recommend that it be completed. During this war, Edwin Stevens built a smaller ironclad gunboat, the *Naugatuck*, and sent her to serve the Union at his own expense. She saw a good deal of action and continued in use as a revenue cutter after the war. When Edwin died in 1868, he left a million dollars to modernize and complete the Battery. The money was spent; the ship was still unfinished; and so she was finally scrapped.

Edwin also left $650,000 and a plot of land in Hoboken to found an institution of higher learning. This bequest gave birth to Stevens Institute of Technology, which still occupies the hill where Colonel Stevens had built his villa. In 1854 Robert Livingston Stevens had replaced the villa by a gray stone mansion with a cupola, called Stevens Castle. This structure long served the college as a social center.

Two of Colonel Stevens' grandsons, Edwin's son Edwin Augustus Stevens, Jr., and James's son Francis Bowes Stevens, also became distinguished engineers and inventors. In the story of American technology, the Stevenses are the most eminent single family.

American railroad builders who imported British locomotives in the 1830s discovered that these machines, though beautifully built, were not well suited to American conditions. Having short distances and plenty of capital, the British spent generously on their rights of way, burrowing and bridging to keep their tracks as straight as possible. Hence their locomotives, with four or six wheels rigidly journaled to the frame, were not meant for sharp curves and steep grades.

In the United States, where capital was scarcer and distances greater, railroad builders could not afford such luxuries. Tracks followed the contour of the ground with little preparation of the right of way and many steep grades and curves. British locomotives had a tendency to run off the rails of such tracks.

Where the British meticulously separated their tracks from road traffic by cuts and embankments, American railroad builders ran their tracks down the main streets of cities. As late as the 1920s, great cities like Los Angeles and Syracuse had main-line tracks in their streets.

The adaptation of the locomotive to American conditions was accomplished by John B. Jervis, chief engineer of the Mohawk and Hudson Railroad. Jervis built a locomotive with six wheels called the *Experiment*. It had a pair of drivers aft, and forward a four-wheeled truck mounted on a pivot so that it could swivel in going around curves.

A few years later, Jervis ordered from the locomotive builder Henry R. Cambell a locomotive for the Germantown Railroad. This engine had a four-wheeled swiveled truck forward and four driving wheels, connected by side rods, aft. Hence the weight of the locomotive was better distributed than before, wear on the track was lessened, and the loose articulation of the wheels allowed the locomotive to snake its way around American curves. This eight-wheeled design became almost standard on American railroads, although many other arrangements of wheels were also tried.

American locomotives developed other distinctive characteristics. Because most of them burned wood in the early decades of railroading, they were equipped with huge funnel-shaped stacks with screens at the top to keep the sparks from setting fire to everything burnable along the right of way.

European locomotive builders, especially the British, preferred to tuck the cylinders down under the boiler, out of sight between the wheels, so that they drove the engine by cranks on one of the axles. On the other hand, nearly all American locomotives had their cylinders in plain sight at the sides of the boiler. This arrangement, if ugly to European eyes, made maintenance easier.

As the century drew towards its close, the heavy loads, long runs, high speeds, steep grades, and inferior coal with which American locomotives had to cope, caused them to evolve along distinct lines. American engines developed boilers much larger than those of their European contemporaries.

They also added more and more driving wheels, up to six

pairs. To get power for hauling mile-long freight trains over the Sierras, American builders adopted a scheme of the French engineer Mallet: the articulated locomotive. In the articulated locomotive, the boiler is mounted on two driving-wheel frames connected by a hinge, so that the locomotive can bend to get around curves.

Most articulated locomotives worked on the compound principle. Steam from the boiler was piped to one pair of cylinders, expanded, and then led to the other pair, where it expanded further before being exhausted. Articulated locomotives were built with two sets of six, eight, or even ten driving wheels.

The process reached its climax in the three locomotives of the P-1 class, built for the Erie Railroad in 1914–16. These had three sets of eight drivers, the last set under the tender; they were compound locomotives with two high-pressure and four low-pressure cylinders. Their power was such that in theory each could have pulled a four-and-a-half mile train of loaded freight cars. They were used mainly as pushers on the Susquehanna grade. They required so many repairs, and their weight so limited the territory on which they could operate, that they were scrapped after only fifteen years of service.

In the twentieth century, some railroads bought three- and four-cylinder locomotives, with extra cylinders working cranks between the wheels, or under the cab. Some built nonarticulated four-cylinder locomotives with two sets of drivers. Meanwhile, European locomotives adopted many features of American practice.

The reign of the steam locomotive was ended around 1950 by the substitution of the Diesel-electric locomotive. The first successful Diesel-electrics were built by a stout, amiable Russian engineer, George Lomonossoff, who looked like Santa Claus and served the Russian railways under the Tsar, under Kerensky, and under Lenin.

During the 1930s and 40s, several American railroads experimented with steam locomotives of radical design: streamlined locomotives, articulated locomotives, high-pressure compound locomotives, turbine locomotives, and turbo-electric locomotives. Some of these worked, but not well enough to prolong the reign of steam. Although the new Diesel-electrics were larger and more expensive than the steam locomotives they replaced, the

Diesel-electrics have so many advantages in availability, instant starting, and low cost of fuel and maintenance that within a few years they practically drove steam locomotives off the rails.

The development of the airplane made people aware of streamlining—that is, giving fast-moving bodies a smooth, tapered shape that would slip through the air with the least resistance. Once the laws of streamlining had been worked out, they were applied to trains, automobiles, and motorboats as well as to aircraft.

In fact "streamlining" became a word in twentieth-century American advertising jargon, meaning in particular modern, graceful, or efficient design, regardless of aerodynamic qualities. Domestic oil heaters, for instance, are advertised as "streamlined" because they are inclosed in neat sheet-iron housings, not because they are designed to fly.

When streamlining became a popular fad in the 1930s and 40s, most people thought that streamlined trains were new. Actually, the idea goes back to 1865. In that year a Unitarian minister of Roxbury, Massachusetts, the Rev. Dr. Samuel R. Calthorp, took out Patent No. 49,227 on a well-designed streamlined train. Dr. Calthorp got his idea by watching racing shells while coaching the Harvard crew for its first race with Yale. Calthorp's patent was broad. The first of its four claims reads:

> 1. Giving to the exterior surface of a railway train a form tapering from the center of the train toward either end, or tapering the engine on the car at the front or rear of the train, substantially as described, for the purpose of diminishing atmospheric resistance.

However, Calthorp never profited from his invention, because it was premature. The world was not ready for it. For one thing, train speeds were much lower than they later became, so that the retarding effect of air resistance was not so obvious. The size of the loss was not widely known. As the wind tunnel had not been invented, there was no way of proving the advantage of the design except by building such a train, which nobody cared to do.

The next streamlined-train patents, Nos. 489,911 and 490,057, were issued in 1893 to Frederick U. Adams. These were much narrower than the expired Calthorp patent. A train called the *Windsplitter* was built under these patents and tried out on the Baltimore & Ohio. There were several minor accidents involving the skirts that extended downwards from the sides of the cars to inclose the trucks, and at last the train was taken out service.

One source of difficulty was that, since the laws of airflow were not yet well known, Adams' design was inferior, aerodynamically, to that of Calthorp. Furthermore, nineteenth-century trains suffered from so many sources of power loss, such as low-pressure boilers and hand firing, that the savings from streamlining were a smaller part of the total costs than they are today.

The first railroads were built to various gages, although Jessop's mine-car gage of 4′ 8½″ dominated. Railroads have been built with many gages, from two to seven feet. The seven-foot gage was devised in 1833 by Isambard Kingdom Brunel, creator of the *Great Eastern,* for the Great Western Railway in England.

In the United States, by the time of the Civil War, at least a dozen different gages were in use. This meant that a day's journey by railway usually had to be broken several times to change trains. During the Civil War, the Union authorized lavish subsidies to the Union Pacific and Central Pacific Railroads to build a transcontinental line. What gage should it have?

Lobbies representing various railroads went frantically to work on Congress, which had authorized President Lincoln to decide the matter. As a result of this pressure, verbal or otherwise, Congress reversed itself and changed the five-foot gage, which Lincoln had chosen on the advice of experts, to the old 4′ 8½″ of Jessop and the Roman chariots. This gage became standard throughout North America and over most of the world, save in a few lands like Russia, India, and Japan. Considering the size and speed of modern rolling stock, a wider gage would have been more efficient in the long run.

The builders of early railroad trains worried about making their trains go at all. By mid-century, this was no longer a problem. Trains were outspeeding the swiftest race horse. The problem was now to stop them.

Cars and locomotives were equipped with handwheels which, turned by brakemen, reeled in chains that forced curved iron shoes against the rims of the wheels. In theory every car had a brakeman who, when the engineer blew certain toots on his whistle, strained at his handwheel until the train stopped. In practice, there were usually not enough brakemen to go round, and trains were stopped in a slow, jerky, and uncertain manner.

Hence the middle decades of the century were enlivened by frightful wrecks, like the airline crashes of today. Trains collided head-on, or ran off broken track ends, or fell off high trestles, or broke in two on steep grades, so that the broken-off cars rolled back down the grade, faster and faster until they leaped from the rails.

George Westinghouse (1846–1914) was a large, stolid-looking youth, born to a carpenter in a small town in upstate New York and reared in Schenectady. In the Civil War he served first as a private in the Army and later as an engineer in the Navy.

After the war, at the behest of his father, Westinghouse entered Union College. However, he proved a poor student, being unwilling to study subjects of no immediate interest. He soon withdrew, though later in life he regretted the lost opportunity. For a while he worked in his father's shop.

One day he watched a train crew spend arduous hours lifting two derailed cars back on the track. He came home with an idea for a device quickly to return such cars to the track. It consisted of a pair of rails to be clamped to the track, from which they led off at any angle, like a derailing switch in reverse.

Failing to interest his father, young Westinghouse found two Schenectady businessmen willing to risk $5000 each on his idea. Soon, at twenty-one, he had a patent and a factory turning out his re-railer for railroads all over the country.

While traveling to Troy, Westinghouse was delayed by a wreck. Two freight trains had collided head-on, although the track was straight and level. The engineers had seen each other in plenty of time. But the brakemen, yanking on handwheels in response to frantic whistle-toots, had not been able to stop the trains.

Westinghouse began thinking of better ways to stop trains. Trains, he thought, could be stopped more quickly and surely if the engineer could apply the brakes throughout the train himself, instead of depending on brakemen.

First, Westinghouse thought of a brake chain extending the length of the train and operated from the engine. He found that this had been tried but had proved unsatisfactory because of its complication and frictional losses.

Then he thought of brakes worked by a cylinder under each car, which in turn was operated by steam pressure from the locomotive. A little investigation showed that the steam would lose most of its pressure on the way by cooling and condensing to water.

Westinghouse continued to mull over the problem. One day in 1866, as he sat in his father's shop, a young woman came in to sell him a subscription to a magazine.

"No, I never read magazines," growled Westinghouse.[8]

Then, relenting, he bought a subscription, starting with the issue that she had proffered. When he read his magazine, he was struck by an article on the Mount Cenis tunnel in Switzerland. This tunnel, he learned, was bored by pneumatic drilling machinery. Air from a compressor, under a pressure of six atmospheres,[4] was piped to a rock drill 3000 feet away.

Compressed air, Westinghouse thought, was the answer to his problem. It would not condense or freeze in the pipes, while transmitting pressure as quickly and as frictionlessly as steam.

Westinghouse moved his car-replacer plant to Pittsburgh to lower his costs and set about promoting his air brake. After a struggle he persuaded a rich young Pittsburgher, Baggaley, to finance the making of a sample. Although many railroad executives told him that his idea was visionary, he persuaded the president of the Panhandle Railroad to let him test his brake, provided that Westinghouse paid all costs and guaranteed the train against damage.

In this version of the device, a steam-driven pump applied air at 60 pounds per square inch to a main reservoir attached to the engine. The engineer admitted this air to a pipe by turning a valve, so that air passed through the pipe, and through flexible couplings from car to car, to the cylinder and piston under the tender and under each car. The piston pressed the brake shoes against the wheels. The old hand-brake wheel was still attached to the brake shoes (as it still is) for use in case the air brake failed. When the engineer turned the brake valve back to its starting position, the pressure reservoir was cut off while the air was released from the pipe and the cylinders.

On the day of the test, the train had just started when it ground to a sudden halt, spilling railroad officials and their guests from their seats. When they scrambled out of the cars, they found that a teamster, whipping up his horses to get across the track before the train arrived, had been thrown from his wagon in front of the locomotive. The engineer gave the brake valve handle a tremendous yank, and the train stopped four feet from the drayman.

After this spectacular demonstration, Westinghouse was on his way. In 1869 he got his first air-brake patent. Soon all the important railroads in the United States had adopted the device. Westinghouse even traveled abroad to sell his brake in Great Britain and Europe.

Westinghouse then developed an even better air brake, which would "fail safe." In this, each car has its own compressed-air reservoir, charged from the locomotive's reservoir, which strives to apply the brakes. The main compressed-air line from the engine counteracts this, holding the brake shoes away from the wheels. If the train breaks, the brakes on the separated cars snap on automatically as the air rushes out of the line.

Westinghouse went on to develop the compressed-air spring and a system of pneumatic railroad signaling. With money pouring in from his companies, he decided to sink a small gas well on his estate in Pittsburgh. He struck a source of gas that blew the tools out of the well with a roar and took weeks to bring under control.

So Westinghouse found himself in the natural-gas business. Again he began inventing. He took out thirty-eight patents in this field, inventing the gas meter, the automatic cutoff valve, and a leakproof piping system.

Having thus become a utilities magnate without really meaning to, Westinghouse went into the manufacture of electrical equipment, though as a capitalist rather than as a technical man. Now a big stout man with a fine white walrus mustache, affable, polite, matter-of-fact, and vigorous, he could be a hard fighter when aroused.

Westinghouse was enraged by a remark of Edison, repeated to him, that he knew nothing about the electrical business and should stick to his air brakes. He fought against Edison in the Battle of the Currents in the 1880s and 90s, pushing the development of alternating currents against Edison's direct current for household and industrial use.

If inventive genius is rare, inventive genius combined with business ability is much rarer. Westinghouse had enough business acumen to found and run several successful companies.

However, the robber barons proved too much for him, J. P. Morgan merged the companies of Edison and Elihu Thomson, Westinghouse's leading electrical rivals, to form the General Electric Company. Then G.E. spent two million dollars suing Westinghouse. This assault so weakened the Westinghouse Company that the panic of 1907 sent it into receivership and cost Westinghouse his control of the company. After a four-year struggle against a group of financial manipulators headed by Morgan, Westinghouse gave up and retired. He continued as long as he lived to invent things, including a steam turbine with a reduction gear, and took out altogether 400-odd patents.

The most useful railroad invention of the heroic age, after Westinghouse's air brake, was Janney's automatic coupling. Eli Hamilton Janney (1831–1912) was a Virginia farmer who served as a Confederate officer and after the war found himself too poor even to run his farm. While working as a dry-goods clerk in Alexandria, Janney got his idea by watching cars being switched.

Before Janney, cars were coupled by a crude link-and-pin system. This required a brakeman to go between the cars and manipulate the coupling while the engineer gently pushed the cars together. As the engineer could not see the brakeman while he did this, and as a locomotive is not a precise instrument anyway, accidents were common. Many brakemen were killed. Lost or mangled fingers, hands, and arms were standard operating risks of the railroad worker.

Janney's coupling consists of a shank to which is attached a hinged knuckle that, opened and pushed against another coupling, closes automatically and is locked in place by a tapered pin that falls through registering holes in the knuckle and shank. When two such couplings engage, it is like two men clasping hands. To uncouple the cars, one of the locking pins is pulled up by a lever on the outside of its car.

Janney whittled his coupling out of wood, patented it in 1868, and with money from friends had a sample made and tried out on the Southern Railway. Then he organized the Janney Car Coupling Company.

It took Janney many years to get his coupling generally adopted. Even after the Master Car Builders' Association approved it in 1888, railroads were reluctant to standardize on a patented article until Janney agreed to waive his rights to the particular contour of the coupling. Then the device became standard equipment on American railroads. Janney retired from the presidency of his company when his first patent expired, but he continued to invent improvements in couplings down to his death.

The Janney coupling saved not only lives and limbs but also time. Hence it was adopted in many lands, such as China, where railroads were built by Americans. In Europe and in lands where the railroads were built by British and other European engineers, the link and pin survive, though passenger trains have a more sophisticated coupling in which the cars are laboriously screwed together by a turnbuckle. The U.S.S.R., however, has adopted an automatic coupling of the Janney type, and is now nearing the end of a long change-over from the link-and-pin coupling.

IV

HENRY, MORSE,

AND THE TELEGRAPH

The steamboat and the railroad enabled nineteenth-century people to travel, as Evans had predicted, "as fast as birds fly." Although these developments also speeded up communication, men wanted to convey intelligence more swiftly yet.

Faster communication might have prevented the useless American War of 1812. The British government repealed its obnoxious Orders in Council before the United States declared war but not in time for the news to reach Washington by ship before the declaration. Transatlantic telegraphy would also have averted the Battle of New Orleans, fought two weeks after the treaty of peace was signed in Europe.

Crude systems of signaling over long distances by light—by mirrors in sunlight and by torches in the dark—go back to ancient times. The researches of Franklin and other eighteenth-century electricians led inventors to think of electricity as a means for such signaling. Many tinkered with wires, batteries, and electrostatic generators. In Spain, Salvá sent electrical messages twenty-six miles from Madrid to Aranjuez by high-voltage discharges from a frictional machine as early as 1798.

Some of these early devices were very odd indeed. Soemmering's, for instance, had a separate cell for each letter of the alphabet. When a letter was transmitted, the little bubbles of electrolytic decomposition streamed up from the corresponding cell.

The semaphore telegraph of the Chappe brothers, using towers, movable semaphore arms, and observers with telescopes, came into use during Napoleon's time. By the 1830s, this system had spread several thousand miles of visual tentacles over Continental Europe.

Of the many who had a hand in the electrical telegraph, Joseph Henry (1797–1878) is second to none in importance. Henry was an upstate New Yorker, noted in youth for indolence and indecision. He failed as a silversmith's apprentice, dabbled in amateur theatricals in Albany, and at sixteen was introduced by one of his widowed mother's boarders to his first scientific book: Gregory's *Lectures on Experimental Philosophy, Astronomy, and Chemistry* (1808).

At once a trumpet blew in young Henry's mind. Away went his sloth and vagueness. He had found his calling.

Henry put himself through Albany Academy by teaching and tutoring. As medicine was the only active scientific profession in the United States, Henry studied medicine. Soon he became assistant to the president of the Academy and began reporting his studies on such subjects as the cooling of air and steam during expansion.

Among the boys he taught was Henry James, who later became the father of the novelist of that name and of the psychologist William James. While Joseph Henry and his boys were experimenting with a fire balloon, the balloon wafted through the open window of a barn. In stamping out the fire, Henry James was burned so badly that he lost a leg. Joseph Henry gave him the tutoring he needed during his long convalescence to get him into Princeton.

In the late 1820s, Joseph Henry became a teacher of mathematics and natural philosophy at the Academy. He also made a geological survey of the surrounding counties under the direction of Amos Eaton, America's foremost teacher of geology. Eaton, who had served a term in prison on a false charge of forgery, had more recently founded the Rensselaer School, later Rensselaer Polytechnic Institute.

Henry also began researches on electricity and magnetism. The electromagnet had just been invented by a Briton, William

Sturgeon. Sturgeon bent an iron bar into the shape of a horseshoe, insulated it by a coating of varnish, and wound a bare wire around it.

Henry wished to increase the power of the electromagnet. But, if he tried to wind too many coils of wire around the bar, the successive loops would touch one another, causing short circuits and decreasing the power of the magnet.

Henry was sitting at home in Albany when he fell into a reverie. Then he startled his friends by slapping the table and crying: "I have it!" like Archimedes with Hieron's crown.

Henry's idea was to insulate the wire itself. Using silken ribbons from his patient wife's petticoat for insulation, Henry wound four hundred turns of wire around his iron core, then four hundred more turns on top of the first lot. He was delighted to find that his electromagnet would lift 28 pounds.

More experiments followed. Henry raised the size of his electromagnets until they lifted the unheard-of mass of 750 pounds. He built the first electromagnet ever to be put to commercial use, for extracting iron from pulverized ore at the Penfield Iron Works.

Henry also experimented with electrical communication. In 1831 he built an electromagnetic telegraph, which rang a small office bell at the end of a pair of wires. The principle was the same as that of the modern electric doorbell.

In 1830–31, Henry built the world's first electric motor. It was the first, that is, if we do not count the experiments of Faraday, Ampère, and others who had caused individual wires to spin around in circles under magnetic influence. Henry's motor was a bar electromagnet pivoted at its center, like the walking beam of a ferryboat. Wires, extending from each end of the bar, dipped into the liquids of a pair of battery cells. The bar rocked back and forth at about seventy-five oscillations a minute. Henry called the device a "philosophic toy" and hoped that a practical use would some day be found for it.

In 1834 came the first rotary electric motors, built by Thomas Edmondson in Baltimore and by Thomas Davenport in upstate New York, at the same time that Watkins in England and Jacobi in Russia were attacking the problem. Davenport, a blacksmith and a brilliantly unsuccessful inventor of the Fitch type, was inspired by seeing Henry's electromagnet at the Penfield Works. As Davenport's armature had but two arms, it revolved jerkily. Nevertheless, it ran. Davenport used it to power the first model electric rail car, an impractical battery-driven affair.

This and other early efforts to build electric locomotives failed because the batteries on which the inventors relied were too heavy, costly, and fragile for the power they gave. The electric motor did not show its possibilities until, fifty years later, the electric generator was invented, to turn the energy of steam engines and hydraulic turbines into electric current on a large scale.

While Henry was developing his motor, making the first iron-core transformer, and discovering the principle of the generator by moving a bar magnet through a coil, Michael Faraday in England was working along the same lines. Faraday and Henry became aware of each other through their publications in scientific journals. Faraday independently discovered the generator effect.

Between 1829 and 1834 the pair independently and at about the same time discovered mutual induction and self-induction. These are the principles, respectively, of the transformer and the spark coil. Faraday is usually given the credit for the first and Henry for the second. As both were modest men, more interested in truth than in personal glory, no quarrels arose between them over priority.

Now Henry began insulating his wires with shellac, thus sparing his wife's petticoats. In 1832 he took a professorship at Princeton, where he taught and investigated for fourteen years. Princeton found him a tall, well-built, healthy-looking man, handsome in a craggy and forbidding way, though mild as milktoast in manner. He never applied for patents on any of his many inventions, later saying:

"I did not then consider it compatible with the dignity of science to confine benefits which might be derived from it to the exclusive use of any individual. In this," he added dryly, "I was perhaps too fastidious."[1]

Henry was vain only about his lack of vanity. He never got angry save when somebody accused him of selfish motives. He had none of the simian passions, sentimental follies, or colorful eccentricities that make a man lively company for his contemporaries and easy copy for his biographers.

In 1836, Henry went to Europe. Faraday, Wheatstone, Sturgeon, and other scientists received him warmly. Charles Wheatstone was a British physicist, a few years younger than Henry and so shy that he could not lecture. Like others, he was trying to make an electric telegraph work.

Once Henry, Faraday, Daniell (inventor of an electric battery), and Wheatstone got together in Wheatstone's laboratory. Wheatstone was trying to draw a spark from current generated by a thermopile. A thermopile is a combination of thermoelectric couples, or thermocouples. Each thermocouple consists of a pair of different metals joined together, with wires attached to the metals on each side of the junction. When the thermocouple is heated, it generates electric current.

Wheatstone, Daniell, and Faraday tried without success to create their spark. Henry asked if he might try. He connected the circuit with an induction coil—a long wire wrapped around a soft-iron core—and got his spark. Faraday jumped up crying:

"Hurrah for the Yankee experiment!"[2]

Subsequently, Henry suggested to Wheatstone the use of the relay to increase his range. Although Wheatstone did not admit this help later, he did get together with Faraday a few years afterwards to persuade the Royal Society to give Henry the Copley Medal, which had previously been awarded to only two Americans, Benjamin Franklin and Benjamin Thompson. Thompson was the American Loyalist who removed to Europe after the Revolution, became Count Rumford, and discovered that heat is the motion of the particles of which a body is composed.

Before returning to America, Henry attended the meeting of the British Association for the Advancement of Science at Liverpool and talked on Leyden jars. At another session, the chairman asked him to say a few words on the progress of steam in the United States. Henry said that some steamboats had done fifteen knots.[3] An economist, the Rev. Dionysius Lardner, accused Henry of being a foreigner from a land whose natives liked to exaggerate. He did not believe that any steamship could go so fast, and he made himself immortal by adding:

As to the project which is announced in the newspapers of making the voyage directly from New York to Liverpool [under steam], it was, he had no hesitation in saying, perfectly chimerical, and they might as well talk of making a voyage from New York or Liverpool to the moon.[4]

The steam voyage across the Atlantic was made by two ships about six months later, and Lardner claimed he had been misquoted.

After Henry left, Wheatstone continued experiments in telegraphy. His system, like others of the time, used dials with needles, which rotated to indicate letters. In 1837 he patented a system with five electric circuits and five dials. This was installed on the Great Western Railway for dispatching trains.

Shortly thereafter a woman was found dying of poison in Slough, a suburb of London. Somebody remembered seeing a man in Quaker garb leaving her house and boarding a train for London. Somebody else thought of the telegraph, and the suburban operator sent a message to the London police. He had trouble with the word "Quaker," as his apparatus had no q. When he spelled it "kwaker" the operator at the other end could not at first understand him. Nevertheless, the murderer, John Tawell, was spotted as he stepped off the train in London, trailed to his home by a detective, and arrested. He pleaded guilty and was duly hanged. Thereafter, nobody denied the usefulness of the telegraph.

Wheatstone improved his telegraph, simplifying it to two needles instead of five. But, after it had been in use for some years, it was swept aside by the still simpler Morse telegraph. Although Wheatstone and Morse developed their systems at about the same time, Wheatstone's was in use first.

Wheatstone thus holds much the same position in telegraphy that Fitch does in regard to the steamboat, Trevithick in regard to the locomotive, and Fessenden in radio broadcasting. He was the first to make the idea do useful work, even though the means he used were soon superseded. This is not to give Wheatstone the sole credit for telegraphy, but to correct the common American impression that Morse did it first and did it all.

Back in New York City, Henry was in Chilton's chemical shop when the proprietor introduced him to a lean, sharp-faced man with fluffy gray hair who had walked in to buy apparatus. This man was Samuel Finley Breese Morse[5] (1791–1872), the most distinguished American artist of his day.

Morse was struggling to perfect an electric telegraph, having conceived the idea independently of the several other telegraphic inventors. He was also having trouble in earning enough money to keep himself and his project going.

To Morse, meeting Henry was a stroke of luck. Henry knew as much as there was to be known about electricity, and he freely advised Morse, asking nothing in return. In the long run, all Henry got for his help was abuse and ingratitude.

In the 1840s, Henry abandoned the study of electromagnetism and went instead into the study of heat, light, and sound. He made many contributions in these fields, all minor. In this respect Henry's life followed the course of that of many scientists. A short period of major basic discoveries is succeeded by a long period of minor contributions and refinements.

Henry was working away happily at Princeton on the measurement of the velocity of projectiles, solid solutions, the molecular constitution of matter, soap films, the variation of electrical charges during thunderstorms, the temperature of sunspots, color blindness, the aurora polaris, the flow of liquids, and sonorous flames, when the United States fell heir to a curious bequest.

James Smithson (1765–1829) was the illegitimate son of Hugh Smithson, first Duke of Northumberland, and Elizabeth Macie, a well-born and wealthy Englishwoman living in France. Smithson spent most of his life in Paris, barely tolerated by English society because of his bastardy. He was an able physicist and mineralogist and a pioneer in microchemistry, after whom the mineral smithsonite (zinc carbonate) is named. He was a member of the Royal Society. His only amusement was gambling. Knowing that, mathematically, he was bound to lose, he prudently limited his bets to small sums.

Smithson left an unusual will, whose wording seems to have been taken from the addresses of George Washington. In case his only heir died without issue, his entire fortune was to go to "the United States of America, to found at Washington, under the name of the Smithsonian Institution an establishment for the increase and diffusion of knowledge among men."[6]

In 1835, the nephew died. Three years later, an American diplomat brought back to Washington 106 bags containing £104,960 in gleaming golden sovereigns.

It took the United States ten years to decide to accept the gift and then to decide what to do with it. John C. Calhoun, the great defender of slavery, thought that such an acceptance would be unconstitutional and beneath the dignity of the United States. When it was decided to accept, John Quincy Adams wanted a national observatory. Others sought a national library or a museum.

Finally Congress passed an act creating the Smithsonian Institution under a Board of Regents composed of various high officers of the government and other prominent persons. The regents asked Joseph Henry, the most distinguished American scientist, to be the secretary, the active executive officer. Henry sighed at leaving research but accepted as a public duty.

Although he cared little for money himself, Henry managed the Institution's funds shrewdly and thriftily. He would have preferred not to buy any building but to rent quarters and spend the income from Smithson's fund entirely on scientific research and publication.

Instead, he found himself saddled with a museum, an art gallery, and a library. The library he gave to the Library of Congress. He was also forced to accept a new building of brown fieldstone ornamented with useless medieval towers.

Henry proceeded cautiously, launching expeditions, researches, and publications. In 1852 Stephen A. Douglas tried to cultivate farm votes by urging that the Institution's funds be used for an agricultural bureau. Henry listened to Douglas' speech and made a forceful reply. Afterwards they met in the hall and apologized for their strong words. Douglas became a friend of Henry and served as regent from 1854 until his death.

When Lincoln came into office, Henry, whose sympathies were with the South, opposed Lincoln without knowing him, while Lincoln suspected that the Smithsonian was wasting the people's money. Acquaintance soon changed their suspicions to fast friendship. During the Civil War, Lincoln sought refuge from the cares of office and the sharp tongue of his wife by going to the Smithsonian at night to help Henry, holding apparatus for him and taking part in experiments with signal lanterns.

The Smithsonian served as the nation's Office of Research and Development during the war. For instance, it promoted the use of balloons for military observation. Henry tried to continue basic research but found this difficult with troops quartered on the grounds, parading and shooting at targets all day.

Henry's own researches included metallurgy, the strength of materials, acoustics, the improvement of lighthouse lights, foghorns, and liquid measurements. He even let Mary Lincoln inveigle him into a séance with a medium named Colchester who claimed to summon up her dead son Willie's ghost. Henry, unimpressed, later learned about the gadget strapped to the biceps, with which Colchester made his mysterious sounds.

Henry was an active organizer of scientists, having much to do in 1847 with the transformation of the Association of American Geologists into the American Association for the Advancement of Science, and with the American Academy of Sciences, organized in 1863 to provide technical help for the Union in the Civil War. After the war, Henry's administrative career continued peacefully, except for a fire in 1865, which destroyed Smithson's effects and Henry's papers. Henry enjoyed travel and honors until his quiet death in 1877.

Samuel Finley Breese Morse got into telegraphy in the following way.

The son of a Congregationalist minister of Massachusetts, Morse went to England to study painting, as the less talented Fulton had done before him. There he fraternized with Samuel Taylor Coleridge and, winning a gold medal in an art competition, stayed right through the War of 1812.

Back home, Morse painted Presidents and other notables but found that even the best artist in America had a hard time earning enough to eat. For three years he lived in New Haven, borrowing from friends and from his neighbor Eli Whitney. After literary and artistic adventures, Morse went to Europe again, hobnobbed in Paris with Fenimore Cooper, and was impressed by the French semaphore telegraph.

On the way home, on the packet *Sully*, Morse conversed with fellow passengers. One was young Charles Thomas Jackson, who later plagued both Morse and Morton. They discussed the recent experiments of Ampère with the electromagnet. A lawyer from Philadelphia asked whether the flow of electricity were not retarded by the length of the wire.

No, said Jackson, it passes instantly over any known length of wire. (This is not quite true, but it was nearly enough right to serve at the time.)

"If this be so," said Morse, "and the presence of electricity can be made visible in any desired part of the circuit, I see no reason why intelligence might not be instantly transmitted by electricity to any distance."[7]

During the rest of the voyage, Morse thought, sketched, and talked about his idea. He began to compile an elaborate numerical code for sending messages which, much later and drastically simplified, became the Morse Code. Nobody told him about the many others, like Wheatstone and Gauss, who were working on the same problem.

For the next few years, Morse taught painting at the University of the City of New York (now New York University). He ran unsuccessfully for mayor of New York on the Native American (anti-Catholic, anti-immigrant) ticket.

He also worked on his telegraph. He consulted with Joseph Henry, with his fellow professor Leonard Gale, and with a former student named Alfred Vail. Vail's father, who owned an ironworks in Morristown, New Jersey, furnished money for the experiments and had instruments made in his shop.

Morse was not so much an outstanding inventor as a promoter of an invention and a manager of inventors. He foreshadows today's organized teams of scientists and engineers, which grind out inventions to order in the laboratories of great modern corporations. He merits credit for pushing his project through to success with great shrewdness, energy, and determination, and for overcoming obstacles that would have stopped most men. For instance, a Postmaster General named Johnson long opposed the telegraph because he thought it would compete with the Post Office Department.

Technically speaking, however, the main contributions to Morse's telegraph were made by Henry and Gale. Of the things that Morse proposed, some became minor features of the system; others turned out to be either old or impractical.

In 1838, Morse and Alfred Vail demonstrated their telegraph to Congress. Then Morse went to Europe to secure exclusive rights there. In England the Attorney General, Sir John Campbell, denied Morse a patent on a false technicality. Campbell, who could always be counted upon to do the wrong thing, dismissed Morse's protest with the remark that Morse ought to be satisfied with his American patent. Morse looked up his rivals Wheatstone and the chemist Davy. Although they were friendly, Morse was not impressed by the devices that they, too, were demonstrating in hope of getting capital.

In France, Morse obtained promises from various governments but no money or contracts. He went to see his fellow painter and inventor Louis J. M. Daguerre and his famous daguerreotype. Daguerre and his partner Niepce[8] had despaired of enforcing a patent infringed as easily as one on their photographic process. They had therefore revealed the process and given up exclusive rights in return for governmental pensions.

Morse brought Daguerre's process back to America and became the nation's first commercial photographer. He hoped to get enough money by painting, teaching, and photography to keep his telegraphic project going. When he asked one of his pupils:

"Well, Strother, my boy, how are we off for money?" the pupil replied:

"Why, Professor, I am sorry to say I have been disappointed, but I expect a remittance next week."

"Next week! I shall be dead by that time."

"Dead, sir?"

"Yes, dead by starvation."

"Would ten dollars be of any service?" asked the astonished student.

"Ten dollars would save my life; that is all it would do."

Strother took his professor to dinner. Morse said as he finished: "This is my first meal in twenty-four hours." Then he uttered the plaint of painters from Polygnotos down:

"Strother, don't be an artist. It means beggary. Your life depends upon people who know nothing of your art and care nothing for you. A housedog lives better, and the very sensitivity that stimulates an artist keeps him alive to suffering."[9]

By 1842 Morse had scraped up enough money to put on another demonstration in Washington. There he sent messages from one committee room to another. His bill for a subsidy of $30,000 squeaked through, although one of those voting for it, Representative David Wallace of Indiana (father of the author of *Ben-Hur*) lost his seat at the next election on charges of wasting the people's money on absurdities.

The bill called for Morse to set up a telegraph line from Washington to Baltimore. Much of the appropriation was wasted because Morse insisted on laying an underground cable. Ezra

Cornell devised a wonderful plow to dig the ditch and lay the cable all at once. Although the plow worked, the cable proved defective.

Then Vail read in a journal that European telegraphers like Wheatstone had found that a bare wire strung on insulated poles worked fine and was not affected by the weather. And so it was done.

At the official opening, on May 24, 1844, Annie Ellsworth, the daughter of the Commissioner of Patents, chose for the first message the words of the prophet Balaam: "What hath God wrought!"[10]

Morse's luck now turned. His sending to Washington the news of the political conventions meeting in Baltimore convinced people that the telegraph worked. Thereafter the story of Morse is one of expansion and improvement, of frantic finance, lurid litigation, and cutthroat competition.

Joseph Henry and Morse fell out as a result of a series of accidents. In 1845 Vail published a history of the telegraph, which entirely omitted Henry. Morse promised to repair the omission but neglected to do so. When Henry was called as an expert witness in the endless litigation in which Morse became involved, he gave a coldly accurate account of the contributions of the various telegraph inventors to the art. His testimony made Morse's scientific contributions look much smaller than Morse would have liked.

Morse, though in many ways a likable man, was also vain, volatile, testy, and temperamental. As time passed, he denied more and more that Henry had helped him. He ended by accusing Henry of lying. "I am not," he said, "indebted to him for any discovery in science bearing on the telegraph."[11] In this case it was not Henry who lied.

In the Civil War, Morse, a man of strong religious and racial prejudices, was a Southern sympathizer and Copperhead leader. He considered slavery "a social condition ordained from the beginning of the world for the wisest purposes, benevolent and disciplinary, by Divine Wisdom."[12]

After the war, however, people forgave Morse his part in this conspiracy, and he ended his days old, rich, and honored. Although never reconciled to Henry, he once made a speech that showed an intelligent grasp of the inventive process:

When the historian has made his search, and brought together the facts, if any one connected with a great invention or discovery has attracted to himself the more concentrated regard or honour of mankind, or of a particular nation, how significant is it that time, and more research bring out other minds, and other names, to divide and share with him the hitherto exclusive honours. And who shall say that it is not eminently just? Did Columbus first discover America, or does Cabot, or some more ancient adventurous North-man dispute the honour with him? . . . It is surely sufficient hon-our to any man that he be a co-laborer in any secondary capacity to which he may be appointed by such a head in a great benefac-tion to the World.[13]

Once it was shown that the telegraph worked on land, the question arose: Why cannot some such device be operated across the seas? In 1842, Morse laid an experimental under-water cable across New York harbor. Three years later, Cornell stretched a twelve-mile line across the Hudson, which worked until an ice floe broke it. Other cables were laid across the English Channel and from Corsica to Italy.

A company was formed to connect Nova Scotia with New-foundland but went bankrupt. In 1854 the promoter, Gisborne, was looking for a way out of his troubles. In New York he met a bony young paper merchant with a fringe of wreath beard under his chin. Cyrus W. Field (1819–92) of Massa-chusetts had made such a success in business that, after nine years of work, he had retired in 1853 at thirty-three.

Gisborne spent an evening at Field's home, talking. After-wards, Field looked at a globe to visualize the route of the system. The idea struck him: Why not go on across the ocean?

Next day, Field wrote two letters. One was to Matthew Fontaine Maury, the American naval officer who founded the science of oceanography. Maury informed Field that a plateau extended across the North Atlantic from Newfoundland to Ire-land. This stretch of sea bottom is deep enough to avoid icebergs and anchors but not too deep to make a cable impractical.

The other letter went to Morse, asking if such a project were electrically practical. Morse came to New York and be-came fast friends with Field. The latter gathered some capi-talists and set up the New York, Newfoundland, and London Telegraph Company. The company had Peter Cooper, builder of the locomotive *Tom Thumb,* as its president and Morse as its vice-president.

Regardless of titles, Field was the driving force of the enterprise. He consulted many leading minds, especially Maury, whom he questioned daily for weeks at a time about cable construction and undersea topography.

So began a thirteen-year struggle that cost twelve million dollars and required Field to cross the Atlantic forty times, when such crossings took the better part of a month and were far from comfortable.

The new company first completed Gisborne's telegraph line to Nova Scotia. They had a taste of the troubles in store the first time they tried to lay a cable across the Gulf of St. Lawrence. The cable was coiled in the hold of a sailing bark, which had brought it from England. As a steamer towed the bark across the Gulf, so violent a storm came up that the captain of the bark cut the cable to save his ship. Lesson one: sailing ships are no good for laying cables.

In 1856 Field went to England to look for capital. He met I. K. Brunel, who proudly showed him the huge hull of the *Great Eastern* rising from her ways. "There is the ship to lay the Atlantic cable!" said Brunel, not knowing that this would come to pass.[14]

Field learned that a new discovery would make insulation of the cable easier. This was gutta percha, the dried latex of a Malayan tree, which is like rubber but more resinous.

Later that year, Field and Morse went to England and organized a new company with British capital, the Atlantic Telegraph Company. One director was a keen but shy and modest Scot, Professor William Thomson of Glasgow, who became one of the century's leading physicists. Edward O. W. Whitehouse, a British physician turned tinker, was official electrician.

Field persuaded the British government to subsidize the enterprise and to lend warships to lay the cable. The United States Congress voted to do likewise after beating down bitter opposition. Most of this came from the South, which was generally hostile to scientific research and technological enterprise.

The cable laying was to be done by two screw-propelled steam warships: H.M.S. *Agamemnon* (the first British steam battleship) and the U.S. frigate *Niagara,* one of the world's largest and fastest warships.[15] Each ship had a smaller escort vessel. As the cable was too bulky for any one ship, half was placed in each of the warships. *Niagara* was to lay her half from Ireland to mid-ocean. Then the ends were to be spliced, and *Agamemnon* would lay the second half the rest of the way.

The fleet set out from Valentia Bay in August 1857, with cheers and speeches. They had gone but 335 miles when an engineer applied the brakes too sharply to the paying-out engine, and the cable broke.

Back they went, to order more cable and improve their equipment. As nobody had ever tried to lay cable on such a vast scale, there was much to learn about making cable and machinery for handling it.

In June 1858, they tried again. They had improved the cable-paying machinery and practiced splicing, buoying, and other maneuvers. This time the ships were to proceed to mid-ocean before laying. There the ends were to be spliced, and *Niagara* and *Agamemnon* would head in opposite directions, paying out cable as they went.

A terrific storm scattered the fleet, but they made their rendezvous and began laying the cable towards the two continents. They were but three miles apart when the cable broke. They rejoined, spliced, and tried again; after ten miles the cable broke once more.

After a third fracture, they returned to Ireland, fueled up, and tried again. This time, despite some desperate moments, the cable was laid all the way across. Messages began to flow.

There was an outburst of celebration: hearty in Great Britain, frenzied in the United States. There were banquets, bands, poems, and fireworks, some of which set fire to New York's city hall and burned up its cupola. Field sold the surplus cable to Tiffany's, which cut it into short lengths for sale as souvenirs. He is said to have made one speech as follows: "I am a man of few words; Maury furnished the brains, England gave the money, and I did the work."[16]

After three weeks of operation, the messages petered out and the cable went dead. Scoffers swore that the cable had never been laid at all; that the whole thing was a gigantic hoax.

The reasons for the failure were not far to seek. The cable had been made in a hurry. Between the expeditions of 1857 and 1858, it had been coiled in the open on the docks at Plymouth, and the sun had melted the gutta percha in places. It had received much rough handling, especially when masses of it were thrown about in the hold of the *Agamemnon* during the great storm.

Finally Whitehouse, a fanatically opinionated man who once faked a demonstration to convince the directors that his receiving apparatus was better than Thomson's, had insisted upon testing the cable with a high-voltage testing set of his own design. This test overloaded the conductor and damaged the insulation. The directors, finding Whitehouse impossible to deal with, fired him, but the damage had been done.

Field refused to give up, even though a warehouse fire and a national depression drove his own private company into bankruptcy. For years he shuttled the Atlantic, rounding up capital, persuading the British government to renew its guarantee, and harkening on the scientists, especially Thomson and Wheatstone, in a five-year search for the causes of previous failures. American capital was dried up by the Civil War. At last, in 1864, Field ordered another cable, nearly twice as thick and more than twice as strong as the first.

Meanwhile Brunel's masterpiece, the *Great Eastern*, had been completed: a 693-foot, 22,500-ton monster, five times the size of any previous ship. She had five funnels, six masts, two paddle wheels 58 feet in diameter, and a 36-ton screw, the largest propeller ever made then or since. Larger ships were not built until around forty years later.

While an engineering triumph, the *Great Eastern* was a commercial disaster. Her inordinate cost, and commercial miscalculations by her owners, bankrupted three companies in the first six years after her launching. Now she belonged to a syndicate headed by Daniel Gooch. Gooch made Field a sporting offer: Let Field use the ship as a cable layer. If she failed, there should be no charge for her use; if she succeeded, the syndicate should receive $250,000 in cable stock.

In 1865 the great ship set out with the cable. There were no highjinks. No joyriders were allowed, and the captain kept iron discipline.

The enterprise, which had begun as a joint Anglo-American effort, had become more and more British as the American participants dropped out. The British had furnished most of the money, men, and ships, and all of the cable. Field was the only American on the *Great Eastern*.

The ship had covered two-thirds of her distance when a defective piece of cable passed through the paying-out machinery. To reel the cable back in, it had to be transferred to a hauling winch at the bow. This machine was not so well perfected as that for paying out. As a result, the cable broke. Several efforts to haul it up from the sea bottom by grapnels failed.

But, with success in sight, nothing could stop Field and his associates. Next year they were back with another cable, which they laid clear across without a single mishap. Then they went back to mid-ocean, recovered the broken cable laid the previous year, spliced a new piece to it, and finished laying it also. So now there were two working cables. From that time on, quick communication across the Atlantic has always been available. Now there are nineteen transatlantic cables.

V

COLT

AND OTHER GUNMAKERS

Whatever damage it may do, war certainly stimulates invention. In the nineteenth century, inventions altered war more drastically than it had been changed in the three preceding centuries.

At the beginning of the nineteenth century, in the Napoleonic period, infantry still marched into battle in step and fought by close-order drill, as had the pikemen and musketeers of Gustavus Adolphus. Cavalry in gleaming helmets and cuirasses still charged with lance and sword. For that matter, except for the boom of cannon and the rattle of musketry, the battles of Napoleon were not too different from those of Alexander and Caesar, who would easily have recognized a Napoleonic battle for what it was.

By the First World War, all this was changed out of recognition. On a twentieth-century battlefield, Alexander or Caesar might mistake the battle for some vast, impersonal convulsion of nature.

This immense change came about mainly as a result of inventions in guns and explosives. The percussion cap took the place of loose powder ignited by sparks from flint and steel. Breech-loading rifled guns, large and small, took the place of muzzle-loading smoothbores. Projectiles changed from balls to cylinders, rounded or pointed in front. At the beginning, a well-trained soldier could fire four shots a minute; at the end, he could squirt out more than a thousand in that time.

Americans played a leading part in this revolution in gunnery. Of these changes, several were old ideas which some new improvement made practical.

For instance, breech-loading guns, rifled guns, and repeating guns had all been tried before. Some of the earliest cannon, in the fourteenth century, loaded from the breech. Because of poor metal work, these guns had a habit of blowing up. Even when they did not explode, the breech could not be made gas-tight. Hence, when the piece was fired, flaming gases spurted out the cracks in the breech.

When hand guns appeared, breech-loading was tried with the matchlocks of the sixteenth century and the wheellocks of the seventeenth, but the same difficulties developed. Although breech-loading made it possible to reload lying down, this advantage was nullified by the blast of flame sent into the musketeer's face.

Rifling—that is, cutting helical grooves inside a gun barrel to make the projectile spin—is also old. Tradition names one Kaspar Koller or Köllner of Vienna, in the 1490s, as the inventor. Rifling much increased range and accuracy. In smoothbores, the ball had to fit the barrel loosely to be loaded into it from the muzzle. Hence, on its way out of the barrel, the ball ricocheted from side to side and took off from the muzzle at whatever angle it happened to be bouncing. Rifling kept the bullet moving in a straight line, and the spin gave it the stability in flight of a little gyroscope.

On the other hand, the bullet had to fit the grooves of a rifle tightly, so that the lands (the parts of the barrel between the grooves) should bite into the bullet. Hence muzzle-loading rifles had to be loaded by hammering the bullet down the barrel with ramrod and mallet. It took so long to reload a rifle that, while rifles were favored by hunters, who could expect to get only one shot anyway, they were not used on the battlefield, where soldiers banged away at one another at close range for hours at a time.

The German-American gunsmiths who developed the Pennsylvania rifle speeded up the loading process by using a smaller bullet wrapped in a patch of cloth or thin leather. Nevertheless, rifles did not come into general military use until mid-nineteenth century, when breech-loading also became practical.

Breech-loading was made effective by three inventions. One was the percussion cap, developed in 1807 by a Scot, the Rev. Alexander Forsyth. This sporting parson got tired of having his flintlock fowling pieces miss fire because the priming powder had gotten wet, or had fallen out of the flash pan, or had blown away, or because the flint had become worn, or out of sheer contrariness. Improved by the British gunsmith Manton, the percussion lock soon took the place of the flintlock in all civilized lands. Thousands of old guns were converted to the new system.

The next improvement was the French Captain Claude Minié's rifle bullet: a cylindrical projectile with a rounded point in front and a soft hollow base. When the gun was fired, the base expanded to fill the grooves of the rifle, thus giving the lands the necessary grip to spin the bullet.

Finally, in the 1840s, two Frenchmen, Houiller and Lefaucheux, combined bullet, gunpowder, and percussion cap in a cartridge case of thin copper or brass. Each claimed to be the true inventor and accused the other of stealing his idea. At any rate, with the new system, the explosion of the charge made the cartridge case expand to seal the cracks in the breech. Therefore no gas escaped, even if the breech mechanism was not air-tight. Again, thousands of older guns were altered into breech-loaders. Although some smoothbore flintlocks saw service in the Civil War, percussion rifles had become pretty general by the end of this conflict.

The main trouble with shooting at people with muzzle-loading firearms was that, if you missed your first shot at a man less than a hundred yards away, he could be upon you with a sword or other hand weapon before you had finished reloading. And, with or without a bayonet, a gun is an awkward thing to defend yourself with at close quarters.

Therefore gunsmiths long sought a means of giving the gunner more than one shot at a time. They built double-barreled guns (effective but heavy) and repeating guns (not so heavy but not very effective).

Repeating guns go back to around 1500, in the arquebus era. Some had a lever action, which, with each stroke of the lever, measured out one bullet and one charge of powder from the magazines in the butt and pushed them into the firing chamber. Such guns were very costly, and the complicated loading mechanism soon got out of order.

Other guns had a revolving cylinder with five or more loaded chambers. Between shots, the gunner turned the cylinder by hand. These revolving pistols and rifles leaked gas through the crack between the firing chamber and the barrel, reducing their effectiveness. Worse, any gun with a lot of loose powder in reserve and an exposed firing pan, which sent out a spurt of flame when the gun was fired, menaced the gunner. There was always a chance that the sparks would set off all the powder at once.

Some of these difficulties were overcome in the 1810s by a Bostonian boilermaker named Elisha Haydon Collier. Collier built revolving pistols and rifles, both flintlock and percussion lock, so designed that the danger of multiple explosion was lessened. Failing to get encouragement in the United States, he went to London and built several score of his repeating guns there. But the cost was so high, and hence the sales so few, that Collier gave up the business.

About the same time, many pistols with two, four, or even six barrels came into use, with various devices for firing each barrel in turn. One design, with six revolving barrels, came to be known in the 1830s and 40s as the pepperbox revolver. Some of these worked by double action: that is, one long, hard pull on the trigger raised the hammer, revolved the cylinders, and let the hammer fall on the percussion cap. This gave quick but inaccurate fire.

About the same time, Henry Deringer of Philadelphia made a line of small, short-barreled, large-bore pocket percussion-cap pistols. Guns of this type, under the nickname of "derringer" (with an extra r) became popular for personal offense and defense in the West. In the late nineteenth century, the derringer usually had two barrels, one over the other. Although they have not been made for several decades, some Colt and Remington .41 derringers have continued in use right down to the present.

The first man to make a really effective and commercially profitable repeating gun was Samuel Colt (1814–62). Born in Hartford, Connecticut, Colt was one of the most venturesome, vigorous, and successful figures of the heroic age of American invention.

Colt's father was a trader who tried several businesses with indifferent success. When young Colt had stepmother trouble (or, to be fair, when the second Mrs. Colt had stepson trouble) the elder Colt packed young Sam off to serve a farmer as apprentice for a year. Colt did well enough as a chore boy but also began a lifetime of fooling with guns and explosives.

Next year, Colt's father put him to work in a textile factory, which he had just established in Ware, Massachusetts. Young Colt, having read about Fulton's submarine mines, set off one of his own in a local pond, drenching the onlookers with muddy water.

Next, Colt's father sent the boy to Amherst Academy. This lasted until one of Colt's explosions burned some school property. The faculty met to consider disciplining the youth. Without awaiting the verdict, Sam Colt came home.

Not knowing what else to do with his son, Christopher Colt sent Sam to sea as apprentice seaman on the brig *Corlo*, Boston to Calcutta. On the voyage, Colt saw a Collier revolver. Conceiving that he could accomplish the same end by a simpler mechanism, he whittled out of wood the parts for a revolving pistol. He got the idea by watching the ship's wheel. This wheel had a clutch, which stopped its rotation in certain positions.

Back home, Colt persuaded his father to finance the building of a couple of samples of his revolver. But the father hired an incompetent mechanic, so that the samples failed when tested.

Meanwhile Sam worked some more in his father's establishment and learned about nitrous oxide from the head of the bleaching department. Presently, to obtain money for more sample guns, he set out as a wandering entertainer, "Dr. Coult," demonstrating the wonders of laughing gas. To avoid ruffling the clergy, who disapproved of all worldly entertainment, Colt advertised his show as "educational." At seventeen, Sam Colt was already a big, powerful, impressive-looking young fellow with a generous portion of Barnum in his makeup.

In the course of his travels, Colt was caught on a Mississippi River steamer during a cholera scare. The passengers insisted that "Dr. Coult" treat them, despite Colt's protests that he was not a doctor of that kind at all. A combination of nitrous oxide, laxatives, and calisthenics banished the symptoms of cholera, but then Colt found himself embarrassed by the reputation of a miracle worker.

In time Colt scraped up enough money to hire a good mechanic, although the mechanic stopped work whenever Colt stopped paying him. In his efforts to keep the work going, Colt even tried smuggling but was caught and lost heavily on the venture.

A trip to London in 1835 procured him British patents on his revolver; his American patents followed next year. Then he organized the Paterson Arms Manufacturing Company to make revolvers in Paterson, New Jersey. Colt himself was to travel about selling these guns. This model, the Paterson Colt, was a .34-caliber, six-shot, single-action, percussion-lock revolver with no trigger guard and a folding trigger that snapped out when the hammer was cocked.

The officers of the company, however, expected Colt to sell enough revolvers at the start and collect enough money from the sales to enable him to live on his commissions alone. They did not wish to lay out additional funds to enable Colt to eat while he campaigned for orders. Colt, on the other hand, envisaged a big, costly promotional campaign, with advertising and publicity, to launch the gun before any were sold.

Colt also wanted to produce the gun by advanced, mechanized methods of manufacture. He wrote his father:

> The first workman would receive two or three of the most important parts, and would affix these together and pass them on to the next who would do the same, and so on until the complete arm is put together. It would then be inspected and given the finishing touches by experts and each arm would be exactly alike and all of its parts would be the same. The workmen, by constant practice in a single operation would become highly skilled and at the same time very quick and expert at their particular task, so you have better guns and more of them for less money than if you hire men and have each one make the entire arm . . .[1]

Thus Colt envisaged not only interchangeable parts, as pioneered by Eli Whitney, but also assembly-line manufacture. However, such a scheme would have required a lot of money for automatic machine tools. This the officers of the company were unwilling to spend. They wished to make and sell some guns—any kind would do—quickly, so that they could start paying dividends. In vain Colt protested that revolvers made by handicraft methods would be too expensive.

Between squabbles with his backers, Colt lobbied in Washington, striving to soften the skepticism of Congressmen with the help of a keg of Madeira. The Army and Navy tested his revolvers; the guns worked fine, but hidebound testing boards found them too complicated for military use. He did sell fifty revolving rifles to the Army in Florida for use against the wily Seminoles, together with a few pistols to individual officers.

Colt also sold a few revolvers to the Texas Rangers for their war with Mexico. This was the Walker Colt, designed after a conference with the Texan purchasing agent, Captain Sam Walker. Despite these sales, the depression of 1837 and the directors' policies drove the company into bankruptcy in 1843.

Colt had wisely insisted upon a clause in his contract providing that, if the company stopped making revolvers, his patents should revert to him. Although the secretary of the corporation tried to steal these patents, Colt got them back by fast and vigorous legal action.

Before the company went broke, Colt had begun working on a proposal to protect American harbors by "submarine batteries"—that is, mines exploded under water by electrical impulses. Colt became friendly with Samuel F. B. Morse, also seeking money from the government for his telegraph. The two traded useful technical hints and helped each other's campaigns by praising each other's inventions.

Over several years, Colt succeeded in prying about a hundred thousand dollars out of Congress for experiments, despite the opposition of John Quincy Adams. Representative and ex-President Adams, despite his keen appreciation of science, deemed the submarine mine "un-Christian." Colt blew up several small vessels in demonstrations. But the government dallied and then withdrew support, just when Colt had his system perfected.

By that time, the resourceful Colt had another iron in the fire. He manufactured waterproof telegraphic cable, organized a telegraph company, and installed telegraph lines under royalty contracts with Morse. In 1843 he laid lines from New York City to Coney Island and to Fire Island Light.

Colt might have become a telegraph magnate but for the Mexican War. Some Texans still carried Colts. At the start of the war, the Mexicans ambushed an American detachment. Only the commanding officer, a Captain Thornton, escaped by shooting his way out with revolvers. General Zachary Taylor ordered Colt's old acquaintance Captain Walker to Washington to buy Colts. Walker caught up with Colt in New York, saying:

"How soon can you get me a thousand of your pistols?"

"As soon as I can build a shop and make them," replied Colt.[2]

Walker wanted the pistols much sooner than that. It was too bad, said Colt, that the government had not made the request a year earlier, when the machinery of the Paterson Company had been sold. They made the rounds of the gunshops of New York, but no revolver could they find for a model. So Colt designed a new revolver and procured the patterns. He contracted to have the first lot made by the Whitney Arms Company, now run by Eli Whitney, Jr., the son of the cotton-gin inventor.

Then Colt organized Colt's Patent Firearms Company in Hartford, rented a building for his factory, and, with the help of his able manager, Elisha K. Root, put his assembly-line ideas into practice.

Mass production, according to the ideas of Whitney and Colt, spread swiftly in America. It was first brought forcibly to the attention of Europeans (who had forgotten the pioneering work of Brunel and Bramah) in 1851, when the Crystal Palace Exposition was held in London. British newspapers waxed sarcastic about the American exhibits, which included no art, only things like cotton, tobacco, rubber shoes, McCormick's reaper, and Colt's revolvers. But the firearms aroused so much interest that the British government sent a commission to America to study the "American system" of manufacture with interchangeable parts.

Colt quickly outgrew his first factory and built another. He ruled his growing industrial empire firmly but with advanced ideas of working hours and conditions. He trotted the globe, drummed up orders from Russia, Turkey, and other foreign governments, became rich, built an ornate mansion, and finally found time to marry his fiancée of several years' standing.

His married life, though happy, was short. In his forties a rheumatic affliction first crippled and then killed him, in the midst of intense production of revolvers for the Civil War. Root became president of the company, which still thrives.

During the cowboy era of 1860–1900, Colt revolvers, especially the 1873 single-action .45 Army model (also called the Frontier model, the Peacemaker, and so forth) became almost standard equipment for cowhands. In more recent decades this gun has spewed blanks on countless motion-picture and television screens, acquiring its own mythos.

Actually, most cowboys were poor shots, because they could not afford enough cartridges to keep in practice. Moreover, the Colt ceased to be accurate after its owner had used it for such cowhandy chores as driving nails and pounding coffee beans to powder—although across a poker table this made little difference. A tale is told of two mortal enemies who galloped into town, dismounted, stalked towards each other in the best cinematic tradition, opened fire, missed with all twelve shots, and rode away again.

In real life such scenes were not common, because a Westerner who really wanted to kill a man was likely to choose the more practical method of ambushing him and shooting him in the back with a rifle. Nor did many Western gunfighters engage in such dramatics as shooting from the hip and fanning the hammer. At least, men who used their guns thus were not around for long. Men who took their shooting seriously obeyed the rule that, if you want to hit a target, you have to aim at it.

Colt's revolving rifles, though used in some mid-century wars, never attained the popularity of his pistols. For one thing, the gas-leakage problem was more serious in rifles, wherein long-range accuracy was important, than in pistols.

The coming of the metallic cartridge brought out a rash of designs for repeating rifles. In 1849, Walter Hunt (who also invented one of the first sewing machines) made a lever-action rifle with a tubular magazine beneath the barrel for the Smith &

Wesson Company of Springfield, Massachusetts. Its mechanism was too complicated and the propellant in its charges (pure fulminate) too weak and erratic for success. In 1850, Lewis Jennings simplified and improved the Hunt rifle. The next year Horace Smith of Smith & Wesson improved it further. These guns were sold in the 1850s as "Volcanic" rifles. The ejecting lever, as in modern lever-action rifles, did double duty as the trigger guard.

In the Civil War, the Union sought repeating rifles. Of the many designs submitted, two proved the most useful. One was an improvement on the Volcanic rifles designed by B. Tyler Henry, the engineer and manager of Oliver Winchester's arms firm in New Haven, which had bought up Eli Whitney's old arms company. This company, after several changes of name, became today's Winchester Repeating Arms Company. It turned out about 10,000 Henry rifles for the Union. Later improvements on Henry's design were called Winchesters.

Even more successful was Christopher Miner Spencer, who had been a mechanic from the age of fourteen. A successful inventor by 1860, he got a patent on a lever-action repeater, organized the Spencer Repeating Rifle Company, and made about 200,000 rifles for Federal and state forces. The technologically backward Confederates, who had to depend almost entirely on single-shot weapons, complained that with these new guns a Yankee could "load up in the morning and shoot all day."

After the war, Spencer found his company losing money. He sold out to Winchester and, in 1869, went into business with Charles E. Billings to make drop forgings. He advanced this art and invented a screw-making machine with an automatic turret lathe. This was a great step forward in the art of automatic machine tools. But Spencer's patent attorney did not understand the inventions and failed to cover the most important feature, the adjustable cams.

The restless Spencer worked as superintendent of another company, then quit to manufacture a repeating shotgun he had invented. When this company failed, he organized the Spencer Automatic Machine Screw Company at Windsor, Connecticut. He divided his time for the rest of his busy life between this company and his directorship of Billings and Spencer, almost down to his death at eighty-nine in 1922.

For several decades, the lever action of the Hunt-Spencer-

Henry type was the world's standard repeating-rifle mechanism, until the German Mannlicher-Mauser bolt action appeared in the 1880s. All the larger nonautomatic repeating rifles in the world today use one system or the other.

Now that they had repeating guns, men were still not satisfied; they wanted guns to squirt bullets like water from a hose. Sixteenth-century attempts at solving this problem were called ribaulds or organ guns. These were carts on which dozens of gun barrels were mounted, all pointing in the same direction and so arranged that they could be fired all at once or in quick succession. Once fired, they could not be reloaded in time to take any further part in the battle.

In 1718, an Englishman named James Puckle got a patent for a repeating cannon on the revolver principle. The cylinder, turned by a crank, held six to nine charges, and the inventor provided cylinders of alternative design to shoot "round balls for Christians, square balls for Turks." Other inventions of rapid-fire guns followed, but none worked well enough to be taken seriously. The metallic cartridge had to be invented first.

The man who first made a practical machine gun was Richard Jordan Gatling (1818–1903). The son of a planter and inventor of North Carolina, Gatling taught school, kept a country store, and invented a screw propeller independently of Ericsson. Then he found his métier as an inventor and manufacturer of agricultural machinery. In 1844 he began making his rice-sowing machine and his wheat drill in St. Louis.

In the winter of 1845, Gatling came down with smallpox on a river steamer caught in the ice on the Ohio. For two weeks he was stuck there without medical care. Recovering, he enrolled at the Medical College of Ohio, in Cincinnati, so as to be able to care for himself and his family in emergencies. Thereafter he was called "Doctor," although he never practiced.

The Civil War found Gatling prospering, with factories in several Midwestern cities and several more inventions to his credit. Like others, Gatling thought that war could be made less destructive by the invention of more destructive weapons, so that fewer men could wreak as much havoc as before.

Out of his musings came, in 1862, a gun like a cannon-sized pepperbox. Ten barrels were rotated about a central axis by turning a crank. Gatling mounted a hopper over the breech. As each barrel passed under the hopper, at the top of its travel, a cartridge fell into its chamber. As the same barrel reached the bottom of its orbit, it was fired, and the empty cartridge case fell out. Thus the gun would go on shooting as long as the gunners kept the hopper filled. A strong gunner could crank out as many as 1200 shots a minute.

Gatling's first experimental guns perished in a fire. His second lot failed to arouse the Ordnance Department, but General Benjamin F. Butler (the one accused of stealing the silver spoons of the ladies of New Orleans) bought a dozen for his James River campaign, in which they fired a few blasts at the rebs. Larger orders followed, but the war was over before the guns could be completed.

Gatling then sold his patents to the Colt company and went back to farm machinery. In his eighties he invented a motor-driven plow and would have put it into production had not death intervened.

The Gatling gun was improved, produced in many sizes and models, and took part in several of the wars of the late nineteenth century. Long after the Gatlings had become obsolete and been retired to courthouse lawns, the American underworld kept the inventor's name alive by calling pistols "gats."

Following Gatling's gun came a number of machine guns fired by turning a crank or by pushing a lever back and forth. But the force required to turn the crank or push the lever made the gun wobble and shoot inaccurately. Moreover, an excited gunner, by pushing too hard, might jam the gun. For the next step in the invention of rapid-fire guns, we must turn to another family of Yankee arms makers.

The Yankee of tradition is supposed to be ingenious. He is considered shrewd and enterprising. He is expected to be an extreme individualist. Seldom have these qualities been shown so well as by the brothers Maxim, inventors of smokeless powder and much besides.

Their father, Isaac Maxim, settled in backwoods Maine when bears still outnumbered settlers. He made a scanty living as a farmer, wood turner, and millwright, and toyed with ideas for an automatic gun and a flying machine. The elder brother, Hiram Stevens Maxim, was born in 1840.

After a sketchy education, Hiram Stevens Maxim worked as a painter and wood turner in Canada and upstate New York, where he became known for beating up the local bullies. He worked as a mechanic in his uncle's engineering works in Massachusetts until a spiritualist medium told the uncle that Hiram was plotting against him.

In Boston he held jobs with several manufacturers, becoming skilled as a draftsman and engineer. He invented an automatic repeating mousetrap, a hair-curling iron, and the automatic sprinkler system. Although he got a patent on the last of these, it profited him not, because the device did not come into use until after the patent had died.

While working for the Novelty Iron Works and Shipbuilding Company in New York City, Maxim invented gas engines and locomotive headlights. He assigned the patents on these to the new Maxim Gas Engine Company and set up a Maxim-Weston Company in Great Britain to exploit his inventions in that land, which was then far ahead of the United States in industrialization.

In 1878, Hiram Stevens Maxim became chief engineer of the United States Electric Company, an ambitious rival of Edison in the electrical field. Maxim developed a method of flashing electric light filaments in a hydrocarbon atmosphere, to lengthen their lives by depositing carbon in the thin spots. He also devised an improved process for making phosphorus pentoxide.

During the 1870s, Maxim lived with his wife and children in the suburbs of New York. Few sons had less conventional fathers than Hiram's son, Hiram Percy Maxim. For instance, the front yard of the first house in Brooklyn had an iron fence with a heavy iron gate. To save the time needed to open and close the gate, Maxim regularly vaulted over it—top hat, full beard, frock coat, and all.

Both Maxim brothers were men of gorillalike strength. When a ruffian demanded money of Hiram Stevens Maxim one evening, the inventor tossed the man over a fence into an excavation and walked calmly on.

They were both, also, notably absent-minded. Hiram Stevens Maxim became so exasperated at his constant loss of gloves, papers, and other possessions that he had stickers printed, reading:

THIS WAS LOST BY A DAMNED FOOL NAMED
HIRAM STEVENS MAXIM
WHO LIVES AT 325 UNION STREET, BROOKLYN.
A SUITABLE REWARD WILL BE PAID FOR
ITS RETURN

A tireless practical joker, Hiram Stevens Maxim once told his son that the sickly little peach tree in the Maxim yard would bear if a dead cat were buried under it. When the boy obtained a dead cat, his father solemnly helped him inter it. When young Percy returned from Sunday school, he found a whole basketful of peaches on the tree, impaled on twigs.

In 1881, Hiram Stevens Maxim went to Paris to show the U. S. Electric Lighting Company's equipment at an exhibition. There Maxim conceived an idea for an automatic gun. Sketches and models followed.

Maxim spent most of the next few years in England, trying to reorganize the Maxim-Weston Company, which was being looted by its British officials. He set up his own laboratory. When the gun was reduced to practice, it had a single barrel, unlike most of the crank-operated machine guns of the time. The recoil of each shot ejected the spent cartridge and moved the next one into the chamber. The gun fired at adjustable speeds up to 666 shots a minute.

Maxim offered the gun to the United States, but the War and Navy Departments rejected it as a mere impractical curiosity. Outraged, Maxim then proffered his gun to the more receptive British. He organized the Maxim Gun Company and traveled about Europe, showing off his gun and keenly relishing the company of kings and ministers. Because of his abstemious habits, the Turks called him "the State of Maine Yankee with no civilized vice."

Later Maxim invented another gun in which the bolt was worked by the pressure of the expanding gas, bled off from the barrel near the muzzle and led back to the breech through another tube. This discovery occurred at about the same time to Maxim, to the Briton Paulson, and to the Spaniard Orbea, in the 1880s. All the automatic pistols, machine guns, and other automatic guns in the world today use one of these two systems: recoil loading or gas-pressure loading.

While Maxim was demonstrating his gun in Austria, the

minister of war asked him to solve the problem of recoil in cannon. Field guns had always leaped back like startled horses when fired, sometimes squashing an unwary gunner. Maxim then invented the hydraulic recoil cylinder, which soon became universal despite the objection of a British officer that "these additions make the gun very ugly."[3]

Yet Maxim was no mere "merchant of death." In later years he waxed indignant over the fact that the world had heaped a fortune upon him for his killing machines but scorned an invention—a bronchial inhaler—that he made to help people.

In 1894, Hiram Stevens Maxim went into aeronautics. He built a steam-driven biplane, the *Flier*, with a 105-foot wingspread, to run on steel rails nine feet apart and 1800 feet long. After the *Flier* had lifted off the rails twice, Maxim, knowing that the machine lacked means to guide it safely in the air, provided a pair of wooden rails to hold it down. He only wanted to learn whether the engines of the time provided the power needed for take-off.

On its last trial, the *Flier* not only left its supporting rails; it also developed so much lift that it broke one of the wooden hold-down rails and soared aloft with the alarmed inventor dangling below it. Before the machine could fly away altogether, the broken rail fouled one of the two propellers, and the flying machine crash-landed. This was one of the experimental steps that led through Langley's aerodromes to the Wrights' success.

In 1896, Maxim merged his armaments firm with Vickers Sons. In 1898, the Maxim gun showed its revolutionary effect on warfare. The warlike Sudanese, under a leader called the Mahdi, had revolted against the misrule of the khedives of Egypt. The British, having puppetized the Egyptian government, set out to conquer the Sudan from the Mahdi's successor in order to reannex it to Egypt.

On August 24, a British-Egyptian army of 25,000 set out for Omdurman, across the Nile from Khartum. Forty thousand screaming Sudanîn charged fiercely upon the British. As the Maxim guns chattered, the onslaughts melted away, leaving the plain littered with thousands of black, white-robed bodies.

The machine gun also profoundly influenced world history. It caused the trench-warfare stalemate on the Western front in World War I. The combination of machine guns and barbed wire so vastly increased the power of the defensive that attackers would lose hundreds of thousands of men in a few weeks to gain a few square miles of shell-churned mud. The horror of that memory affected the foreign policies of the British and French governments between the two World Wars. It partly accounts for the craven and addle-witted helplessness with which these governments watched the rise of the Nazi menace in the 1930s.

In 1900, meaning to live the rest of his life in Britain, Hiram Stevens Maxim took out British citizenship. Next year, Queen Victoria knighted him. He retired in 1911 and died in 1916.

And now for the other Maxim brother. Born in 1853, and christened Isaac, he so disliked the name that as an adult he called himself Hudson Maxim.

After an education as scanty as his older brother's, Hudson Maxim became a schoolteacher. The school agent explained that, as Maxim's predecessor had been thrown through the schoolhouse window by his pupils, Maxim's first task would be to thrash the biggest boy in the school. At the first recess, Maxim challenged the young lout to a wrestle and threw him. After that he had no trouble.

Later, Hudson Maxim went into partnership with a friend and sold a cure-all liniment while his partner sold ink and lectured on the pseudo-science of phrenology. They built up a business in Massachusetts, dealing in stationery, penmanship books, and printing.

When the typewriter and the fountain pen spoiled this business, Hudson Maxim received a letter from his brother Hiram, asking him to come to England to work for the Maxim Gun Company. So Hudson Maxim went to work for his brother, married an English girl, and traveled between Great Britain and the United States representing the Maxim Gun Company. A self-made Jack-of-all-trades like his brother, he got a job in explosives engineering. Thereupon Hiram Stevens Maxim demanded:

"You must quit inventing anything whatever relating to naval and military matters, and have nothing to do with war materials, or you must get out of this house and I'll make things hot for you."[4]

Hudson, as peppery a character as Hiram, defied his brother. Although this quarrel was patched up, the two broke for good in 1898 and never spoke to each other again. Both were too aggressive and self-willed to work together. And, despite his charm and his boyish japes and enthusiasms, Hiram Stevens Maxim was bitterly jealous of competitors for fame and fortune.

One source of dispute was the invention of smokeless powder and the perforated grain. Hiram Stevens Maxim claimed to have made both inventions in 1885–86, but Hudson claimed them also, and historians side with Hudson.

From the Chinese invention of gunpowder about 1200 to the mid-1800s, the only explosive was gunpowder, made of sulfur, charcoal, and saltpetre, finely ground and carefully mixed. The only real improvement was the fifteenth-century discovery of "corning." This meant making the powder into paste with wine, drying it into cakes, and breaking the cakes into lumps called "grains." The grains could be sorted according to size, to control the speed of the explosion.

In 1845, the German chemist Schönbein soaked strands of cotton in a mixture of nitric and sulfuric acids. He put the strands on the stove to dry and went to dinner. While he was gone, his laboratory blew up. Thus, unexpectedly, he had discovered cellulose nitrate or guncotton.

This was the first of a series of explosives made by *nitrating* various substances—that is, adding to each molecule a group of atoms of oxygen and nitrogen by treatment with nitric acid. The family includes nitroglycerine, blasting gelatine, and trinitrotoluol or TNT.

At first, these nitrogen explosives could not be used as propellants in guns. When gunpowder explodes, it burns and gives the projectile a gradual push out the barrel. In the nitrogen or high explosives, on the other hand, all the molecules in the charge break down almost simultaneously. The explosion releases so much energy so quickly that the projectile has no time to leave the gun, which consequently bursts.

In the 1880s, several chemists experimented with means for slowing down the explosion of high explosives. The Maxims (among others) succeeded with adulterants like sawdust and petroleum jelly. The new explosive was quickly adopted by all modern armies because it gives off much less smoke than conventional gunpowder and fouls the barrels of guns less with unburned residue.

The perforated grain is a piece of smokeless "powder" (actually on amberlike solid) in the shape of a cylinder with seven holes drilled lengthwise in it. While the size of the grain varies, a typical artillery grain is about the size of a finger-joint. The shape controls the surface exposed to the air during burning and, hence, the rate of burning. As the outer surface decreases in area, the inner surfaces around the holes increase, so that the total area stays about the same. Thus the gas pressure can be controlled during the projectile's flight along the barrel.

In 1891, after Hudson Maxim finally broke with his brother, he went to work for the Columbia River Manufacturing Company, which made explosives at Squankum, New Jersey. When this company failed two years later, Hudson Maxim organized the Maxim Powder Company and took over the Squankum plant. He took out many explosives patents, to which his brother stubbornly refused to buy British rights.

In one experiment, Hudson Maxim blew off his left hand. Another explosion blew his assistant to pieces while Maxim was out of the laboratory.

In 1897, Hudson Maxim sold his company to the E. I. du Pont de Nemours Company, for which he worked as a consulting engineer. He invented maximite, an explosive of the picric acid class for high-explosive shells, and sold the rights to the U. S. Government.

In 1901, Hudson Maxim won a competition at Sandy Hook with a 12-inch armor-piercing shell against the Gathman shell. The latter was an 18-inch projectile carrying 500 pounds of guncotton, designed to explode on impact, outside the ship's armor. Gathman's shell did little damage; Maxim's went through the armor plate, exploded on the way, and blew the plate to bits.

During the First World War, Hudson Maxim served as chairman of the Committee on Ordnance and Explosives of the Naval Consulting Board. During his last years, until his death in 1927, he lived with baronial gusto in a castle at Lake Hopatcong, New Jersey. He was once persuaded to appear as King Neptune in the Atlantic City beauty pageant. Once was enough, as he hated crowds and smells.

When Hiram Stevens Maxim removed to England to live, he left his wife and children in New York. In Britain he took up with his secretary, so that his wife divorced him; and he in due course married the secretary. One member of his abandoned family, his son Hiram Percy Maxim, also became a distinguished engineer.

Despite the feud between his father and his uncle, Percy Maxim kept on good terms with both. He helped to make the automobile practical in the early 1900s and later went into ordnance work. In 1908 he invented his silencer, which found two diverse applications. One was as a silencer for rifles; the other was as a muffler for automobile exhausts. He inherited the family's keen sense of humor and before his death in 1936 wrote two hilarious books of reminiscence, *Horseless Carriage Days* and *A Genius in the Family*, the latter a memoir of his uninhibited father.

VI

McCORMICK

AND FARM MACHINERY

The middle decades of the nineteenth century saw the working out, in detail, of some of the principles that have ruled American patent law ever since. For instance, where does one draw the line between what is a patentable invention and what is not? Section 101 of the patent law states:

> Whoever invents or discovers any new and useful process, machine, manufacture, or composition of matter, or any new and useful improvement thereof, may obtain a patent therefor, subject to the conditions and requirements of this title.[1]

Before 1953 the wording was: "Any person who has invented or discovered any new and useful art, machine, manufacture, or composition of matter . . ." As the courts had long since decided that "art" meant "process," the Patent Codification Act of 1952 changed the wording to make the meaning plainer.

Almost every word of Section 101 and its predecessors has been fought over in court to determine its exact meaning. For, no matter how careful legislators are in their use of words, the variety of things and events is so vast that no word or phrase can be applied forever without interpretation.

For instance, is a newly discovered law of nature patentable?

That question was settled by the tragic case of Morton's discovery of anesthesia. As with most laws, cases arise in which the application of the patent law seems to have an unjust result. Morton's use of ether as an anesthetic is a case in point.

The patent in question, No. 4848 to Morton and Jackson, was taken out on November 12, 1846, by William T. G. Morton (1819–68), an active-minded young dentist practicing in Boston. Morton had invented an improved dental plate. But, to install this plate, any surviving teeth had to be pulled out. To make this procedure painless, Morton experimented with anesthetics.

For thousands of years, men had sought methods of killing pain. These included alcohol, narcotics, and even hypnotism. None had proved satisfactory. The anesthetic properties of chloroform and ether had been noted; and in 1842 a backwoods physician in Georgia, Crawford W. Long, removed a small tumor from the neck of a patient under the influence of ether. Long performed several other minor operations under ether; but, being an easygoing and retiring man, he did not try very hard to publicize his painless operations.

Morton, just out of the nation's first dental school, the Baltimore College of Dental Surgery, was in partnership with Dr. Horace Wells. Wells, also interested in anesthesia, tried nitrous oxide, but a public demonstration with it failed. Then a private patient died under its effects. The horrified Wells gave up dentistry and tried various enterprises such as touring with a troupe of singing canaries.

Morton, however, persisted in his search for a safe pain-killer, using ether. Thinking that he saw a fortune in the idea, he called upon another Bostonian, Charles Thomas Jackson. This Jackson was a geologist by profession and a dabbler in other sciences. Although a man of ability, he thought himself much greater than he was and caused trouble all his life by trying to make others think so as well. He claimed to be the true inventor of Morse's electric telegraph and Schönbein's guncotton.

When he visited Jackson, Morton cautiously asked questions and borrowed apparatus without revealing his discovery. Having proved that ether worked in dental operations, he made arrangements with Dr. John C. Warren of the Massachusetts General Hospital for a demonstration of ether. On October 16, 1846, Warren publicly removed a facial tumor from a patient under

Morton's anesthesia and said to the assembled physicians: "Gentlemen, this is no humbug."

Hearing of this, Jackson called on Morton to demand $500 for his advice. Morton did not have the money. However, he was not sorry to get Jackson into the enterprise, as Jackson had an established scientific reputation. They agreed that the patent should be taken out in both their names and that Morton should pay Jackson ten per cent of the earnings of the invention.

The use of ether spread rapidly, despite some delay while a dispute as to whether the Bible allowed anesthesia was ironed out in Scotland. The quotation that decided the case in favor of anesthesia was Genesis ii 21: "And the Lord God caused a deep sleep to fall upon Adam . . ."

Many physicians called Morton unethical for trying to make a fortune out of his discovery instead of giving it free to the world. In his own profession of dentistry, however, Morton was not being any more unethical than other dentists of his time.

The Morton-Jackson patent was granted with the following claim:

What we claim as our invention is the hereinbefore described means by which we are enabled to effect the above highly important improvement in surgical operations, viz: By combining these with the application of ether, or the vapor thereof, substantially as described.

Morton, however, had little success in collecting royalties on his patent, as he had no way of knowing when some physician in a distant place pressed a spongeful of ether to his patient's nose. Morton therefore asked the United States Government for a grant of money instead. He might have obtained it, too, had not the paranoid Jackson popped up to claim credit for the whole discovery and to call Morton a "quack doctor" of "infamous character."

Morton and Jackson fought each other like crabs in a bucket for the rest of their lives. Morton got some medals, an honorary degree, and a little money. But, when $50,000 was raised for him in England, Jackson and his partisans raised such an uproar that the money was all returned to the donors.

In addition, Wells, hearing of Morton's fame, decided that he, too, was the sole and original inventor. He made emotional speeches in which he accused Morton of stealing his idea until at last he killed himself in a fit of insanity. His widow added her claim to the confusion, and Crawford Long also added his.

To crown Morton's misfortunes, when he sued one infringer, the court found his patent invalid on the ground that it claimed a monopoly on a law of nature. The decision (Morton v. N. Y. Eye Infirmary) said:

A bare principle, called by one a law of nature, is not patentable. The discovery may be brilliant and useful and yet not patentable. Every invention may in a certain sense, embrace more or less discovery, for it must always include something that is new; but it by no means follows that every discovery is an invention. It may be the *soul* of an invention, but it can not be the subject of the exclusive control of the patentee, or of the patent law until it inhabits a *body* any more than a disembodied spirit can be subjected to the control of human laws.[2]

Some of Morton's misfortunes were due to the fact that he, too, showed a trace of paranoid characteristics. Although he had been doing well as a dentist and maker of dentures when struck by his great idea, he gave up his practice then and never worked for his living again. He spent the rest of his life campaigning for the fortune that he thought the world owed him. When he and his family were reduced to starvation, his admirers passed the hat for money to keep Morton going a while longer.

After serving as a volunteer anesthetist in the Union Army in the Civil War, Morton, poor and worn out, retired to a farm. Pursuing his feud to the end, in 1868 he died of apoplexy, brought on by reading an article upholding Jackson, and left his family destitute.

Jackson's victory did him no good either. He went violently mad and spent his last seven years in an asylum.

The principle that patents shall not be granted on laws of nature has held good from that day to this. It is, however, a distinction easier to state than to apply. After all, if it be a law of nature that if you make a patient breathe ether you can cut him up without pain, it is also a law of nature that if you assemble a certain combination of wires and electrical cells you can send telegraphic messages.

Some scientists feel that, as their discoveries often do quite as much for human welfare as the devices of inventors, they should be allowed to profit from them also. One country, Portugal, does protect the interests of scientists in this manner by allowing patents on scientific discoveries.

Other scientists join Franklin and Henry in asserting that scientists should be above vulgar material rewards. Perhaps the answer to that argument was given long ago by the Greek philosopher Protagoras. Hearing that his colleague Socrates was condemning his fellow-philosophers because they lectured for money, Protagoras said that he knew of no reason why philosophers were not as much entitled to eat as other people.

The patent law allows an inventor to patent an *improvement* on a process, machine, manufacture (that is, a manufactured object), or composition of matter. The government, when it grants the patent, sends the inventor a document called a letters patent, bedight with ribbons and seals. The granting clause of a letters patent reads:

"Now, therefore, these letters patent are to grant . . . the right to exclude others from making, using or selling the said invention throughout the United States."

Before the revision of the law in 1952, this granting clause said that the patent granted, instead: "the exclusive right to make, use and vend the said invention." If taken literally, this phrase led to anomalies. The inventor already has the right to make, use, and sell his invention, patent or no patent—unless his invention is already dominated by a prior patent owned by another person. In the latter case, the later inventor does not have the right to make, use, or sell the invention without the prior patent owner's permission. Therefore the later inventor's patent cannot really give him the right to make, use, or sell anything, regardless of what it says.

A case that helped to give the granting clause a reasonable interpretation was that of Howe v. Singer. Elias Howe, Jr., (1819–67) was a young mechanic working for a maker of precision instruments in Boston. In the 1840s he conceived the idea of a sewing machine. He solved a problem that had driven inventors nearly mad for years, that of imitating the movement of the human hand in sewing.

Howe did this by combining the action of two needles on opposite sides of the fabric. Moreover, the needles had holes in their points instead of in their butts, as needles had always had since cave men made them of bone in the Old Stone Age.

In 1846, Howe took out Patent No. 4750 for an "Improvement in Sewing Machines." For years, however, he had little success with his invention. During a poverty-stricken sojourn in England, he sold his British rights for £250.

When Howe got back from England in 1849, he found that several manufacturers had started to make sewing machines more or less like his. He sued the most aggressive and successful of these, Isaac Merrit Singer, who had made important improvements in Howe's original design.

Singer's lawyer tried to show that Howe's design had been anticipated by other inventors. But in 1854 Judge Sprague decided that these previous efforts were abandoned experiments and so had no effect on the legal status of later inventions.

An abandoned *invention*, on the other hand, becomes public property and cannot later be patented by somebody else. There is no easy rule for drawing the line between the two. If the rules had been applied to steamboats, the boats of Jouffroy, Rumsey, and Symington might be deemed abandoned experiments, but that of Fitch would be an abandoned invention which Fulton could not have later claimed.

However, understanding of patents had come a long way since the days of Fulton and Fitch. Despite what Singer's patent said about granting him the exclusive right to make, use, and vend the improvements described therein, it was evident that he could not make, use, or sell these improvements without violating Howe's previous exclusive rights. Likewise, Howe's patent gave Howe the exclusive right to exploit his original basic invention but said nothing about his right to do likewise with Singer's improvements, based though they were on Howe's invention.

Under the final interpretation of the law, therefore, each had the right to prevent others from making, using, or selling the particular invention or improvement claimed in his patent. Howe could stop Singer from making any sewing machines on Howe's principle, dominated by Howe's basic patent. Singer could likewise stop Howe from exploiting Singer's improvements.

Instead of fighting it out to the death, Singer and Howe agreed on a contract, under which Singer paid Howe license fees for making sewing machines. The other manufacturers fell into line also when Howe offered them similar contracts. Howe was more interested in making a good living from his invention than in megalomaniac dreams of being the world's sewing-machine emperor. And so, albeit no great businessman, he managed to die rich.

Again, is it patentable invention to take two old things and combine them? That depends. If the old parts perform a joint function, their union may be a patentable combination. But, if each continues only to do what it had done before, the union is an aggregation and unpatentable.

For instance, in 1858, Lipman took out Patent No. 19,783 on an article of which millions have been sold since: a pencil with an eraser mounted on one end. The claim of the Lipman patent reads:

> But I *claim* the combination of the lead and India-rubber, or other erasing substance, in the holder of a drawing pencil, the whole being constructed and arranged substantially as set forth.

Reckendorfer in 1862 took out an improvement patent on this same invention. But when Reckendorfer, who owned both patents, sued Faber for infringement (Reckendorfer v. Faber) the Supreme Court declared both patents invalid for lack of invention. There was, said the court, no joint function performed by the pencil and the eraser; each performed the same function as before. The pencil was still a writing instrument and the eraser was still an eraser. Therefore the pencil and its eraser formed an unpatentable aggregation:

> A handle in common, a joint handle, does not create a new or combined operation. . . . It may be more convenient to turn over the different ends of the same stick than to lay down one stick and take up another. This, however, is not invention within the patent law, as the authorities cited fully show.[8]

This decision has been criticized as overstrict in its definition of "joint function." The great commercial success of the article, say the court's critics, implies that inventive genius had been required to conceive it. The decision was not unanimous; three justices dissented. The case may be deemed a borderline case, with good arguments on both sides.

Another case that went into the making of modern patent law was a case involving Cyrus Hall McCormick (1809–84), the reaper inventor and magnate.

Of all kinds of men, farmers have been, throughout history, the most conservative. Hence most inventions have been made either by nomads or by city-dwellers; peasants have created few if any. Nevertheless, the forces released by the Industrial Revolution soon swept the farmers of the nineteenth century along with the rest of humanity on a course of headlong technological change.

Early American farming was especially backward. European travelers were astonished by its crudity. Faced with a vast extent of cheap land, a shortage of labor, and a lack of transportation to make it worth while to raise a surplus for sale, American farmers had had to change their methods. In place of the more intensive cultivation of the Old World, they adopted the opposite—extensive cultivation, we might call it. This method looked wasteful and careless but served its purpose. In making this change, they forgot many of the intensive methods of their ancestors and had to learn them over again when conditions came more nearly to resemble those of Europe.

Until the nineteenth century, almost nothing was done to improve agricultural equipment. The plow was still a heavy pointed piece of wood, which, hauled by several oxen, dug an irregular furrow and did not even try to turn the earth. In 1797 Charles Newbold of New Jersey patented a cast-iron plow with a curved moldboard to turn the sod. Newbold devoted his life and his fortune of $30,000 to the promotion of his marvelous plow but got nowhere. Farmers said that the iron would poison the soil or encourage the growth of weeds.

Jethro Wood followed Newbold with an 1819 patent on a cast-iron plow whose parts were detachable so that they could be replaced when worn. Farmers overcame their superstitions and began to use the plow, whereupon a host of imitators and infringers sprang up like the weeds that iron plows were supposed to foster. Wood made a little money. He spent most of it in lawsuits but at least had the satisfaction of seeing several thousand of his plows in use before his death.

When men began to plow the plains, iron plows were found to have one fault: the sticky soils stuck to them. Two Midwestern blacksmiths, John Lane and John Deere, independently invented plows with steel wearing surfaces, which overcame this fault. The only steel they could use for this purpose was saw steel—at first, actual saw blades; later, sheets of this steel imported from Germany.

Finally James Oliver, a Scottish-American iron founder, developed an iron plow with a face hardened by chilling in the mold when it was cast. The most successful of the plow inventors, he died in 1908, the richest man in Iowa.

Most of the ideas of these inventors of plows had been anticipated by European inventors in the eighteenth century. But oblivion had swallowed these inventions, born ahead of their time.

During the nineteenth century a number of inventors, American and European, improved that ancient device, the harrow, for breaking up lumps on the surface of the ground. This was more efficient than hiring a laborer to break up the clods with a hoe, or by stamping on them—"clodhopping," as it was called.

They also invented seed-planting devices called drills. But the inventions that most increased the farmers' productivity were those having to do with harvesting.

Wheat, on which the first Mesopotamian civilization was founded six or seven thousand years ago, vastly raised the number of calories of food that a man could produce. But there is a bottleneck in the growing of wheat. It all ripens at once in a given area and must be harvested within about a week—ten days in perfect weather, four in bad. If it stands longer, the seed falls to the ground and is lost.

Hence, under American conditions of cheap land, it was no trick at all for a farmer, even with the crudest methods of plowing and sowing, to raise a stand of wheat larger than he could harvest. Before mechanical harvesting, by working himself and his family day and night, and hiring such hands as could be lured to the task, an able and well-off farmer could, at most, harvest about five acres of wheat. This was enough to feed two families: his own and one other. As there were always many marginal farmers who were either not able or not well off, most of the people of any self-supporting area had to be farmers, because they did not produce enough surplus food to feed a number of people equal to their own. Nowadays a one-family farm can produce enough food for a dozen families.

To increase the amount of wheat that could be reaped in the short time available, the farmers of Roman times enlarged the sickle to a scythe. Some large farms in Gaul even used a kind of header (that is, a device to cut the heads only from the wheat stalks) pushed by oxen, with an arrangement of fingers and slots in front to catch the heads of the wheat.[4]

But the Middle Ages saw a retrogression in Western European farming techniques. The scythe disappeared and was not revived until the seventeenth century.

An eighteenth-century Scottish invention, the cradle, speeded up the harvesting process a little. The cradle, a set of long curved wooden fingers attached to the scythe parallel to the blade, gathered the wheat into neat bundles as it fell.

The early nineteenth century saw more than a dozen inventors, in Europe and America, struggling with the idea of a mechanical harvester. They put the horse behind the vehicle, which made him balky; before it, which caused him to trample much of the grain; and beside it, which made it run in circles. They tried various combinations of fixed and moving blades, working like sickles, scissors, and razors.

The most promising cutter was that developed about 1826 by another Scot, the Rev. Patrick Bell. This consisted of two metal strips, one fixed and the other oscillating back and forth against it. Each blade had a set of deep teeth or sharpened fingers. As the machine moved forwards, the metal strips cut the grain in the same way that the barber's clippers cut your hair.

However, Bell found little encouragement. A mob of farm laborers, seeing in his machine the end of their profitable harvest-time work, demolished it. Years later, however, when Bell had gone back to his parish of Carmylie, the farmers of Scotland collected a thousand pounds for him, in recognition of the benefit that he had conferred on Scottish agriculture.

One of the harvester tinkerers was Robert McCormick, a farmer of Scotch-Irish parentage. Born in Pennsylvania, he settled in Virginia and prospered. He came to own 1800 acres, two grist mills, two sawmills, a smelting furnace, a distillery, and a blacksmith shop in which he did his own smithery.

During the boyhood of his son, Cyrus, Robert McCormick worked on a harvester, as well as a hemp brake and other devices. The harvester never did work; but when the elder McCormick gave it up, the younger (who had already patented a hillside plow) was ready to take up the task.

With the help of his father and of an intelligent Negro slave, Jo Anderson, Cyrus McCormick got the pilot model of his harvester ready for a public trial by the harvest season of 1831. In its crude state of design, it still cut as much grain as six laborers could cut with scythes, or as much as twenty-four peasants could cut with sickles.[5]

The harvester combined a number of elements, all old in themselves but never before assembled in so practical a combination. These were the reciprocating knife with sawlike teeth; the parallel strip of steel with fingers or guards (as in Bell's machine) against which the teeth of the moving knife cut the stalks; the reel (something like that of a modern lawn mower) which pushed the stalks back against the knife; the platform on which the grain fell to be raked off in swaths; a heavy wheel directly behind the horse, to carry most of the machinery; mounting the cutter to one side of this wheel, so that the horse could walk in the stubble previously cut; and a partition or divider at the outer end of the cutter bar to divide the standing grain from that to be cut.

Next year, McCormick demonstrated an improved reaper before a crowd at Lexington, Virginia. The first trial failed because the field was too hilly. But another farmer offered his flatter field for the trial, which was a triumph—except that nobody ordered any reapers.

McCormick advertised his reapers at fifty dollars apiece; still no takers. During the 1830s, he and his father made most of their money as ironmongers. The panic of 1837 crushed the McCormicks. Cyrus and his father lost half their land and kept the rest only by mortgaging it heavily and borrowing from friends. Cyrus McCormick's creditors could have demanded his reaper patent (issued in 1834) but did not because they deemed it worthless.

In 1840, somewhat desperate, Cyrus McCormick at last began to sell a few reapers. First a stranger rode in to buy one; then came two farmers from forty miles away to buy another. In 1842 McCormick sold seven, in 1843 twenty-nine, and in 1844 fifty, for $100 apiece. All were made in the McCormick blacksmith shop at Walnut Grove, Virginia.

McCormick was a long way from being rich. But, except for the usual commercial hazards of labor opposition, embezzling subordinates, and failures of delivery, he at last had a going business.

In 1844 he took $300 and set out on a trip west. Passing through Ohio, Michigan, Illinois, Wisconsin, Iowa, and Missouri, he saw his first prairies and realized that here lay his future. If his device worked after a fashion among the tumbled hills and small farms of the Atlantic coastal region, how much better would it work on these vast flatlands!

First, McCormick licensed others to make reapers in this region. This did not work out well because some of his licensees made defective machines.

Resolutely, McCormick moved his business to Chicago and set up a factory in partnership with William B. Ogden, who had been Chicago's first mayor and had made a fortune in real estate. Both men were too domineering to work together for long. Next year, before any quarrel arose, McCormick bought back Ogden's share of the business.

In these days, McCormick was a huge man, tall and powerful, with thick dark hair and beard and an incongruously squeaky voice. He was sober and formal in dress and manner, ponderous in conversation, and ruthlessly intolerant of opposition. Although several rival inventors of harvesters were as original as he, he overcame and outsold them all by his shrewdness in business and by his invincible drive and energy.

McCormick introduced, or adopted in its early stages, several business practices that were rare or unknown at the time, but which became usual later. For one, he sold his reapers with a written guarantee. If one failed to meet specifications, he took it back and returned the buyer his money. He sold at a fixed, published price at a time when haggling over every purchase was still common. He made lavish use of advertising and publicity. He appointed district agents and built a storage warehouse in each district, so that reapers were ready to sell to farmers who wanted them in a hurry in time for harvest. He sold on credit, in return for time payments. He promoted field tests to stir up interest in the reaper.

These tests flourished for forty years. Competition at tests was so severe that salesmen tried to sabotage competing machines. Failing that, they sometimes drove their rigs into one another like Messala and Ben-Hur in hope of disabling an adversary. Field trials died out after they had become mere circus stunts, in which reapers were driven against saplings and other unrealistic obstacles.

McCormick's earliest competitor was Obed Hussey, a one-eyed sailor from Maine who settled in Cincinnati. Hussey was a brilliant but erratic inventor, given to fits of profound lethargy. Before he entered the harvester field he had invented a corn grinder, a sugar-cane crusher, a machine for grinding hooks and eyes, and an improved candle mold.

When a friend asked Hussey why he did not build a reaper, Hussey exclaimed: "Why, isn't there such a thing?"[6] and set to work. He got a patent in 1833, half a year before McCormick obtained his first reaper patent. Then Hussey made his reapers in Cincinnati. His reaper was smaller and simpler than McCormick's, and it worked better as a grass mower than it did on wheat. In some elements of the combination Hussey anticipated McCormick; in others, such as the use of the reel, McCormick was ahead.

Bitter competition sprang up between Hussey and McCormick. They held a number of public contests, which McCormick usually won by a narrow margin. Later Hussey sued McCormick for infringing his patent and collected handsome damages. Both tried to have their patents extended, McCormick by a furious and costly fifteen-year legal effort which he carried up to the Supreme Court. But in each case the application for renewal was defeated because all the other reaper makers combined to lobby against it.

Hussey continued to make reapers for many years. However, his business dwindled and fell farther and farther behind that of McCormick. He lost out to McCormick because he lacked McCormick's intense business drive and because he stubbornly refused to add improvements made by others to his machine. McCormick, on the other hand, was alert to buy up any patents that could be applied to his business.

In 1858, Hussey sold his reaper business. He was working on a new invention, a steam plow, when he was killed by a train in 1860. The steam plow was a system of pulling a plow back and forth across a field by cables powered by a stationary steam engine. It had some vogue on the small fields of England in the nineteenth century, before the arrival of the tractor. But it never caught on in the United States, where conditions did not favor it.

When his basic patent expired in 1848, McCormick had not yet made any real fortune from his reaper. After that he had to depend mainly on his business acumen, although he took out patents on improvements in 1845, 1847, and 1858. The last was on an automatic raking attachment to rake the cut wheat off the platform. Thereafter McCormick left inventing to others and devoted himself to the business and legal sides of his enterprise.

When McCormick's reaper was exhibited at the Crystal Palace Exhibition in London, in 1851, the *Times* waxed caustic. It described the device as "a cross between an Astley chariot" (a kind of carriage), "a wheelbarrow, and a flying machine." America, the paper went on, was "proud of her agricultural implements which the English manufacturers would reject as worthless."[7]

One spectator was John J. Mechi, whose Italian father had been barber to mad George III and who himself had gained a fortune from a patent razor strop. Mechi now made a hobby of scientific farming. He arranged a test of the reaper on a patch of his land.

One other reaper was tried but failed, as it broke down the wheat instead of cutting it. An onlooker suggested that Mechi stop the trial before all his grain was ruined.

"Gentlemen," replied Mechi, "this is a great experiment for the benefit of my country. When a new principle is about to be established, individual interests must always give way. If it is necessary for the success of this test, you may take my seventy acres of wheat."[8]

The McCormick reaper then cut seventy-four yards in seventy seconds. Mechi led three cheers, swinging his beaver in the rain. The reaper got a first prize at the Exposition and a Council Medal. Even the *Times* changed its tune to say:

"The reaping machine from the United States is the most valuable contribution from abroad, to the stock of our previous knowledge, that we have yet discovered. It is worth the whole cost of the Exposition."[9]

Like most of the reaper inventors, McCormick was a rampant individualist—a tooth-and-nail fighter who never compromised or co-operated with an opponent. After Hussey, his next most formidable competitor was John H. Manny. In 1854, McCormick sued the firm of Manny & Emerson for $400,000 for infringing his improvement patents. All of McCormick's competitors got together to finance Manny, since, if McCormick could beat Manny, he could beat them all.

Each side hired a high-powered battery of lawyers. As the case was originally to be tried in Springfield, Illinois, the Manny forces thought it wise to include a local lawyer, Abraham Lincoln. Then the parties agreed to transfer the case to Cincinnati.

Lincoln was no longer really needed, but nobody told him that. Besides, he needed the thousand dollars. He arrived in Cincinnati, dressed any old way as usual, to find that the Manny group had hired the brilliant, self-assertive, and irascible Edwin M. Stanton. Stanton, seeing the quaint-looking Lincoln, remarked for all to hear:

"Where did that long-armed baboon come from?"

When he heard that either he or Lincoln would make the closing speech, he exploded: "If that giraffe appears in the case, I will throw up my brief and leave."

Stanton had his way; Lincoln silently swallowed his feelings. The main point at issue was the divider that separated the standing grain from that to be cut. Both McCormick's improvement patent of 1847 and Manny's patent of 1851 showed a divider with an upward curve, although there were minor differences between the two designs. McCormick's lawyers demanded an interpretation of the McCormick patent broad enough to include Manny's design, since the McCormick improvement had been made first.

Stanton, on the contrary, argued that patent rights must be interpreted "in the light of the state of the art at the time of the invention patented." As dividers for harvesters already existed before either man made his improvement, each patent could dominate only a narrow part of the inventive field, namely, the specific design shown in each patent. Therefore McCormick's patent did not dominate Manny's harvester, and Manny was not guilty of infringement.

Lincoln listened intently from the back of the courtroom. Later he remarked: ". . . it would have been a great mistake if I had spoken in this case; I did not fully apprehend it . . . I am going home to study—to study law."[10]

Although Manny died during the trial, and although McCormick appealed to the Supreme Court, McCormick lost his case. He then hired Stanton to handle his next lawsuit. Years later, when he became President, Lincoln chose Stanton as his Secretary of War in recognition of the brilliance and energy that he remembered from the Manny-McCormick trial.

Litigation was McCormick's fun. In 1862 McCormick, his wife (a New York girl half his age whom he had married four years before), a couple of small children, and a couple of servants took a train from Philadelphia to Chicago. The baggage master demanded $8.70 for 200 pounds of surplus baggage. McCormick refused to pay and left the train. He ordered his baggage taken off, but the conductor refused to hold the train. Away went the vast mass of trunks and suitcases.

McCormick stormed in upon the president of the Pennsylvania Railroad, who wired orders to Pittsburgh to take McCormick's baggage off the train. McCormick and his family went on to Pittsburgh, where they found that the trunks had nevertheless gone through to Chicago. The next day, arriving at the Fort Wayne Station in Chicago, McCormick learned that the baggage had been stored in the freight station, which had been struck by lightning and burned to ashes.

The furious McCormick sued the railroad for $7193, the value of the baggage. He won a judgment for $12,000, but the railroad appealed all the way up to the Supreme Court, which ordered a new trial. McCormick won again, but again the railroad appealed. The Baggage Case became one of the nation's leading sporting events. Five times the case reached the Supreme Court. The last time, the court told the railroad to stop fooling and pay up.

The railroad still evaded payment for three years, until after McCormick was dead. Then it paid $18,060.79, the value of the baggage plus interest, to his estate, to the great satisfaction of his widow. It made no difference that McCormick had spent many times that amount in the suit; it was the principle of the thing.

As a Chicago millionaire, McCormick, a devout Presbyterian, founded Northwestern Theological Seminary. He also bought a paper, *The Interior,* which he made into a religious weekly. When not running his business with the help of his brothers or writing theological articles for his paper, he dabbled in politics. He ran for office on the Democratic ticket several times, once for the United States Senate, but was never elected. His heavy personality failed to charm the masses, while his rigid adherence to principle alarmed the politicians, who tolerated him only because of his generous contributions to the party.

In the Civil War, McCormick was a moderate Southern sympathizer who favored a negotiated peace. He did not let his sympathies interfere with business, however. The reaper, by releasing for service in the armies thousands of men who would otherwise have had to stay behind to work as farm hands, was a major factor in the Union victory. Thus, while a Yankee, Eli Whitney, invented the device on which the cotton slave-empire was based, a Southerner, McCormick, created the means by which it was struck down.

McCormick's iron nerve faltered only once, when the Chicago fire of 1871 burned up his harvester factory. His wife reached Chicago two days later to find McCormick wearing a half-burned hat and overcoat. He asked her: should he rebuild or retire? Rebuild! said Nettie McCormick, a lady with much of her husband's forcefulness. He did and soon was making harvesters faster than ever.

After McCormick died, his son of the same name approached George W. Perkins, a Morgan partner, for capital to expand. Perkins engineered a merger of six makers of agricultural machinery, of which the McCormick company was the biggest. Thus the International Harvester Company was formed to monopolize the industry.

This trust was attacked by the government for violation of the Clayton Act in 1912. After three years of litigation, the trust was forced to split up again by selling three of its lines. The reduced International Harvester Company has continued to thrive down to the present and, in memory of ingenious Jo

Anderson, McCormick's slave assistant, has always insisted upon equal treatment for its Negro employees.[11]

The farmer's task is not over when his wheat is cut. Somebody has to gather it into bundles which, after sunning for a few days, are then collected to be threshed. In 1858, in Illinois, two brothers named Marsh patented a reaper with attachments to make binding easy. The cut wheat was carried by a conveyor up to a shelf. Behind the shelf the worker stood, riding on a platform, and bound the stalks by hand as they piled up in front of him. The Marsh brothers built up a business which prospered until a commercial accident put an end to it; a company to which they had sold an interest in their business failed. After ups and downs, both brothers finally prospered in other lines of work.

The Marsh harvester still did not bind the sheaves mechanically. It only made it easier for a human binder to do so. If you are not familiar with knot-tying machines, try to imagine how one could work. You must admit that it seems impossible.

But the late nineteenth century was the heyday of the mechanical engineer and inventor. There was no problem, it seemed, that could not be solved in the way of making machines do the work of men. From mid-century on, a host of inventors worked on machines to tie grain in bundles with wire or string.

In 1874 a farmer and mechanic named C. B. Withington called at McCormick's home in Chicago one evening to explain his invention of a mechanical wire binder. The colossus of Chicago had been awake most of the previous night thinking about his business problems and fell asleep during Withington's discourse. When he awoke, the offended inventor had left. Eager not to let slip a profitable opportunity, McCormick sent an emissary to Withington's home in Wisconsin to fetch him back. McCormick adopted the idea at once and made 50,000 Withington machines.

But wire had shortcomings. It got into cattle feed and killed the animals that ate it. It cluttered the farmyard and tripped the farmer. It got into the threshed wheat. It cut the farmer's hands. String, though harder to manage mechanically, was much better agriculturally. John E. Heath of Ohio had some small success with a twine binder in the 1850s.

John F. Appleby did better in Wisconsin. As a soldier in the Civil War, Appleby whittled out a model of an automatic feed for rifle cartridges, got a patent in 1864, sold it for $500, and saw it promptly resold for $7000. This experience determined him to be a professional inventor. After several years of tinkering, he got a twine binder to work and sold the rights to William Deering. Deering became McCormick's leading competitor, until McCormick hired another mechanical genius, Marquis L. Gorham, to invent another twine binder.

Meanwhile a host of other inventors developed threshing machines, machines for harvesting and binding corn, and machines for processing an entire crop. These enormous "combines" were pulled at first by scores of horses or mules, then (especially in California) by huge steam tractors. As the twentieth century began, the internal-combustion revolution reached the farm, and gasoline tractors took the place of steam-driven machines. The mechanization of agriculture has gone on amain ever since. We are still in the midst of an Agricultural Revolution as far-reaching in its effects as the Industrial Revolution, which preceded it and of which it is an outgrowth.

VII

ERICSSON

AND THE MODERN WARSHIP

Fulton's devil-on-a-sawmill was the first of several inventions that revolutionized naval warfare in the nineteenth century. If Lord Howard of Effingham, who beat the Armada in 1588, had stepped aboard the U.S.S. *Constitution*, he would have felt right at home. On a twentieth-century warship, however, he would have been utterly lost.

Besides steam, several other changes comprised the warship revolution. These included iron construction, armor, rifled cannon firing explosive shell, and the turret. When all these inventions had been assimilated, a warship—say, the *Oregon* of the Spanish-American War or the *Bismarck* of World War II—no more resembled her predecessor the *Constitution* than a man is like an ancestral lungfish, slithering through a Paleozoic swamp.

However, these changes were not adopted everywhere as soon as they appeared. It took half a century to convince naval men that all warships should be steam-propelled. Everybody has heard that the battle between the *Monitor* and the *Virginia* was the world's first fight between two armored warships. It is not so well known that this was also the world's first serious combat between two warships depending on steam alone for their motion.

The world's first steam warship was Fulton's *Demologos,*

renamed *Fulton* after her creator's death. After the first *Fulton* blew up in 1829, the United States built a second "floating battery," also called *Fulton*, powered by steam and armed with the new Paixhans shell-firing gun. She performed extensive tests in the 1830s, slowly convincing the Navy that shell guns and steam were both here to stay.

Meanwhile the British and French navies began acquiring steamships—at first, steam merchantmen, bought for use as auxiliaries and sometimes fitted with a few small guns. Most naval men did not believe that fighting ships would ever be driven by steam, although they admitted that steamers would be useful for towing becalmed sailing warships. Although a steam vessel could move in any direction, regardless of wind, the advantages of steam in the 1830s were not overwhelming.

For one thing, the steam engines of that time were horribly inefficient. They weighed about a ton per horsepower and used so much fuel that not until 1836 could a ship cross the Atlantic under steam power alone. Earlier ships could not carry enough fuel. The engines often broke down; and even when they worked, they did not drive their ships so fast as a good suit of sails.

For another thing, all the earlier steamers applied their power by means of paddle wheels. The wheels took up much of the space on the sides of the ship needed for guns. Also, be a steamer ever so nimble, this would do her little good if the first shot smashed a wheel and stopped her. The wheels were not only vulnerable in themselves, but they also caused the boilers and engines to be mounted high up, so that they, too, were exposed to shot and shell.

But steam engines improved. The invention of the screw propeller got rid of the paddle wheels. In the 1840s the leading navies added sail-and-steam frigates—the ancestors of the modern cruiser. In the 1850s came the first sail-and-steam battleships, and the British and French converted a number of sailing frigates and battleships into steamers.

Iron construction proved almost as revolutionary as steam. Although men had long known that a vessel of thin iron would float, such construction was not possible in earlier times because of cost. In the eighteenth and early nineteenth centuries, British metallurgical inventions—Darby's coke furnace, Cort's plate rolls and puddling furnace, and Neilson's hot-blast furnace —made iron cheap enough for shipbuilding. Wilkinson's 8-ton iron canal boat *Trial* began operations in 1787, and an iron steamer, the *Aaron Manby*, plied the Seine in 1822.

In the 1840s, navies cautiously bought a few small iron auxiliary ships. Iron not only was stronger than wood for a given weight of material and less bulky, but also made possible the building of much larger ships. Brunel's *Great Eastern* could not have been built of wood, as the needed internal bracing would have practically filled the ship.

Iron had its shortcomings, however. Iron bottoms became badly fouled with weeds and barnacles. The first tests of guns against iron ship plates, in 1840, showed that the shot not only went through but also sent jagged iron splinters flying.

However, while wood stood up better than iron to solid round shot, this did not prove true when the projectile was Colonel Henri Joseph Paixhans' new explosive shell. As one of Napoleon's artillery officers, Paixhans had seen plenty of shooting. In the peaceful 1820s and 30s, he perfected an explosive missile to be shot from cannon. He also cultivated political influence so that he could be sure his ideas were given a fair trial.

For centuries, bombs had been thrown from very short guns called mortars. This was a tricky business. The bomb was placed in the mortar, fuze uppermost. The gunner first lit the bomb fuze and, when that began to sizzle, touched the linstock (a staff holding a lighted match) in his other hand to the touchhole of the mortar. If the mortar went off, well and good. But sometimes the fuze of the bomb went out before the bomb reached its target. Worse, the mortar itself might miss fire, so that the gunner had to leap madly for cover before the sputtering bomb exploded.

Paixhans devised an elongated projectile, shaped like the bullet of his colleague Captain Minié. This "shell" had a band of soft metal around its base to make it fit the gun barrel tightly and give something for the rifling to grip. Inside the shell was a charge of gunpowder, and on the tip of the pointed nose was a hammer and a percussion cap. When the shell struck the target, the hammer was driven back against the cap. *Boom!*

Paixhans tried out two of his guns against an old wooden line-of-battle ship at Brest in 1842. The shells not only blew the wood to splinters but also set the hulk on fire.

Guns also improved in other respects. Brittle cast iron gave way to wrought iron and then to steel. Rifling became more and more common. In 1850 an American naval officer, John A. Dahlgren, devised an ingenious gage by which he could measure the pressure at any point inside a gun barrel when the gun was fired. With this new knowledge, a gun could be made thickest where the stress was greatest, without wasting metal.

Several gunmakers, especially Krupp in Germany and Armstrong in England, learned to make a gun barrel out of two or more steel tubes. An outer tube was heated so that it expanded and was slid over the inner tube. When the outer tube cooled, it shrank and gripped the inner tube with tremendous force. Such guns could fire heavier charges than one-piece guns of the same size.

When Colonel Paixhans saw the results of his test, he declared that ships would have to put on iron armor. Except for the never-finished Stevens Battery, little was done with this suggestion at first. For one thing, it was not yet possible to roll iron plates thick enough to make effective armor. When engineers fired at samples of armor built up of thinner plates bolted together, the shot went right through.

In the 1850s, a French invention made it possible to roll four-inch plates. Then the British and French navies began building armored warships. For the Crimean War, the latter made three armored floating batteries, the *Dévastation, Tonnante,* and *Lave.* Having neither engines nor sails, they had to be towed into position, but they knocked to pieces the Russian forts at Kinburn on the Black Sea without damage to themselves.

The British and French also built sail-and-steam frigates with belts of armor along the sides. The French *Gloire,* finished in 1859, was followed by the British *Warrior* in 1861, and other armored ships. Some were of iron and some of wood, but iron slowly took the place of wood as the lesson of the battle of Sinope sank home. Here, on the south shore of the Black Sea, at the outset of the Crimean War, a Russian squadron attacked a Turkish squadron. The Russians knocked the wooden Turkish ships to matchwood with explosive shells as easily as Paixhans had destroyed his wooden hulk eleven years before.

When the American Civil War broke out in 1861, the United States Navy had nothing to compare with the *Gloire* or the *Warrior*. There were five unarmored steam screw frigates, of which the *Merrimack* was burned and scuttled at the Norfolk Navy Yard to keep her out of rebel hands. There were twenty-eight steam sloops and gunboats, driven some by screws and some by paddles. And there was a straggle of sailing vessels left over from former decades.

Luckily for the Union, the Confederates started out with nothing. The rebs improvised gunboats and commerce raiders out of merchant ships. The Union bought up scores of civilian craft—steamers, ferries, tugs, anything that would float and carry a gun—and built scores of small warships to back them up. Federal expeditionary forces seized a chain of island strongholds along the coast. From these bases the Federals began to strangle the commerce on which the Confederacy relied for its munitions.

Shortly after the war began, two Confederates, a Lieutenant Brooke (who knew about the Stevens Battery) and the naval constructor John L. Porter began an ironclad ship. They raised the hull of the *Merrimack* from the bottom of the James estuary. They cut down the hull almost to the water line, erected over it shedlike casemate of massive timbers, and began to lay upon it a roof of 4-inch iron bars, re-rolled from railroad rails.

The Federals heard from their spies about the monster, renamed *Virginia*. Three months after the war started, Secretary of the Navy Gideon Welles got an appropriation for ironclads and appointed a board to consider designs. Some strange ones came in, including an iron rowing galley and a ship sheathed in rubber from which the shot was supposed to bounce.

Two ships were authorized: the frigate *New Ironsides* and the corvette *Galena*. The former, an imitation of the British *Warrior*, was a squarish 4120-ton wooden screw ship with a single thick funnel rising from her flush deck, and broadside guns shooting through a belt of heavy armor. Though slow, she proved one of the Union's best, giving and taking more blows than any other ship in American naval history.

The smaller *Galena* did not turn out so well. Before she was started, her designer, C. S. Bushnell, met an iron founder, Cornelius H. Delameter. The latter urged that Bushnell take his figures to Delameter's old friend and associate Ericsson in New York for checking. Ericsson was a Swedish-American engineer who had once built ships but had been driven out of the naval construction business as a result of an accident and a case of personal enmity.

John Ericsson (1803–89) was born in Värmland, in the mountains of west central Sweden. A friendly troll once told his grandfather's hired man that the farm would produce two boys whose fame should overspread the world.

John Ericsson and his brother Nils grew up to be eminent engineers, though only John became world-famous. At the age of fourteen, working on the Göta Canal as an engineering cadet in the Swedish Navy, he turned out the work of an adult draftsman.

Then Ericsson joined the Swedish Army as an ensign. He became a handsome youth of medium height, with broad shoulders, large hands and feet, blue eyes, and curly brown hair. His strength was enormous; at eighteen he strained his back by lifting a 600-pound cannon to show off. His energy was equally phenomenal. When he was surveying for the Army he was paid on a piece rate, and he worked so fast that he was carried on the rolls and paid as two men, lest his earnings seem excessive. He was volatile, hot-tempered, and opinionated.

For a time Ericsson was betrothed to an aristocratic Jemtland girl. As Swedish betrothal was a kind of companionate marriage, the union produced a son. Then, however, it was decided that Ericsson was too poor, and the girl married another.

In 1826 Ericsson went to England on leave to look into engineering prospects. He liked them so well that he resigned his commission and threw himself into the hazardous life of an inventor, in partnership with John Braithwaite, whose family had been engineers since 1695 and whose father had invented the diving bell.

One of Ericsson's first jobs was to design a surface condenser for the engines of Captain John Ross's ship. Felix Booth, a London distiller, had provided the money for Ross to make an Arctic expedition.

Ross kept his destination secret. Therefore Ericsson, supposing the condenser to be for military use, designed it so that it was quite unsuited to Arctic exploration. Ross threw the condenser overboard in the Arctic and, on his return, blamed Ericsson for his failure to find the long-sought Northwest Passage. Ericsson angrily wrote to Ross, accusing the captain of "forgetfulness of justice and candor" in dealing with him and Braithwaite; Booth had to intervene to prevent a duel.[1]

During the next few years, Ericsson produced many significant inventions. One was the steam fire engine, the ancestor of all those lovely horse-drawn fire engines, which older readers remember clattering about the streets of cities with brightly polished metal work.

Ericsson's engine did good service at some conflagrations in the early 1830s. In fact, it worked too well in a sense. There were no water mains. The way to fight a fire was to dig a hole in the street, wait for it to fill with ground water, and then squirt this water by hand pumps. Ericcson's engines, throwing two tons of water a minute, pumped the hole dry faster than it could refill.

Moreover, the fire brigades of the time hated the fire engine as robbing them of their work. Finally they incited a mob to destroy the engine. Ericsson built two more in England, one of which served in Liverpool and one in Berlin.

Another accomplishment of Ericsson was the design of a locomotive for the Liverpool and Manchester Railway competition at Rainhill in 1829. In preliminary trials the Ericsson-Braithwaite entry, Novelty, worked up the then astounding speed of 31.9 miles an hour—much faster than its leading rival, Stephenson's winning Rocket. But, in the final runs, Ericsson's Novelty sprang leaks in its boiler, which forced him to withdraw it.

In the early 1830s, Ericsson made the first forced-draft fan for a steamship, the Corsair (Liverpool to Belfast). He invented a pneumatic recording sounding lead, in which depth was measured by the height to which water ascended in a column against the pressure of air.

One of Ericsson's inventions was his "caloric"[2] or hot-air engine, to which he devoted many years of experiment and much of the money that he made from other inventions. This is an engine in which hot air is compressed, heated, and expanded. In these cylinders it drives pistons like those of a reciprocating steam engine. The hot-air engine avoids the loss of energy that goes into the boiling of water—the "latent heat" required to turn water at 212 degrees F into steam at 212 degrees.

On the other hand, the hot-air engine must do much more work in compressing air than a steam engine needs to do in pumping water into its boiler. Furthermore, a hot-air engine is larger in proportion to its power than a steam engine. In the 1850s Ericsson built a hot-air ship, the *Ericsson*. For a while Ericsson thought he had made the steamship obsolete. But the *Ericsson*'s 220-horsepower engine had four cylinders, each fourteen feet in diameter, which left little room inside the ship for anything else. Hence the experiment was not repeated.

As time went on, the hot-air engine was found to be useful for running things like pumps and cotton gins. It was simple and reliable and never blew up because somebody had forgotten to keep the boiler filled. In the later nineteenth century it became quite popular in isolated installations, such as country houses and sugar plantations in Cuba, so that for some years Ericsson got a modest income from caloric-engine royalties.

The screw propeller was an old device, with which Fitch, Bushnell, Colonel Stevens, and Fulton had all experimented. In the early nineteenth century, engineers disagreed as to what form it should take: a single helical plate, circling the shaft several times, or separate blades; and if the latter, how many?

In 1835, Captain Ericsson began work on the screw propeller problem. The design that he patented two years later (just ahead of an English farmer named Smith who independently invented a screw of the continuous-helix type) had six or eight blades radiating from the same point on the shaft, like the petals of a flower, with a hoop or drum to brace them. He also conceived the contra-rotary propeller, used on many large modern aircraft.

Ogden, the United States consul at Liverpool, put up the cash for Ericsson to build a 45-foot screw boat on the Thames. When Ericsson proposed to sell it to the British Navy, the Lords of the Admiralty declined because, they said, a boat with the propulsion at the stern could not be steered. (No doubt they were thinking of the false analogy of a man's standing on the stern of a boat and pushing it with a pole.)

So, in the summer of 1837, Ericsson demonstrated the *Francis B. Ogden* to the Lords of the Admiralty. He took them for a ride, towing the Admiralty barge up and down the Thames and showing that his boat steered beautifully. Their lordships thanked Ericsson politely, went away, and sent him word that the screw "would never do."[3] They could not buy his boat, they explained, because a ship so propelled would be impossible to steer.

A month later, the Admiralty adopted Smith's less efficient propeller. Furthermore, Ericsson's patent was declared subservient to Smith's, because Ericsson had put off applying for a patent for five years and had finally done so only on Ogden's insistence. Unfortunately, great creative genius seldom goes with the sort of tidy, prudent common sense that watches every penny and takes advantage of every safeguard.

As a result of the Admiralty's decision against Ericsson's propeller, Braithwaite and Ericsson failed. Ericsson, after a stretch in debtor's prison, was released as a bankrupt. Braithwaite found another partner, while Ericsson took a job as superintending engineer on a railway. Meanwhile Ogden had taken out American patents for him on his propeller and other devices.

Ogden also introduced Ericsson to Lieutenant Robert F. Stockton, executive officer of an American warship. A rich and politically potent New Jerseyite who had invested his family's fortune in the Delaware and Raritan Canal, Stockton was looking for capital in Europe to enable his canal company to weather the depression of 1837. He was brilliant, garrulous, charming, selfish, and treacherous.

Being an engineer and inventor also, Stockton argued steamboats with Ericsson, who insisted that paddle wheels were no good for warships. He, Ericsson, had invented a better system: his screw propeller, whose use enabled the engine to be mounted below the waterline.

Stockton said he had heard of this screw thing, but that it would not work, because the necessary gearing used up too much of the engine's power.

"Not with my screw," retorted Ericsson, sketching as he spoke. "It has no gearing; the engines work directly upon the propeller shaft in the bowels of the ship." And he told about the *Francis B. Ogden.*

Stockton saw the little ship. He and Ogden put up another thousand pounds, wherewith Ericsson built the 70-foot *Robert F. Stockton* on the Mersey. In 1839 she arrived in New York, creating a sensation, and went into service on Stockton's canal as a tug. She tugged efficiently for twenty-five years.

Then the British Patent Office wrote Ericsson asking if they might have the *Stockton*'s engines when the ship wore out, to exhibit in the Patent Office Museum. At this time the *Stockton* was owned by the Stevenses. When the Stevenses heard of this request, they had the ship scrapped and completely melted up, lest somebody other than Colonel John Stevens get credit for developing the screw propeller.

In 1836 Ericsson had married a handsome English girl of nineteen, as strong-minded as he. In 1839 he moved to New York, where he set himself up in engineering and naval construction; she followed. But Amelia Ericsson soon tired of the United States and of being neglected for engines. She returned to her relatives in England.

Ericsson continued to support her; they wrote friendly letters alluding to plans for reunion. But, as she would not leave England, nor he America, nothing came of these plans, and Amelia died in 1867 without ever seeing her husband again. They evidently got on better with an ocean between them, and Ericsson was sometimes heard to growl that he was not fitted for domestic life. He formed a liaison with another woman in New York, but so discreetly that little is known about her.

In New York, Ericsson lived in a whirl of activity. He built another steam fire engine for New York City and with Stockton's help got into the fields of ordnance and naval construction. He formed an agreement with the construction firm of Hogg and Delameter, by which he furnished engineering ideas in return for a share of the profits, if any. The agreement lasted all his life and kept him solvent when his own bull-headedness would have landed him in the poorhouse a dozen times over.

In 1839 the United States Navy, for the first time in a decade, received money for new construction. The progressive elements wanted steam warships, while the board of naval commissioners who were supposed to be technical experts swore they "would never consent to see our grand old ships supplanted by these new and ugly sea monsters."[4]

By some sharp political log-rolling, the progressive elements got three steam warships authorized. One, the paddle frigate *Mississippi*, was a notable success. She carried Commodore Matthew Calbraith Perry to the opening of Japan to American commerce in 1853—a feat which was much lauded then, but which ninety years later seemed to have been a little hasty.

Another steam warship, the *Union*, flopped. The dream of a Lieutenant Hunter, she had a pair of paddle wheels turning about *vertical* shafts in recesses in her sides. She made almost three miles an hour in smooth water.

The third was the screw frigate *Princeton*,[5] built at the Philadelphia Navy Yard under Stockton's supervision, with an engine designed by Ericsson. Instead of cylinders, this engine had a pair of expansion chambers shaped like quarter-cylinders. Inside each, instead of a piston, was a valve hinged at one edge and swinging back and forth like a door in the quarter-cylinder. Thus Ericsson saved space.

For armament, the *Princeton* carried twelve 42-pounders on pivots down the centerline. Thus each gun could shoot either to port or to starboard, whereas with the old system of broadside mounting a gun could shoot to one side only.

The ship also mounted two big 12-inch rifles of the Paixhans type, one at the bow and one at the stern, one made by Ericsson and one by Stockton. They were built up of wrought iron, with which ordnance men were experimenting as a substitute for cast iron. When fired, Ericsson's rifle "Oregon," which he had brought with him from England, developed a crack near the breech. Ericsson had three massive iron bands shrunk on over the breech, to guard against bursting. Stockton's rifle, the "Peacemaker," was of thicker iron to begin with.

Now the worm of jealousy began to gnaw at the partnership of Stockton and Ericsson. When the *Princeton* was fitting out for sea in 1843, Stockton sent the Navy an enthusiastic report on the new ship, in which he carefully said nothing about Ericsson. On trials the *Princeton* fully lived up to her designers' expectations.

In February 1844, Stockton brought his splendid new ship

up the Potomac to give governmental dignitaries, from President Tyler down, a demonstration. All went well until the guns were fired. The "Peacemaker" blew up, killing the Secretaries of State and Navy and a gabble of Congressmen and wounding everybody else on deck.

When the court of inquiry met, Stockton demanded that Ericsson come to Washington to testify in his defense. Ericsson, who had disapproved of Stockton's gun from the start, refused to come. Stockton was exonerated on grounds of "unavoidable accident," but cherished a lifelong grudge against Ericsson.

Then Ericsson sent the Navy a bill for $15,080 for his engineering work on the *Princeton.* The Navy Department referred the bill to Stockton, who after a long delay wrote: "I must say that, with all my desire to serve him, I cannot approve of his bill; it is direct violation of our agreement as far as it is to be considered a legal claim upon the department."

Nine days later, Stockton wrote another letter, asserting that he had not needed Ericsson at all, but that this "ingenious but presumptuous mechanic" had "thrust himself upon me." Their understanding had been that Ericsson was to help in designing the engines for the glory alone; Stockton had permitted the Swede to take part in the work merely as a favor.[6]

So the bill was not paid. Fourteen years later Senator Stephen R. Mallory of Florida urged payment of Ericsson. But nothing was done, even after the Civil War when Ericsson, as the *Monitor's* sire, was being showered with medals and testimonials as a savior of the nation. The bill has not been paid to this day.

Forced out of naval construction, Ericsson turned to other enterprises. He experimented with anthracite fuel for locomotives. He invented a hydrostatic gage for measuring the volume of fluids under pressure. He invented the reciprocating fluid meter, the rotary fluid meter, the alarm barometer, the pyrometer for measuring high temperatures, a hydrostatic weighing machine, steam pumps, and a salt-water purifying still. His income ranged from $40,000 to $80,000—in those days excellent earnings. However, having little more financial sense than most inventors, Ericsson spent his money freely, mostly on engineering research, and gave it away generously.

In 1848 Ericsson became an American citizen, although he always retained a sentimental love for Sweden. He led a Spartan life. When busy on some project he was likely to sleep on a drafting table with a book for a pillow. He drank a lot, but only as a lubricant, having no time for sprees or parties. Proud of his youthful vigor, he dyed his hair—what little was left of it—when it began to gray.

Ericsson had begun to think about armored ships as early as 1826. He sent Napoleon III a plan for such a ship in 1854; but nothing came of it, although the French ruler did authorize the building of the armored floating batteries of the *Dévastation* class.

When the Civil War broke out, Stephen R. Mallory, who as Senator from Florida had wanted Ericsson's bill paid, became the Confederate Secretary of the Navy. Although much abused, he seems to have been a man of some knowledge and energy.

Mallory authorized Brooke and Porter to raise and armor the *Merrimack*. But there was only one foundry in the South that could roll the iron for the armor. Hence work was slow, and the Union had time to catch up.

Such was the state of affairs when Cornelius S. Bushnell, who had contracted to build the *Galena*, came to see Ericsson. Ericsson ran over Bushnell's figures and grunted that they seemed all right. But he, Ericsson, had a better idea for a floating battery, if Bushnell had time to look at it.

Ericsson rummaged through the litter in his office and pulled out a cardboard model and some drawings. The model was of a flat, narrow elliptical plate with a bump in the middle. The bump, Ericsson explained, was an armored turret carrying two heavy guns. The turret would rotate in battle, halting to fire when the guns faced the foe, turning again until the guns pointed away and then halting to reload, thus making it hard for the enemy to shoot into the turret ports. Built of 9-inch armor, the turret would be invulnerable to any guns in existence.

Would that thing ride the seas? Bushnell wanted to know. Surely, said Ericsson; in his boyhood he had seen timber rafts on stormy lakes in Sweden ride steadily through seas that laid conventional ships on their beam ends.

Bushnell suggested that Ericsson submit his design to the Navy Department, but Ericsson growled that he had had enough of the Navy's ingratitude. Besides, he had already written to Lincoln and to the Ironclad Board and received no answer. Bushnell borrowed the model, took it to Washington, and saw Lincoln, who agreed to come to a meeting of the Ironclad Board next day. At the meeting, Lincoln whittled a stick and remarked:

"All I have to say is what the girl said when she stuck her foot into the stocking. It strikes me there's something in it!"

Captain Davis of the Ironclad Board, on the other hand, would have none of it. Although chosen for his receptiveness to new ideas, he told Bushnell: "You can take that little thing home and worship it, as it would not be idolatry, because it is in the image of nothing in the heaven above or on the earth beneath or in the waters under the earth."[7]

There was no decision until Bushnell got Ericsson to come to Washington to explain. Then Lincoln and Welles said to go ahead. Ericsson's contract was hardly fair. Although the ship was highly experimental, Ericsson had to build it at his own risk. The Navy would not pay unless it worked perfectly.

Ericsson fell to in the Greenpoint shipyard like Thor smiting the giants of Jötunnheim. To make the fires draw, he invented a system of forced draft. To provide air for the cramped crew, he invented a system of forced ventilation. As shot for the 11-inch guns were too heavy to manhandle into the turret, he invented the ammunition hoist.

Although the original design called for a dome-shaped turret, for ease of manufacture Ericsson changed this to a cylindrical turret shaped like a birthday cake. He even invented a water closet which (if the user remembered to turn the valves in the right order) would flush a toilet against the pressure of water outside. This system is still used in submarines.

The turret itself had been invented before by an upstate New Yorker named Theodore R. Timby, who produced a caveat to prove it. Bushnell had rounded up two capitalists, with whom he formed a company, the Battery Associates, to build ships designed by Ericsson. When Timby appeared, the Battery Associates bought the rights to his turret patent, though Ericsson claimed that neither he nor Timby invented the idea of the revolving turret. The idea, he said, went back to the previous century.

In February of 1862, a hundred days after Ericsson began work, the *Monitor* was ready for her trials. Everything went wrong. The engine worked badly. A Naval engineer, Alban C. Stimers, disabled the turret mechanism by turning the compressor wheels the wrong way. The rudder had been over-balanced so that the ship steered erratically. Newspapers, to whom inventors were still fair game, had fun over "Ericsson's folly."

Ericsson rushed about, rebuilding and reinventing. The Navy wanted to put on a new rudder, but Ericsson roared: "The *Monitor* is mine, and I say it shall not be done! . . . Put in a new rudder! They would waste a month in doing that; I will make her steer in three days."[8] And he did.

Even so, the Confederacy got its ironclad out first. On the morning of March 8, 1862, the *Virginia* slid out of the Norfolk Navy Yard and headed towards the squadron of Union warships blockading the entrance to Chesapeake Bay. Her casemate, looking like a barn roof afloat, ended in a pair of conical structures like the turrets of a Norman castle. Ten guns, including two 7-inch rifles, poked through the ports in sides and ends. Her bow ended in a wedge-shaped ram, like those of the galleys at Salamis and Actium. Five Confederate armed civil craft followed her.

As *Virginia* neared the blockaders, around two o'clock, gliding silently under a cloud of black smoke, the Union ships opened up. Paying no attention, the monster headed for the best-armed of her foes, the sail sloop *Cumberland.*

The *Cumberland* gave *Virginia* a broadside from the raking position. A score of iron balls rebounded clanging in a shower of sparks from the iron hide. *Virginia's* ram crunched into her victim's side, making a hole like a porte-cochere. Her bow gun boomed, killing ten men on the *Cumberland.*

As the ships slewed, *Virginia's* iron beak broke off. *Virginia* swung clear and turned, shooting deliberately as water rushed into the *Cumberland.* The Union gunners kept firing; one shot smashed a gun muzzle and wounded Confederate Admiral Franklin Buchanan.

But it was no use. The *Cumberland* sank until nothing was seen but her masthead and flag, and a few swimming survivors.

Farther out, the sail frigate *Congress* had run aground while shaking out her sails and was being pounded by the smaller Confederate ships. Three Federal steam warships, hastening to the scene of action, also ran aground. *Virginia* took a convenient position and raked the helpless *Congress* until the wreck blazed from end to end against the evening sky. Then the *Virginia* went home.

In Washington, the Cabinet met in wild excitement, Secretary of War Stanton crying: "It is not unlikely that we shall have from one of her guns a cannon ball in this room before we leave it!"[9]

During that momentous day, the *Monitor* plodded towards Hampton Roads. A ferocious storm sent the two tugs to cover that were towing her. The crew had a miserable time. Some expert at the Brooklyn Navy Yard had changed the system of sealing the turret base so that water poured in and all but drowned the machinery. The storm almost sank the vessel herself, as so low-built a ship, with a mere eighteen inches of freeboard, had little buoyancy to spare.

But the awkward-looking little craft survived and reached the Chesapeake on the evening of March eighth, in time to hear the guns and see the *Congress* burning in the distance. A pilot boat brought word that, besides the loss of the two sloops, the armed Federal steamer *Whitehall* had been destroyed by an accidental fire and the steam frigate *Minnesota* was still aground.

On the morning of the ninth, *Virginia* came down again, heading for the helpless *Minnesota*. The *Monitor* slid out from behind the frigate. At first the Confederates thought her a floating water tank; then, as she closed with flag flying, gave her a broadside. The projectiles bounced off, skipping over the quiet sea. The birthday cake revolved. Out came the two 11-inchers to give a violent double blow that threw half the *Virginia's* crew off their feet.

For two hours they banged away, neither able to knock the other out. *Monitor's* guns were designed for 30-pound powder charges, but the Navy Department, fearing another blowup, limited loads to fifteen. As for *Virginia*, she carried only shell for her heavy rifles as she had expected to meet only wooden ships.

Monitor still had the best of it, smashing another gun and shooting off *Virginia's* funnel, so that the ram's speed dropped. On the *Monitor*, Engineer Alban Stimers sweated over the turret gear, which worked badly because it had been allowed to rust. But it spun the turret fast enough to keep *Virginia* from hitting the ports.

Virginia tried to ram, but the *Monitor*, her wooden hull protected by the broad iron overhang, slithered aside. *Virginia's* gunners aimed at *Monitor's* little pilot house and burst a shell against the iron shutters, temporarily blinding her captain, Lieutenant Worden. *Monitor* yawed out of control, but Worden's second took his place and she steadied, knocking plates and rivets loose on the Confederate's carapace. *Virginia's* captain asked his gunnery officer:

"Why are you no longer firing, Mr. Eggleston?"

"I can do her as much damage by snapping my fingers every three minutes."[10]

Virginia limped home to Norfolk, never to fight again. The Confederates blew her up when they evacuated Norfolk before the advance of McClellan's army, to the grief and rage of the people of Norfolk at the loss of the "iron diadem of the South." *Monitor* fought against the Confederate forts on the James and sank in a gale the following winter.

The *Virginia* and the *Monitor* were by no means the first armored ships, or even the first armored ships to fire shots in anger. What the battle of Hampton Roads did was to give the idea of armoring ships a boost, so that it was adopted more swiftly than it might have been.

This boost in turn was due to the misleading fact that the two ships had hammered each other at close range for two hours without effecting a single death or serious injury. Had the *Monitor* been using full charges, or the *Virginia* solid shot in her heaviest guns, the result might have been different—perhaps resembling what happened to the C.S.S. *Atlanta*, a ram like the *Virginia*.

In the summer of 1863, off Charleston, the *Atlanta* met the Federal monitor *Weehawken*, designed to carry two 15-inch bottle-shaped Dahlgren guns in her turret. One was not ready in time, so she bore one 15- and one 11-inch gun. The first two 15-inch balls stove in the armor, spreading death and destruction, and the ram surrendered.

Despite the battle of Hampton Roads, ships could not be made invulnerable. No matter how thick the armor, a big enough gun could get through it. But it was not necessary to make ships invulnerable. It was enough that an armored ship could always destroy an unarmored one of comparable size. So, during the Civil War, both sides built armored ships as fast as they could.

The rebels built rams along the original Brooke-Porter lines— powerful ships, but liable to engine troubles at critical moments. The Confederates suffered from the South's technological backwardness and from having a government of landed gentry. These, like the fumbling British ministry in the American Revolutionary War, knew little and cared less about mechanical matters.

The Federals built dozens of "monitors," as all later ships of this type were called. Some had two turrets and other experimental arrangements. In 1863, worried about rebel rams on the inland waters, the Navy Department asked Ericsson to design a well-armored monitor that should mount a single gun and draw no more than four feet of water. Ericsson reported that it could not be done; there would have to be either more draft or less armor.

Stimers, the "old, able and cantankerous"[11] naval engineer who had worked the *Monitor's* turret at Hampton Roads, said he would build the shallow-draft monitors if given money and authority. He got both; but alas! when the first of the class, the *Chimo*, was launched, she sank to the bottom with a gurgle. One of Stimers' draftsmen had calculated her weight on the basis of kiln-dried oak. But wartime shortages had eaten up all the kiln-dried oak, so the twenty ships were made of the denser green oak.

The Navy Department called in Ericsson, who redesigned these nonfloating ships; but the war was over by the time they had been rebuilt. Then they were quietly left to rot, as the United States went through another long period of naval neglect.

The United States kept some of its Civil War monitors clear through the Spanish-American War and even built four more in 1903, but none saw battle again. The real importance of the *Monitor* design was revealed when the British and French navies mounted Timby's turrets on regular ocean-going warships. After experiments showed that sail rigging got in the way of turret guns, the British built the *Devastation* of 1873 with two turrets and no sails at all. From that design evolved the twentieth-century battleship, with two to seven turrets, all on the centerline and bearing two to four guns each. The battleship ruled the seas for three-quarters of a century, until airplanes reduced it to a secondary role and then nuclear explosives and guided missiles made it obsolete.

Down through the First World War, the guns of cruisers continued to stand in a row around the edge of the ship in the old broadside fashion. Guns of destroyers and cruisers and the small guns of battleships were mounted naked or fitted with shields whose protection to the crews was negligible.

By the Second World War, however, navies mounted all but light antiaircraft guns in turrets; and small warships as well as large carried their main guns on the centerline as Ericsson's monitors and the *Princeton* had done.

After the Civil War, Ericsson gave a pair of 15-inch guns for the Swedish monitor *John Ericsson*. He built two gunboats for Spain, which helped to defeat the efforts of the Cubans to revolt from Spanish rule and so indirectly contributed to the causes of the Spanish-American War. In the celebrated cruiser competition of 1869, Ericsson's *Madawaska* made 13.5 knots. This was excellent speed for the time, second only to the phenomenal twenty-three of Isherwood's winning *Wampanoag*. But the *Madawaska* vibrated so badly that she could hardly hit anything with her guns. Ericsson built a torpedo boat, the *Destroyer*, which discharged its weapon from the first submerged torpedo tube. But Congress refused to appropriate money for her purchase.

Around 1870 Ericsson, now an ornery sixty-seven, withdrew from active engineering and lived on his income, which ran around $19,000. He worked on solar engines, which converted the sun's heat into power by steam or by hot air.

Dwelling in a decaying ward at 36 Beach Street, in New York City, old Ericsson became so set in his ways that he would not read a typewritten letter; his secretary must needs copy it in longhand. He would not ride the El. He never saw Central Park and would never have seen Brooklyn Bridge had not his secretary driven him over it without telling him in advance. He was sure the telephone was a hoax; though when Edison became famous, Ericsson admired him. He speculated about God's being a "great mechanician," evolved erroneous theories of the source of the sun's heat, and destroyed most of his personal papers.

In 1889 he died. His son Hjalmar Elworth, who had become director general of the Swedish railways and visited his father briefly in 1876, had died without issue two years before. Ericsson's estate was split among many relatives, friends, and associates.

Although he had come out of the Civil War worth over a quarter-million, Ericsson's estate had shrunk until he had only $7500 in cash. However, the posthumous sale of the *Destroyer* to Brazil for $75,000 made possible the payment of Ericsson's legacies.

In 1890 the United States, with all the pomp it could muster, sent his remains back to Sweden on the new cruiser *Baltimore*. This was one of the nation's first warships of the type that evolved from the ironclad monsters of Hampton Roads.

Of the other naval developments of the heroic age, submarine mines had been experimented with by Bushnell, Fulton, Colt, and various Europeans. In the Civil War both sides used them, especially the Confederates, who sank eighteen Federal ships by this means.

The oceanographer Matthew Maury, commissioned in the Confederate Navy, spent a year in experiments with mines. He also vainly advocated a program of many small gunboats, each carrying two big guns. At last, disgusted by what he considered Mallory's weak and sluggish management of the department, he had himself ordered to Europe to buy ships for the Confederacy.

The Civil War also saw the use of the spar torpedo, an explosive charge on the end of a long pole mounted on the bow of a ship. The torpedo boat pushed the charge against the side of its victim and exploded it. Thus Lieutenant Cushing sank the rebel ram *Albemarle* in 1864.

The self-propelled torpedo, which became a dominant weapon in the twentieth century, was invented by a Briton, Whitehead, in the late 1860s. Whitehead's crucial invention was a gadget that kept the torpedo running at a predetermined depth, neither diving to the bottom nor leaping out of the water like a hooked tarpon.

Both sides in the Civil War tried submarines. The Federals bought a French submarine, the *Alligator*, but lost it in a storm before it was used. The Confederates built several submarines of the Fulton type, driven by crews turning cranks and bearing spar torpedoes. All were named *David* for Goliath's nemesis. The first *David* stuck in the mud of the bottom and suffocated her crew. Fished up, she was tried as a surface torpedo boat but had so little reserve buoyancy that she sank four times more, killing the crew each time. At last, in 1864, she sank the Federal corvette *Housatonic* off Charleston but sank herself for the last time in the process.

Later in the century several governments experimented with submarines. France led the world for a while with its compressed-air *Plongeur* of 1863, but two of the most effective submarine inventors worked in the United States.

One was John P. Holland (1840–1914), a stout, jolly Irishman who came over in the seventies boiling with hatred of Great Britain, whose maritime rule he hoped to destroy by inventing a practical submarine. He had read Jules Verne's *Twenty Thousand Leagues under the Sea* and knew about the submarines of Bushnell and Fulton.

While teaching in a Catholic school in New Jersey, Holland built his first submarine, a cigar-shaped vessel two by sixteen feet, with a space in the middle for him to sit and turn the screw by pedaling. He meant to affix a mine to the bottom of a hostile ship and go away as Bushnell had tried to do.

With several thousand dollars from the anti-British Fenian Society, Holland built more submarines, each larger and more effective. He worked out the use of water ballast and horizontal rudders. By 1881 he had an underwater vessel, driven by a petroleum engine, which could dive in a few seconds.

In the 1890s he began building submarines for the Navy, albeit with difficulty because the naval technicians insisted upon changes that caused the failure of his first boat to meet specifications. His *Holland*, completed in 1900 with a gasoline engine for surface cruising and a storage battery for diving, was far ahead of any other submarine of the time.

Holland sold several more submarines to the government before he retired from his company in 1904. His Anglophobia abated with time and prosperity, he sold his British patent rights to the British government.

Holland's rival for the first United States contract for a submarine was Simon Lake of Pleasantville, New Jersey, whose main interest at first was in submarines for undersea salvage work. His *Argonaut Junior* was a 14-footer with wheels for traveling on the bottom and a lock in the bow by which a diver could leave the craft to work on a wreck. Lake's second boat had a 5-horsepower engine and got its air from a hose to the surface. Later Lake devised the conning tower, which survives as the dorsal finlike structure atop all modern submarines. He worked actively as a submarine builder throughout the First World War.

VIII

KELLY

AND STEEL REFINING

It is fun to imagine what would happen if we could resurrect some ancient worthy—a Caesar or a Leonardo da Vinci, for instance—and show him about the present-day world. What would he say to it all? No doubt, like Merlin in C. S. Lewis's novel *That Hideous Strength*, he would be as much taken aback by the lack of personal service as by the traffic and gadgetry. If, before beginning his tour, we told him that science and invention had revolutionized the world since his day, he might rejoin:

"I suppose you have everything made of gold and silver now?"

"Well, not exactly," we would say. And when the ancient has taken his tour, he might well exclaim:

"Oh, I see! You have everything made of *steel!*"

For steel, while never so valuable as gold and silver, was still costly enough in the days of Caesar and Leonardo da Vinci so that its lavish use in the modern world would astonish them. How did this change come about?

The story forms part of that of American invention, for Americans played a large part in it. On the other hand, it is a story in which, as in the case of the automobile, we cannot separate the American contributions from the European. The story leaps back and forth across the Atlantic like a tennis ball across a court.

To begin with, what is iron? What is steel, and what is the difference between iron and steel?

Iron is one of the hundred-odd elements that make up the universe; and, moreover, one of the earth's commonest elements, comprising about five per cent of the earth's crust. It does not usually occur in a pure form in nature, because it is chemically active. Unless it is very pure, when exposed to moist air it combines with oxygen to form ferric oxide or rust.

In nature, most iron occurs in the form of oxides and carbonates. These ores are turned into metallic iron by heating with carbon and limestone. The resulting iron, however, is seldom pure. It nearly always contains a small amount of carbon. The commercial substances that we call "iron" and "steel" are iron-carbon alloys. These alloys vary in their properties, depending upon the amount of carbon.

First, there are irons with very little carbon—less, usually, than one-tenth of one per cent. These irons are called "wrought" or "malleable" iron. They are tough and can be hammered out thin, but they are relatively soft: not much harder, in fact, than brass. Blades of wrought iron hold their edge no better than those of copper. When heated red, wrought iron becomes soft and doughy, but it does not really melt until a temperature of over 2800°F is reached.

Second, there are irons with a high carbon content, from two to four per cent. These are called "cast iron" or "pig iron." Their properties differ from those of wrought iron. When heated to red heat, they do not soften as wrought iron does. Instead, they melt quite sharply at about 2250°F. When solidified, cast iron is much harder than wrought iron. But it is also brittle, so that it cannot be shaped by hammering.

Cast iron is so called because things made of it are usually given their final form by melting and pouring into a mold. Wrought iron, on the other hand, cannot be cast, because in its molten form it is not fluid enough to fill the mold completely. However, it can be shaped by hammering, which cast iron cannot be; hence the name, meaning "worked" or "hammered" iron.

Between wrought iron and cast iron are the steels, whose carbon content is usually between 0.3 per cent and 1.7 per cent. To some degree these alloys combine the hardness of cast iron with the workability of wrought iron, and they are stronger and springier than either. Their melting points are also intermediate. Hence most of the iron that we see in commercial use today—for office buildings, bridges, railroad rails, railroad cars and locomotives, ships, automobile and truck frames, and so on—is in the form of steel.

Besides wrought iron, steel, and cast iron, there are intermediate forms of iron and many alloys of iron with other metals. These alloys all have their special properties.

Before men knew how to smelt iron from its ores, they sometimes beat pieces of iron meteorites into tools and weapons. Actual smelting began in Asia Minor about 1500 B.C., and the art became widely known by 1000 B.C.

All the early iron would be classed today as wrought iron. The method of smelting was to dig a pit in a hillside, line it with stone, fill it with iron ore and wood or charcoal, and set the fuel on fire. When the fuel had all burned up, a porous, stony, glowing mass would be found among the ashes. This was fished out and hammered, compacting the iron and squeezing out the impurities in a shower of sparks. The finished lump, called a "bloom," was about the size and shape of a large sweet potato.

In time men learned to make the fire hotter by blowing on it with a bellows and to build a permanent furnace of brick instead of merely digging a hole in the ground. Steel was made either by smelting iron ore with a large excess of charcoal, or by packing a piece of wrought iron with charcoal and cooking it for days, until the iron absorbed enough carbon to turn into steel. As these processes were costly and uncertain, and the founders knew nothing about the chemistry of the metal they were working with, steel for many centuries remained a scarce and expensive metal. It was employed only in such vital uses as sword blades.

Other advances were the addition of a flux such as limestone to the mixture of ore and charcoal, to absorb the impurities in the ore; the invention of tongs and hammers to handle heavy lumps of metal; and the tempering of iron objects by heating to just the right degree and quenching by plunging into water. In classical times, two of the world's main iron centers were Austria and India, from which good steel was exported all over the civilized world. Elsewhere iron was made and consumed locally in small amounts.

During the Middle Ages, iron-smelting furnaces were made larger and taller. By the fourteenth century, German and Belgian furnaces became so large—ten to fourteen feet high and heated by water-driven bellows—that it was now possible to dissolve enough carbon into the iron to transform it into cast iron, which flowed freely out in liquid form. These late medieval founders turned out either wrought or cast iron at will, in masses of hundreds of pounds per charge.

The use of coke, begun unsuccessfully by Abraham Darby in 1709, permitted the building of even taller furnaces. Coke, being stronger than charcoal, was not so liable to be crushed by the weight of the charge. About the same time, ironmongers began the practice of remelting iron in a special furnace, called a finery furnace, to improve its purity.

However, cast iron still comprised only a small fraction of the total iron produced (five per cent in 1750). Steel still had to be made by a slow and uncertain process of persuading wrought iron to take up extra carbon.

In the late eighteenth century, two more steps were taken towards the mass production of steel. Several scientists discovered the relation between the quality of different kinds of iron and the percentage of carbon in them.

The other advance was the puddling furnace of Henry Cort (1740–1800) who also built the first successful rolling mill. In Cort's improved finery furnace, one compartment contained cast iron; another, a coal fire. The gas from the fire passed over the iron and melted it, while excess air oxydized the carbon in the mixture and converted cast iron to wrought iron. A workman called a puddler kept stirring the molten iron with a long pole until it solidified.

Cort was on the verge of success when a strange misfortune befell him. A man from whom Cort and his partner had borrowed money to enlarge their plant turned out to have embezzled this money from the British government. The government, ignoring Cort's pleas to be allowed to pay the money back from his earnings, confiscated Cort's iron works and his patents, so that Cort was poor for the rest of his life.

William Kelly (1811–88) was the son of a man who had come to America from Ireland and made good in business in Pittsburgh, which in Kelly's youth was becoming known as an iron-producing center.

Kelly was a tall, well-built man with a drooping mustache and a spaniel-like expression in his mild blue eyes. For a time he worked as a traveling salesman for the business run by his brother and his brother-in-law. In the course of his travels he married Mildred Gracy, the daughter of a Kentucky tobacco merchant.

Seeing iron ore in the neighborhood of Eddyville, Kentucky, where his wife's family lived, Kelly persuaded his brother to sell out their share of the business in Pittsburgh and join him at Eddyville. There, in 1846, with money borrowed from Kelly's father-in-law, they bought a furnace and 14,000 acres of timberland and began to smelt and refine iron.

At first they did well, especially with a process that Kelly had invented for making sugar kettles larger than those in use. As he could not persuade the local whites to work in a foundry, Kelly had to rent about three hundred Negro slaves from their owners. This went against Kelly's grain, because he disapproved of slavery. Furthermore, the slaves often escaped across the nearby Ohio line, and then Kelly had to reimburse their owners.

To avoid the use of slaves, Kelly persuaded ten workers to come from China. The Chinese—the first in the United States—delighted him with their industry, and he would have imported more had not legal obstacles prevented.

Then, however, Kelly and his brother began to run into the law of diminishing returns. When their surface ore gave out, they found that the subsurface deposits near their furnace were contaminated by black flint, and that the next best surface deposits were too far for economical hauling. Also, they had turned all the nearby timber into charcoal, and the nearest supply was now seven miles away.

Kelly at that time used the conventional finery furnace for refining cast iron to wrought iron. This furnace, however, used large quantities of charcoal. If Kelly wanted to stay in business, he had to find a more economical method.

Kelly was watching his finery fire one day when he started up. He saw that a spot in the molten mass of iron had become white-hot, though there was no charcoal near it—just a steady current of air.

Kelly grasped the idea that, once pig iron was molten, and a current of air was directed at it, the carbon and other impurities in the air would furnish the fuel to keep the mass above the melting point. Meanwhile the oxygen in the air, combining with the carbon in the iron to form carbon dioxide, reduced the carbon content of the iron and turned cast iron into steel or wrought iron.

Kelly began to talk excitedly about his discovery. His family thought him mad and sent for a physician. After all, they had always blown on their coffee to cool it, not to heat it. But Dr. Higgins listened patiently to Kelly's explanation and sided with the ironmonger.

Kelly also gave a demonstration of his process before some of the other Kentucky ironmakers. With an improvised apparatus, he showed that blowing air through molten pig iron made it hotter than ever and also lowered its carbon content. A blacksmith beat a horseshoe and some nails out of the resulting low-carbon iron and nailed the shoe to the foot of a horse, which he could not of course have done with cast iron. The ironmakers shook their heads, remarking:

"Some crank'll be burning ice next."

The obstacles to Kelly's use of his "pneumatic process," as he called it, piled higher and higher. His father-in-law demanded that he either give up this visionary project or pay back the money he had borrowed to start his iron works. A customer wrote him from Cincinnati:

"We understand that you have adopted a new-fangled way of refining your iron. Is this so? We want our iron made in the regular way or not at all."[1]

In addition, Kelly's shortage of ore became serious. To keep his backer and his customers satisfied, he pretended to drop his "air-boiling process" and went back to traditional ironmaking. But, with the help of a pair of English ironworkers, he secretly set up a furnace in the forest three miles away and continued his experiments when no one was looking.

By 1851, Kelly had his first pneumatic furnace working. This was a square brick structure four feet high, with a cylindrical chamber and holes in the bottom to admit the air. His main difficulty lay in blowing the air through fast enough. Otherwise the molten iron ran down into the holes and stopped them up.

Bit by bit, Kelly improved his furnaces, of which he built seven. In 1856 he heard that an Englishman, Henry Bessemer, had taken out an American patent for a similar process. Kelly, who had not bothered with patents, now filed a patent application. The Patent Office therefore declared an "interference." This is an investigation to determine who, of two inventors claiming the same invention, is the true and first inventor and so entitled to a patent.

In this case, the Patent Office decided that Kelly was first with the general idea of refining molten pig iron by blowing air through it. On the other hand, Bessemer had devised a sophisticated apparatus for carrying out the process. This was a crucible mounted on trunnions. It could be tilted up to the vertical position after it had received its charge of molten iron, to let the air bubble up through the melt, and then tilted down to a horizontal position again to pour off the refined iron. Bessemer had priority on this device, which became known as the Bessemer converter.

However, Kelly was not destined soon to make money from his basic patent. The panic of 1857 ushered in a depression that slaughtered commercial companies in droves. To get a little ready cash and to avoid complete loss of his patent rights, Kelly sold his patent to his father for a thousand dollars, with an understanding that his father would either sell the patent back some day or bequeath it to his son. Then Kelly went bankrupt.

In 1860 the elder Kelly died suddenly without having changed his will. As a result, Kelly's patent descended to Kelly's sisters. These women, deeming their brother William a vague, unbusinesslike character, kept possession of the patent for several years. At last they were prevailed upon to transfer it back to Kelly in trust for his children.

Meanwhile Kelly, released from bankruptcy, went to the Cambria Iron Works in Johnstown, Pennsylvania. There he persuaded the manager to let him use a corner of the yard for experiments. Having built an egg-shaped converter of the Bessemer type, he announced that he would again demonstrate his process. A couple of hundred workmen gathered to watch.

The puddlers, whose occupation would be threatened if the method succeeded, passed remarks about the "Irish crank." Kelly told the engineer:

"I want the strongest blast you can blow."[2]

Taking him at his word, the engineer hung a weight on the safety valve of the blowing engine and let it rip. The resulting blast sent the entire contents of the converter flying out in a volcano of sparks and molten metal. For days "Kelly's fireworks" were the joke of the county.

Then Kelly staged a second trial with a more moderate blast. When sparks began to fly from the converter, he ran about, picking them up with tongs and hammering them on an anvil.

For half an hour the little lumps of iron shattered at the first blow. At last one of them flattened, showing that the iron had lost enough carbon to become malleable. Kelly shut off the blast, poured out the contents of the converter, and hammered a small piece of the solidified iron out into a thin sheet. The joking died.

At last Kelly had arrived. In 1862 he formed a company with the help of some financial backers.

Now, however, he came up against the fact that, while he had control of the basic patent on the pneumatic process, Bessemer—or rather Bessemer's American associates—controlled Bessemer's American patent on the tilting converter, which made the process practical. Now let us look into the career of Henry Bessemer.

Bessemer (1813–98) was born in Hertfordshire, England, the son of an Englishman of remotely French descent. The elder Bessemer, a successful metal worker and type founder, moved to the Netherlands and then to France, whence he fled back to England to escape the Revolution. Henry Bessemer spent most of his boyhood in his father's shop and, when he finished school at seventeen, went to London to seek his fortune. Here he made a good living by skilled metal work, such as embossing.

About 1833, Henry Bessemer invented a perforated die by which the date could be impressed upon a stamp. This was to stop people from soaking the stamps off documents in order to use them over, a petty misdemeanor common at the time. Bessemer gave his invention to the British government free, on the understanding that he was to be given a good, permanent, governmental job.

But the promise was not kept. Convinced that he had been swindled, the outraged young inventor became thereafter extremely aggressive in the protection of his rights.

Bessemer continued to invent. From his fertile brain came a glass polisher, a ventilator, a sugar-making process, a method of making waste plumbago into pencil leads, a process for casting type under pressure, a type-composing machine, a process for making a kind of plush, and methods of making bronze powder and gold paint.

In 1854 Bessemer had a talk with Napoleon III, who complained of the quality of iron used in cannon. He would do something about that, said Bessemer. Back in London he began a series of experiments in iron metallurgy, of which he knew but little.

In 1856, Bessemer noticed that a pig of iron on the edge of the pool of molten metal in his furnace had not melted away as it should. Poking at the pig, he found that it was a mere shell. The iron had melted out of the inside, leaving the outer surface.

Bessemer at once looked into the matter. The iron on the outside of the pig, he reasoned, must have had its carbon removed by the current of air from the furnace. Lowering its carbon content had raised its melting point and made it into wrought iron. From this he leaped to the idea of refining molten pig iron by blowing air through it, just as Kelly had done years before.

To make sure that he was not fooling himself, Bessemer consulted an engineer whom he knew. The engineer persuaded Bessemer to present an account of his process at a forthcoming meeting of the British Association for the Advancement of Science. Reactions were mixed, but some were impressed. After all, Bessemer was known as a successful inventor. Several ironmakers took out licenses to use Bessemer's process.

Disillusion awaited them, however; their first attempts failed. Bessemer was berated and denounced. Giving back their money to those who asked for it, Bessemer embarked on a costly two-year program of research to find out what was wrong. At last his chemists gave the answer: Bessemer's process produced good wrought iron if, and only if, the ore was very low in phosphorus. If there was much phosphorus in the ore, the iron would be no good.

Bessemer now offered more licenses, but nobody would take any because of his previous failure. At length, in 1859, he set up his own ironworks at Sheffield.

The Kelly-Bessemer process (so-called because the two men discovered it independently) began with high-carbon pig iron and, by burning out the carbon, changed the substance first into steel and then into wrought iron. If the blast were stopped at just the right point, steel would be made. In practice, however, it did not prove possible to shut off the blast at just the right time.

So, practically speaking, both Kelly and Bessemer continued to make wrought iron. They could make wrought iron in larger quantities and more cheaply than had been the case with the older methods, but it was still soft wrought iron. Steel remained a scarce and costly material.

The next step towards the mass production of steel was taken by the Welsh metallurgist Robert F. Mushet (1811–91). In 1848, Mushet began experiments with spiegeleisen,[3] an alloy of iron, carbon, and manganese. About 1856 he obtained a sample of iron refined by Bessemer's process. He observed that it was "burnt," that is, injured by overheating. When melted and mixed with molten spiegeleisen, however, it regained its former quality.

Starting from that point, Mushet worked out a process of steelmaking. First, all the carbon was burnt out of molten pig iron, as in the Kelly-Bessemer process. Then a small quantity of spiegeleisen was added to the melt. The manganese combined with any oxygen that had remained in the iron, while the carbon raised the carbon content of the iron to the exact percentage required for steel of the quality desired.

Mushet took out a number of patents, the most important of which was the British patent of September 22, 1856. Kelly's backers bought the rights to Mushet's American patent, and things looked bright for Mushet.

But Mushet fell victim to another of those extraordinary misfortunes that lie in wait for inventors. In the course of some obscure financial deal, he turned his main British patent over to a trustee, and the trustee neglected to pay the tax due the British government on this patent in 1859. (Great Britain, like many nations, collects annual taxes on the patents it issues; the United States does not.) Hence Mushet's patent lapsed, and British ironmakers—the ones who most counted—were free to use his process without payment. Mushet spent the rest of his life, if not exactly poor, in modest circumstances, while Bessemer became one of the world's richest men.

Mushet took out a number of metallurgical patents, on the alloying of steel with titanium, tungsten, and chromium, and invented self-hardening tungsten tool steel. A reserved and self-reliant man, he never visited any ironworks except his own. He suggested to Bessemer that the latter really ought to pay him a royalty for the use of his process, whether legally obligated to or not. This the hard-bitten Bessemer would not do.

However, hearing that Mushet was hard up, Bessemer paid him a pension of £300 a year during the last years of his life and approved giving Mushet the Bessemer Medal of the Iron and Steel Institute in 1876.

Meanwhile, Bessemer's American patent rights had been bought by a group of ironmakers of Troy, New York, headed by the brilliant engineer Alexander L. Holley. As has already been mentioned, Kelly's group in Johnstown, Pennsylvania, controlled the pneumatic process, while the group headed by Holley controlled the American rights to Bessemer's tilting converter, which made the process practical. Each could stop the other from using the invention dominated by its own patent.

Instead of fighting each other to the death, the two groups arranged a merger in the late 1860s. The Bessemer group got seventy per cent of the stock of the new company. (Historians of technology still argue over the question of whether Kelly was fairly treated and how much credit for modern steelmaking methods he ought to have.)

In 1870, Kelly and Bessemer applied for renewal of their American patents. The American steelmakers, wishing to use the inventions without payment, opposed these renewals vigorously. Kelly's patent was renewed but Bessemer's was not. Kelly could have extorted more money from his company for use of the renewed patent, but this he high-mindedly refused to do; he allowed the previous terms to stand. He had received about $30,000 in royalties up to that time, and during the life of the renewed patent he made $450,000 more.

So William Kelly did not do badly, although it irked him to have the steel made by his process marketed as "Bessemer steel." The company did so for commercial reasons, as Bessemer was the better-known man and British steel was still more important than American.

Kelly also suspected to the end of his life that one of the English workmen who had helped him back in his Eddyville days, and who had suddenly quit his job and returned to England, had been Henry Bessemer himself. Bessemer (now a stout, bald, grim-looking man with sidewhiskers, piercing eyes under shaggy brows, a blob of a nose, and a wide, rattrap mouth) snorted at this story. He had never, he said, been in America in his life. All the time he was supposed to be working in Kelly's backwoods finery he was, as many people could attest, hard at work on his own inventions in London. We can be reasonably sure that in this matter Bessemer spoke truthfully.

In his sixties Kelly settled in Louisville and indulged his taste for quiet, comfortable, scholarly living. He increased his fortune several times over by founding a successful axe-blade factory and engaging in real estate and banking. Thus he showed that he was by no means so simple in business matters as his sisters had thought.

Bessemer, now "Sir Henry," having been knighted by Queen Victoria in 1879, also retired from steelmaking but kept up his restless activity. He experimented with solar furnaces and built a fine astronomical observatory. The most spectacular invention of his late years was an anti-seasickness cross-Channel steamship. This vessel had its first class passenger saloon hung on gimbals so that, in theory, the saloon would stay upright no matter what the ship did. However, the scheme did not work very well, and Bessemer soon scrapped the ship.

Nor were the inventions of Kelly, Bessemer, and Mushet the whole story. The process of steelmaking was further refined by the Swede Göransson, who developed a method of closely controlling the air blast; by Alexander Holley, who devised important accessories for the converter; and by other steel engineers. And the Kelly-Bessemer process itself was partly displaced a few years later by the open-hearth steel process, invented by the Siemens brothers of Germany and England and improved by the Martin brothers of France.

As a result of these advances, steel soon replaced wrought iron in cannon, railroad rails, boilers, ship plates, and many other applications; and thus the steel industry became the colossus of the modern industrial world.

IX

MERGENTHALER, SHOLES, AND WRITING MACHINES

We have all seen cartoons showing a cave man squatting before a boulder on which he is laboriously chiseling pictographs. Some of us may recall Macaulay's little joke about the Assyrian poet who published three walls and a bridge in praise of his king.

Of course, the ancients did not really chisel ordinary writings, such as letters and expense accounts, on stone, any more than we do. They wrote with pens or brushes on sheets of papyrus or leather or palm frond, or with styli on tablets of wax-covered wood or slabs of soft clay. Stone was for monuments, as it still is.

But, whether the writer used a reed brush or a goose-quill pen, and whether he wrote on parchment or silk or paper, writing was still a laborious business. Speech flows along at about ten times the speed of ordinary longhand writing.

The slowness of writing became especially bothersome when a published work had to be copied over a number of times. Such copying was not only slow, but also so inaccurate that a major branch of modern scholarship has to do with the tracing and correcting of copyists' errors in ancient manuscripts.

The great step forward in speeding up writing was that taken in Mainz, Germany, in 1450 by Johann Gutenberg, with his invention of movable type—unless, as some maintain, Gutenberg stole the idea from Laurens Janszoon Coster.

For many centuries, people had been stamping impressions—seals, textile patterns, woodcut pictures—on receptive surfaces. Books were even printed from wooden blocks in China centuries before Gutenberg. Gutenberg's invention was not printing, but movable type. That is, he made a separate slug of type for each letter, so that the appropriate letters could be assembled to print a piece of copy and then broken up and distributed back in their pigeonholes after the job was done. So began the mechanization of printing.

Since mechanical writing was invented so long ago, it shows, in modern times, the characteristics of an old technical art. Although many inventions are still made in the field, they are likely to be small improvements rather than big basic advances. So many inventors strive for given improvement at the same time that one succeeds by only a small margin over his nearest competitors.

The art of printing was assimilated to the Industrial Revolution by a German, Friedrich Koenig, who built a steam press in Germany in 1811. Failing to find backing, he came to England, where the publishers of the *Times* of London hired him to build two steam presses for them. The first press had to be assembled secretly to avoid threatened violence by the pressmen.

When the press was ready for work, in 1814, the pressmen were told to wait for some expected news from abroad. Then John Walter, the publisher, walked in with an armful of papers, saying: "The *Times* is already printed by steam!"[1] Since he added that he would continue to pay the displaced pressmen until they found other jobs, there was no riot.

Other improvements in presses followed. One of the most important was the cylinder press, developed by several inventors between 1790 and 1850. In this press, instead of two flat surfaces (one bearing the type and one the paper) which are forced together like the jaws of a vise, one flat surface is replaced by a large cylinder. As the cylinder revolves, the flat surface rolls back and forth beneath it. The type may be set up either on the flat surface or on the cylinder.

The main American contributions to printing were made in the 1840s by the Hoe family. In 1803 Robert Hoe (1784–1833) landed in New York from Leicestershire. After nearly dying of yellow fever, Hoe married and went into business with his two new brothers-in-law. These were carpenters named Smith, who built printing presses and type cases. In time Hoe took sole charge of the business. He built steam-powered cast-iron presses in place of hand-operated wooden ones, adopted many other improvements, and finally worked himself to death.

He left three sons, Richard March Hoe, Robert Hoe, and Peter Smith Hoe. These brothers worked closely together; they even owned a single carriage in common. Richard was the inventor of the group.

As the demand for newspapers still outran the ability of the presses to furnish them, Richard Hoe invented an improved cylinder press: one in which both type and paper were carried on cylinders, with no flat bed at all. The type was set in curved forms around the main cylinder, while the paper was pressed against it by two smaller cylinders. The rate of production of the press was at once increased from one to two thousand copies an hour. Presses with four, six, eight, and ten paper rolls followed.

Other inventors added other methods of speeding up the printing of newspapers, such as printing on a continuous strip of paper and later cutting it into sheets. They invented machinery for folding the printed papers and methods of reproducing and printing pictures. The descendants of the Hoes continued to run the family business, and R. Hoe & Company, Inc., flourishes to this day.

Down to the late nineteenth century, all this mechanization of printing did not touch one of the most laborious, time-consuming steps in the process: setting the type and redistributing it afterwards. Until 1886, nearly all type was set by hand. The little letters all had to be picked out of their cases, one by one, as they still are in printing Chinese and Japanese.

Beginning in 1822, several inventors undertook to build machines to set type. Some even worked fairly well. In all, however, the type had to be justified by hand. That is, each line had to be spaced out so that it was exactly the same length as all the other lines in the column. And the type had to be redistributed by hand after it was used.

The most spectacular effort to solve the typesetting problem was that of James W. Paige of Hartford, Connecticut. Paige spent twenty years, beginning in 1873, and over two million dollars in perfecting this monstrosity. Mark Twain (whose *Tom Sawyer* was the first book composed on a typewriter) lost a fortune in Paige's machine, which weighed three tons and had 18,000 parts. The basic patent No. 547,860 had 163 sheets of drawings with 471 figures, and 146 claims. Two Patent Office examiners went insane during the prosecution of this application and the many applications that Paige filed on improvements.

When completed, the Paige compositor was a marvelous piece of machinery but commercially useless. Only Paige himself ever fully understood the mechanism. Therefore, every time it got out of adjustment, Paige himself had to be fetched to fix it. Only two were ever built, and both were soon retired to museums. Paige ended his days in the poorhouse.

The man who solved the typesetting problem was a native of Württemberg, Ottmar Mergenthaler (1854-99). Mergenthaler landed in Baltimore in 1872 and went to work for a cousin named August Hahl, who ran a machine shop in Washington. Young Mergenthaler proved handy and ingenious, working on the instruments ordered by the United States Signal Service for observing the weather and building models ordered by inventors to accompany their applications for patents.

At this time the official reporter for the United States Senate was James O. Clephane, who, trying to record the floods of fustian rhetoric poured out by the legislators, had long and earnestly wished for a practical writing machine. Clephane and some friends backed a West Virginian named Charles Moore, who had invented a machine for printing words on lithographic stone. The machine was brought to Hahl's shop (now located in Baltimore) to get the bugs out of it. But nothing, it seemed, would make it work.

Mergenthaler then began to build his own machines. He tried out Clephane's suggestion, of a machine to press letters into a strip of papier-mâché. This strip could then be used to cast type, somewhat as in the stereotype process. But the scheme did not quite work.

After more experiments, Mergenthaler hit upon his great idea. This was a machine carrying a lot of different letters in the form of metal matrices, to be set in a line and used as a mold to cast one whole line of type at once. The matrices were selected by the operator by means of a keyboard. They were dropped down tubes and mechanically lined up. A refinement by Mergenthaler automatically justified the type by making the blank matrices between words in the form of wedges. Then molten metal was poured into the mold so formed.

When the type metal had hardened, the cast slug dropped out. The matrices were separated and carried back mechanically to their rack at the top of the machine. A system of keying caused every matrix to drop into its proper compartment. Meanwhile the compositor set the next line. The cast slugs were assembled in trays called galleys for the press. When they had been used, they were melted up again.

Mergenthaler soon began making and selling his typesetting —or, to be more exact, typecasting—machines. The first one was set up in 1886 in the offices of the New York *Tribune*, whose editor, Whitelaw Reid, suggested the name "Lin-o-type." Mergenthaler prospered, but he overworked and succumbed to tuberculosis at the age of forty-five.

His contemporary Tolbert Lanston invented the other principal kind of typecasting machine, the Monotype. In the Monotype the operator, at one machine, punches symbols on a strip of paper tape by means of his keyboard, and this strip of paper, fed into another machine, effects the actual typecasting.

A typecasting machine does not take the place of pen and pencil; for, while one could compose original copy on a Linotype, this would be entirely impractical. Ever since the early eighteenth century, inventors have essayed to create a real writing machine, on which the writer could compose directly. They sought a machine that should not only write faster than a pen or pencil but that should also turn out good, uniform, legible copy, not the scrawl into which longhand degenerates with haste or carelessness.

Early writing machines sometimes tried to write longhand mechanically, imitating the movement of a pen in the hand of the writer. Such inventions worked no better than the first efforts at sewing machines, which strove to duplicate the motions of the housewife's needle.

By mid-nineteenth century, a number of European and American inventors were at work on the problem. Some produced machines that worked after a fashion, although none functioned well enough for commercial sale. Some of these inventors' ideas, however, are still used in modern typewriters.

In 1867 there lived in Milwaukee a tall, slender man with flowing hair and a dreamy air, Christopher Latham Sholes (1819–90). Sholes worked as Collector of Customs. The job was a political sinecure given him because, as editor of the Milwaukee *Sentinel*, he had supported Lincoln in 1860. It provided a modest but steady income and lots of spare time, which Sholes used in editing his paper and tinkering with inventions.

Sholes devised the method of getting newspapers to subscribers by printing their names on the margin. He also thought of a machine to print consecutive numbers on tickets and on the pages of books. His friend Carlos Glidden suggested:

"Mr. Sholes, why can't you make a machine that will print words as well as figures? If you can make a paging machine, you ought to make a writing machine."

"I can," said Sholes. "I have thought about it a great deal and I am going to try it as soon as I get through with this paging machine."[2]

Sholes accordingly rigged up a single telegraph key which, when pressed, actuated a lever. This lever forced a brass letter *w* up against a sheet of glass.

Sholes went to the local telegraph office to borrow a sheet of newly invented carbon paper from the operator, Charles Weller. Back at his office, Sholes slid the carbon paper and a sheet of ordinary white paper under the glass and pressed the key. Sure enough, the letter *w* appeared on the white paper.

Sholes then went into partnership with Glidden and a mechanic, Samuel W. Soulé, to make a complete writing machine. Soulé suggested converging type bars, all striking in the same place.

They struggled with the invention for five years. The peculiar arrangement of the typewriter keys—QWERTYUIOP and so on—was based upon the arrangement of letters in a printer's case. Charles Weller, now a court reporter in St. Louis, bought the first complete machine and used it in his business.

Sholes wrote many letters on his typewriters, one of them to a Pennsylvanian businessman named James Densmore. Sholes had met Densmore years before but had not liked this large, red-faced, hairy man with a loudly belligerent manner. Now, however, Densmore sought out Sholes and his partners and asked if he might join the firm. That would be fine, they said, if he would pay developmental costs. So Soulé dropped out and Densmore took his place, cajoling and bullying Sholes to keep him hard at work on his balky invention.

The typewriter (Sholes thought up the name) now looked like a practical writing machine and even acted like one for a while. But a few weeks of hard use always broke the machines down. So complex a mechanism, with so many little levers and shafts and wheels, was in particular need of careful engineering study to cure its weaknesses and adapt it to mass production.

One steady customer was James O. Clephane, the reporter in Washington who later helped Mergenthaler. Clephane ruined one typewriter after another. He cursed their shortcomings by letter until even the saintly Sholes lost his temper and cried: "I am through with Clephane!"

"This candid fault-finding is just what we need!" roared Densmore. "Where Clephane points out a weak lever or rod, let us make it strong. Where a spacer or an inker works stiffly, let us make it work smoothly. Then, depend upon Clephane for all the praise we deserve."[3]

They took their problem to Thomas Edison's laboratory in Newark. Edison, then becoming known as an inventor of multiple telegraphs and stock tickers, made some improvements and built a dozen typewriters for Sholes.

In 1872 they approached the Remington Arms Company in Ilion, New York. The Remingtons were delighted, as the gun business was not good in the years following the Civil War. They proposed to buy the entire rights to Sholes's machine and offered the partners their choice of $12,000 in cash apiece or a royalty.

Densmore took the royalty, became rich, and built another line of typewriters of his own. The Remingtons failed to find the mass market they expected and were forced to sell their typewriter company in 1886. Then, as so often happens with a new invention, people began to realize its true value after the pioneers had lost fortunes trying to promote it. They saw that the typewriter was the perfect instrument for business correspondence and records. Business picked up, and by 1895 the typewriter boom was on. Many makes appeared, often circumventing the Sholes patent by changing the arrangement of keys and type bars.

Sholes took the $12,000 offered him and went on living in the modest way he always had, making a few more improvements in typewriters. He does not seem to have cared much about money. He remarked:

"All my life I have been trying to escape being a millionaire, and now I think I have succeeded."[4]

He did not have much time left, as he had been middle-aged and tubercular when he began his work on the typewriter. In his last years he traveled for his health on money furnished by Densmore, whom he survived by a year.

One objective, however, Sholes did achieve. He believed that the typewriter could provide genteel jobs for women, and it did on a scale far beyond anyone's imaginings. It was, in fact, one of the biggest factors in the emancipation of women. So marked was the social revolution brought about by this one invention that Sir James M. Barrie wrote a one-act play on the subject, *The Twelve Pound Look*. Ethel Barrymore once played in it, portraying Kate, the woman who had been freed by a £12 typewriter from servile dependence on a tyrannical husband.

X

BELL

AND THE TELEPHONE

One cold wet day in March 1875, Joseph Henry, now seventy-eight, was working in his office in the Smithsonian Institution when a caller brought in an apparatus. The caller was a tall, slender, shabby young Scot with bushy black hair, long drooping sidewhiskers, and a courtly manner. He was Alexander Graham Bell (1847–1922), a teacher of speech as his father and grandfather had been. He had come to Washington on borrowed money to see his patent attorney about his gadget, and he was staying with a friend to save the cost of a hotel.

All afternoon the old man and the young one tinkered. Henry said:

"You are in possession of the germ of a great invention, and I would advise you to work at it until you have made it complete."

"But," protested Bell plaintively, "I have not got the electrical knowledge that is necessary to overcome the difficulties."

"Get it," said Henry, no man to waste words.[1]

Bell went out and got it. Born in Edinburgh, Bell had been educated there and in London. He left home to become a teacher of elocution in British schools and made some small discoveries about the nature of vowels. In London he met Sir Charles Wheatstone, one of the inventors of the telegraph, who fired him with a passion for science.

Bell also met Alexander J. Ellis, president of the London Philological Society. Ellis showed him, in his home, some of the experiments of the great German physicist Helmholtz on the nature of sound. For instance, he demonstrated that tuning forks could be kept in vibration by electromagnets in such a way as to imitate human vocal sounds. From this demonstration Bell got the idea of sending the human voice electrically by wire.

Then Bell was attacked by tuberculosis, this scourge of the nineteenth century which afflicted so many great men of the time. One modern medical theory holds that tuberculosis actually stimulated the genius of these men by causing them to run a constant slight fever.[2] Be that as it may, the white plague killed Bell's two brothers; and Bell's doctor advised a complete change of climate.

Bell accordingly emigrated to Canada, where he taught the Mohawks a system of phonetic symbols called "visible speech," which his father had invented.

Bell's father, lecturing in Boston, proudly referred to his son's exploits. So the Boston Board of Education wrote to Bell, asking him to come to Boston and introduce his system of teaching deaf mutes at a recently opened school.

Bell came. Besides teaching at the School for the Deaf, he gave private lessons to a five-year-old deaf-mute boy, George Sanders. He boarded at the Sanders home, where he was allowed to use the cellar for experiments.

From time to time, Bell would awaken George's father Thomas Sanders, a prosperous leather dealer, in the middle of the night to try out some new electrical scheme. If Sanders thought he heard any improvement in the strength of the signals over Bell's wires, Bell would do a kind of Iroquois war dance and go back to bed.

Bell also fell in love with another deaf and dumb pupil, Mabel Hubbard, who had lost her hearing from scarlet fever as a small child. He did not tutor Mabel himself but advised her father on her instruction.

The father, Gardiner G. Hubbard, a lively and enthusiastic lawyer, had a long record of promoting worthy causes. Sometimes he was rich; sometimes poor. To him Bell confided his ambitions to build, first, a musical telegraph, over which as many messages could be sent at once as there are notes on a piano; second, to transmit speech by wire.

Hubbard and Sanders agreed to finance the musical telegraph. But at first they balked at the telephone, which they deemed impractical. The word "telephone" had already been in use for some time, but it was generally applied to devices like speaking tubes.

In Germany, Philipp Reis had for several years been working on another variant of the musical-telegraph idea. This was a device in which the vibrations of a musical note, causing a diaphragm to vibrate and thus making and breaking an electrical circuit, transmitted a similar note over wires. Reis also called his device a "telephone" and has a statue to this day with an inscription describing him as the inventor of the telephone, although his device could not transmit audible speech at all.

Bell soon saw that a telephone to send vocal sounds had a much wider potential appeal than any kind of multiple telegraph. But Sanders and Hubbard insisted that he keep on with the musical telegraph. So, to please them, he worked on both.

Bell's task was, first, to make a continuous current in an electrical circuit vary in just the way that the pressure of the air against the transmitter varied as the sound waves from the speaker's mouth struck it, and then to turn these electrical waves or pulsations back into sound waves at the receiver end of the circuit. Earlier experimenters, like Reis, who used discontinuous currents, got nothing but buzzing sounds.

The receiver proved the easier task. If the wire of the circuit be wound around a U-shaped iron core to make an electromagnet, and a thin metal diaphragm be mounted close to the ends of the magnet, variations in the current cause the electromagnet to pull the diaphragm with varying force. Hence the diaphragm vibrates and sends out sound waves.

It proved much more difficult, however, to arrange a diaphragm or a piece of clock spring so that its vibrations, responding to sound waves in the ambient air, should cause the current in the circuit to vary. Obtaining the ear of a corpse from a surgeon he knew, Bell tried using it as a transmitter. Then he tried various combinations of thin diaphragms and vibrating metal strips.

Bell knew something about diaphragms, for he had already worked with a device he called the phonautograph to help his deaf pupils. This had a diaphragm attached to a stylus, so that when a pupil spoke into it the stylus made a wavy line. The deaf person could compare the wavy line made when he pronounced a word with that made by a normal speaker and thus correct his mistakes.

Bell's assistant, the brilliant young mechanic Thomas A. Watson, told how they neared success:

> On the afternoon of June 2, 1875, we were hard at work on the same old job, testing some modification of the instruments . . . I had charge of the transmitters as usual, setting them squealing one after the other, while Bell was retuning the receiver springs one by one, pressing them against his ear as I have described. One of the transmitter springs I was attending to stopped vibrating and I plucked it to start it again. It didn't start and I kept on plucking it, when suddenly I heard a shout from Bell in the next room, and then out he came with a rush, demanding, "What did you do? Don't change anything. Let me see!" I showed him. It was very simple. The make-and-break points of the transmitter spring I was trying to start had become welded together, so that when I snapped the spring the circuit remained unbroken while that spring of magnetized steel, by its vibration over the pole of its magnet, was generating . . . a current of electricity that varied in density within hearing distance of that spring.[3]

Ten months of hard work followed until Bell's matured plan took shape. Bell and Watson strung wires down two flights of stairs to the ground floor of Williams' Electrical Shop in Boston. After more adjustments, Watson, on March 10, 1876, heard Bell, who had just spilled acid on his trousers, say:

"Mr. Watson, please come here; I want you."

Watson bounded up the stairs, crying: "I can hear you! I can hear the *words!*"

Later Watson, no doubt thinking of Morse's magniloquent opening telegraph message, remarked: "Perhaps if Mr. Bell had realized that he was about to make a bit of history, he would have been prepared with a more sounding and interesting sentence."[4]

At noon on May 10, 1876, in Fairmount Park, Philadelphia, Ulysses S. Grant, President of the United States, threw away his cigar and nodded to Dom Pedro de Alcántara—Emperor Pedro II of Brazil.

The emperor, a scholarly, broad-minded, widely traveled man who insisted on seeing everything, had been touring the United States. In Washington he had dropped in on Simon Newcomb at the Naval Observatory. In Boston he had asked Alexander Graham Bell for advice on conducting the first Brazilian school for deaf mutes, which he had organized near Rio de Janeiro. Thirteen years later he was thrown out by his subjects, who resented his freeing their slaves.

Together the two bearded, middle-aged politicians walked along a red carpet on the floor of Machinery Hall at the Philadelphia Centennial Exposition, which celebrated the hundredth anniversary of the Declaration of Independence. They came to the great Corliss engine, so called for George H. Corliss, the American engineer who invented a celebrated quick-acting valve gear and who built this particular monster. President and emperor heaved their weight on the levers.

With a sigh, a hiss, and a groan the world's largest steam engine turned its thirty-ton flywheel. Grant and Pedro shook hands. Outside, the sun came out from behind the threatening clouds; bands burst into music; Philadelphia's mightiest foghorn boomed.

This exposition of the arts and sciences of all nations had been two years in preparation. The great steam engine drove the other machines by a banyan-grove of slapping belts. Everywhere were machines for sawing, grinding, cutting, pumping, spinning, knitting, and so on.

In invention, as represented at the Exposition, the United States and the German Empire were quickly pushing to the front. In the fine arts, both were outshone by Great Britain. American art was represented by things like a statue of Iolanthe made of butter by a lady in Arkansas, which partly melted every day and had to be patted back into shape after hours. The German arts consisted mainly of busts of the Kaiser, Bismarck, and Field Marshal von Moltke made of every sculptural material from bronze to soap.

The British had sent a fine art exhibit, which they housed in a special building of stone. One of their most popular pictures was the well-known painting by Briton Riviere, "Circe and the Friends of Ulysses." A samite-clad Circe sits on her porch while before her eighteen hogs stand, wallow, and beg for food. The story was told of a rustic's standing in front of this painting, reading the title from his catalogue, and exclaiming:

"Well, if that ain't the roughest thing on old Grant that ever I see!"[5]

Everybody who could, went. Eight-year-old Robert Andrews Millikan, who later measured the charge of the electron and discovered cosmic rays, was there with his parents.

Another visitor was a garrulous youth of twenty-three, Elihu Thomson (1853–1937).[6] He was small and slight, with a thin square-jawed face and a mustache that dwarfed his other features. He taught chemistry at Philadelphia's Central High School and spent most of his time at the Exhibition hanging around the small exhibit that the Belgian electrical inventor Théophile Gramme had sent over from Paris.

This consisted of a small steam engine driving a Gramme dynamo, which operated an electroplating machine, lit an arc light, and ran a motor which in turn worked a pump. A discouraged French operator kept calling over the din: *"Voyez la puissance électrique!"*

Bell's backer Gardiner Hubbard was one of the Centennial Commissioners. Hubbard used his influence to get a small table for Bell in the exhibit of the Massachusetts Department of Education. Bell set up his brain child, but for six weeks it lay there without attracting attention. Hubbard, however, persuaded the judges to promise to spend a few minutes on it.

On a Friday late in June, the deaf Mabel Hubbard took a train to see the Centennial. Bell, who saw her aboard the train, explained that he could not go along. Thereupon the girl burst into tears, and the tenderhearted Bell excitedly leaped aboard the moving train without a ticket.

Thus it came about that on Sunday, June 25, Bell was manning his exhibit at the Centennial when the judges appeared. On this day the building was closed to ordinary visitors.

The judges, tired and hungry and sweating in long formal coats of heavy broadcloth, did not reach Bell's section until 7:00 P.M. The party included Joseph Henry, Bell's later rival Elisha Gray, Sir William Thomson (whose engineering had made the transatlantic cable practical), and Dom Pedro of Brazil, with his empress and a retinue of courtiers.

The sweltering judges were ready to call it a day. One picked up the telephone receiver, looked at it blankly, and put it down. Another made a small joke at Bell's expense. Then the burly Brazilian emperor recognized Bell and strode over, beaming through his square blond beard. "How do you do, Meester Bell? And how are the deaf mutes of Boston?"

Bell said how sorry he was that they weren't going to inspect his apparatus until next day, when he could not be there because he had to return to Boston to give an examination at the School for the Deaf.

"Ah!" said Dom Pedro. "Then we must look at it now."

Presently Bell and the judges were reciting Hamlet's soliloquy across the width of the building by telephone and exclaiming as they recognized each other's voices. Henry said:

"This comes nearer to overthrowing the doctrine of the conservation of energy than anything I ever saw."

Thomson, his monocle agleam, cried: "It *does* speak. This is the most wonderful thing I have seen in America!"[7]

The demonstration went on for hours. Learning that Bell's invention had arrived after the deadline for eligibility for awards, Thomson and Henry procured a special certificate of merit for it.

Hubbard then set out to promote the invention. He arranged for Bell to give a series of lecture-demonstrations. Bell delivered the first of these before the Essex Institute of Salem, while Watson stayed in the laboratory in Boston to furnish the entertainment. Bell described the invention, and Watson sent songs and music over a pair of borrowed telegraph wires. Another demonstration spanned the 250-mile stretch from New York to Boston.

When newspapers persisted in their doubts, Bell and Watson held a three-hour conversation over the telegraph line from Boston to the Cambridge Observatory. Each took careful notes of what he said and heard. The *Boston Advertiser* ran the story with the words spoken and recorded in parallel columns; there were just enough errors in transmission to make the show convincing. The first money that Bell made from his invention was a thousand dollars from ten of these lectures.

With this money, Bell married Mabel Hubbard and went to Europe for his honeymoon, while Hubbard pushed the invention at home. Charles Williams, in whose shop Bell had developed the invention, had a friend named E. T. Holmes, who ran a burglar-alarm business in Boston. Holmes suggested linking telephones to his wires.

Hubbard at once lent Holmes twelve telephones. Holmes went to six banks and nailed up a telephone in each. One banker made him take his "playtoy" out, but the others remained and were used by the bankers, whose wires all ran to a crude switchboard that Holmes had rigged up in his office. This was the world's first telephone switchboard.

Sixteen months after the invention, there were 778 telephones in use. Then Hubbard organized the Bell Telephone Association, with Bell, Sanders, and himself each owning three-tenths of the stock and Watson one-tenth. Sanders furnished what little capital was used. Although the company was busy enough, it was not for a long time profitable. In fact, Sanders kept putting money into it until he was $110,000 in debt. Salaries to the officers were apt to be paid late or not at all, while Watson's notebook contained entries like *"Lent Bell fifty cents,"* or *"Lent Hubbard twenty cents."*

At one time the entrepreneurs offered all their rights to the Western Union Company for $100,000. President Orton refused: "What use could this company make of an electrical toy?"[8]

But when its subsidiary, the Gold and Stock Company, reported that several of its stock tickers had been superseded by telephones, Western Union suddenly became interested in the new art. It organized the American Speaking-Telephone Company, with a capital of $300,000. The new subsidiary hired three leading electrical inventors—Thomas A. Edison, Amos E. Dolbear, and Elisha Gray—to develop its own telephones. Western Union also passed these men off to the general public as the original inventors of the telephone.

Hearing this, several of Sanders' rich relatives decided that there must be something to this newfangled thing after all. They came forward with capital to prop up the faltering Bell Telephone Association. Hubbard soon found himself leasing telephones at the rate of a thousand a month.

Hubbard wisely decided that the company needed a man with more experience in organizing than himself. At this time Theodore N. Vail, a cousin of Morse's associate Alfred Vail, had been reorganizing the United States Government's mail service.

Hubbard persuaded Vail to leave the government and work for the Bell company as general manager. Vail proved as much a genius in his way as Bell was in his.

Meanwhile, Edison invented the carbon microphone, which greatly increased the volume of sound transmitted. The principles of the carbon microphone are, first, that graphite conducts electricity (even though not so well as metals); second, that if two pieces of graphite are pressed together and a current sent through them, the amount of current increases as the pressure between the two pieces is raised.

Therefore, if pieces of graphite are placed behind the diaphragm of a telephone transmitter and a current is passed through them, sound vibrations, making the diaphragm vibrate, cause changes in the current passing through the pieces of graphite, because with each vibration the diaphragm pushes the pieces of graphite together more tightly and then lets them fall apart again.

The new transmitter so improved the telephone's performance that it cut into the Bell company's business until a Bostonian named Francis Blake invented a transmitter as good as Edison's. It turned out later that Edison had been anticipated with the general idea of a variable-resistance transmitter by Emile Berliner, a German immigrant then clerking in a dry-goods store in Washington. Berliner invented such a microphone, with metallic contacts instead of carbon ones, two weeks before Edison. The Bell company bought Berliner's patent and sued users of Edison's microphone.

After fourteen years of litigation, the Circuit Court of Appeals held (American Bell Telephone Co. v. National Telephone Mfg. Co. *et al.*) that, while Berliner had indeed been first with the variable-resistance transmitter, his patent did not dominate Edison's carbon microphone.[9] Judge Colt's point—a dubious one to my way of thinking—was that Berliner had not specifically disclosed what the judge deemed to be the essential principle of the microphone: that of having the electrodes in initially loose contact. As Berliner's device was of little worth compared to Edison's, no more was heard of Berliner's microphone, although Berliner himself went on to a successful career in other inventive fields.

Several other inventors were close behind Berliner and Edison in developing the microphone. This sort of thing happened more and more towards the end of the nineteenth century. Inventors became so numerous and so well informed, by comparison with their struggling predecessors, that as soon as any promising line of technical development opened up, a swarm of inventors would rush into it, racing one another to be the first to exploit its possibilities.

Meanwhile Western Union's chief electrical expert, Frank L. Pope, made a six-months' study of the Bell patent and reported: "I am entirely unable to discover any apparatus or method anticipating the invention of Bell as a whole, and I conclude that his patent is valid."[10]

The heads of Western Union brushed aside this opinion and told Edison, Dolbear, and Gray to invent a telephone that should circumvent Bell's patent. Then Western Union sued the Bell company for infringing Gray's patent, asserting that Gray was the true inventor of the telephone.

Elisha Gray was a professor at Oberlin College and a successful inventor who made over five million dollars from his patents. In 1874, like Bell, he was working on a musical telegraph. The day that Bell applied for his patent, Gray filed a caveat in the Patent Office on the same subject.

A caveat was a declaration, not that the inventor had made an invention, but that he believed himself to be on the verge of making one. Filing a caveat gave the inventor an effective filing date earlier than that on which he filed a complete patent application, thus giving him an advantage in litigation. Caveats were abolished in the United States in 1909, although they still obtain in Canadian patent law.

Gray got his patent in due course and maintained to his dying day that he was the true inventor of the telephone. But, as Gray's own partner once said of him, "Of all the men who *didn't* invent the telephone, Gray was the nearest."[11]

During Western Union's suit against the Bell company, the chief lawyer on the Western Union side, George Gifford, became convinced in his turn that the Bell patent was impregnable. At his advice, Western Union settled the case out of court. Western Union conceded the priority and validity of the Bell patent and agreed to withdraw from the telephone business, while the Bell company would buy Western Union's telephone division and agree for its part to leave telegraphy alone.

In 1881 the Bell company paid its first dividend, of $178,500. Sanders sold his stock for a little less than a million dollars but soon lost most of the money in a Colorado gold mine. Hubbard retired and devoted himself to the National Geographic Society. Watson (who as the chief—and for a long time the only—engineer of the Bell system had taken out sixty patents of his own on telephonic improvements) became a shipbuilder.

As for Alexander Graham Bell, he gave all his stock to his wife on their wedding day and went back to teaching deaf mutes. He declined an offer of $10,000 a year from the Bell company to stay on and invent for them, saying he could not invent to order.

In the following years, 125 competing telephone companies were formed, defying the Bell patent. Most of them were intended as mere stock-jobbing operations. They fought the Bell company by rumors and by agitation and by lobbying against monopolies, in spite of the fact that a telephone system, whether privately or publicly owned, is destined by its very nature to be a monopoly. The Bell company fought 600 lawsuits, carrying five to the Supreme Court. Except for two small contract suits of no importance, it won every one of them.

When Bell left the business, an enormous number of inventions and improvements were still needed to make the telephone as efficient as it is today. One Bell engineer, Charles E. Scribner, alone took out over 600 patents on telephone switchboards and their parts.

One of the main improvements, after the carbon microphone, was the loading coil for long-distance lines. The first long-distance lines were of copper as thick as a pencil, which made them very costly.

This problem was solved by Pupin's loading coil. Michael Idvorsky Pupin (1858–1935) was an iron-muscled Serb from the Banat who arrived in New York as a raw youth of fifteen with a fez on his head and five cents in his pocket.

Pupin worked his way through Columbia University, studied in England and Germany, and became a professor at Columbia. He was one of the early experimenters with tuned inductance circuits and with X rays after these were discovered by Roentgen in 1895. Pupin invented the fluorescent screen used in X-ray work.

Pupin's most profitable invention was the discovery that, by loading a telephone line with inductance coils at intervals, the signals could be made to reinforce themselves. Thus a thin, economical wire with these coils would transmit speech over long distances as effectively as a thick wire without them.

But the accomplishment for which Pupin became best known was a brisk and colorful autobiography, *From Immigrant to Inventor*, which became a classic of American literature.

Meanwhile, Alexander Graham Bell bought a baronial estate in Nova Scotia, where he bred sheep. He built a laboratory to help the deaf and became very active in and generous to scientific organizations. Thus in 1883 he founded *Science*, the organ of the American Association for the Advancement of Science, and supported it for several years.

At his winter home in Washington, Bell gave regular intellectual soirées on Wednesday evenings. Hither as regular visitors came many American scientists, including John Wesley Powell, the gnomish little geologist who had lost an arm in the Civil War and later conquered the Colorado River; Simon Newcomb the astronomer; and Spencer Baird, the zoölogist who succeeded Henry as head of the Smithsonian Institution, of which Bell became regent in 1898.

Bell also became an aviation enthusiast. He gave money and moral support to Samuel P. Langley in the latter's pioneering aeronautical researches. He gave $50,000 to an Aerial Experiment Association which he founded and which built early experimental airplanes in competition with the Wrights. Aileron control of the modern type came out of this group's researches.

In the First World War, still active, Bell and his young associate Frederick W. Baldwin, the Canadian engineer who invented the hinged aileron, built a motor boat of radical design, called a "hydrodrome," for naval use. It was a cigar-shaped vessel, which rode on ladder-shaped hydrofoils. An airplane engine and propeller pushed it along at the then unheard-of speed of 71 mph.

In 1915 the first transcontinental telephone line was opened. As part of the ceremony, Bell in the East and Watson on the Pacific Coast spoke over it as they had thirty-nine years before. Bell: "Mr. Watson, please come here; I want you."

Watson replied: "It would take me a week now!"[12]

EDISON

AND THE ELECTRIC LIGHT

The Centennial Exposition, with Gramme's dynamo and Bell's telephone, displayed the buds of the electrical revolution. Seventeen years later, at the World's Columbian Exposition of 1893 in Chicago, the revolution was in full bloom.

Gone was the forest of slapping belts, replaced by quiet little electric motors. The grounds were lit by incandescent electric light bulbs.

The Westinghouse Company had received the contract to light the grounds. To circumvent Edison's patents, its engineers developed a "stopper lamp" based on the patents of Moses Farmer and Hiram Maxim for lamps with ground-glass plugs to keep the air out. These lamps did not last so long as the Edison lamps, which were sealed shut in the making, but they burned long enough for the purposes of the Exposition.

By now telephones were commonplace, even though the user had to ring Central by turning a crank and to shout into the instrument to make himself understood. Streetcars were becoming numerous. Electrical exhibits at the Exposition included a high-frequency coil that threw a five-foot spark with a deliciously terrifying crackle.

At the Exposition, the International Electrical Congress met, with electrical scientists from overseas. Most famous of these was the leonine Prussian sage, Hermann Ludwig Ferdinand von Helmholtz (1821–94). Helmholtz had covered a wide range of sciences: physiology, optics, hydrodynamics, and meteorology. Along with Mayer, Joule, and William Thomson he helped to found the law of the conservation of energy. He also made an early measurement of the speed at which electromagnetic waves (including radio, light, and X-ray waves) travel through space.

Edison was there, but not as a delegate. He thought, perhaps rightly, that some scientists disdained him as a mere tinkerer. But at the banquet, when Edison and Samuel Insull, his secretary at the time, were sitting quietly at their own table, Helmholtz made a point of stepping down from the speaker's table to shake hands with Edison. The diners set up a cry of "Edison! Edison! Speech!"

Edison never spoke in public, because his voice was not suited to the task. It was a high-pitched, flat, deaf man's voice, not agreeable to listen to. Edison rose twice, bowed, and sat down. Then little Elihu Thomson got up and said:

"Well, if Tom will not speak, Thomson will have to."[1]

In the great electrical revolution of the last third of the nineteenth century, nearly all the basic theory (aside from Joseph Henry's contributions) was developed in Britain and Germany by Faraday, Maxwell, William Thomson, Helmholtz, and Hertz. Of the basic inventions, the generator was almost entirely European in origin.

The electric motor was partly American and partly European. After the abortive attempts of Henry, Davenport, and others, the main contributions were those of Charles G. Page of Salem, Massachusetts, and of Robert Davidson of Scotland, both around 1840.

However, all the early motors had to rely upon batteries for their power. For heavy duty, batteries were too heavy, expensive, and fragile. So the general use of the motor had to wait for the generator.

The biggest breakthrough in electric motors, when they became not only workable but also profitable, came in 1873. In that year the Belgian-born Zénobe Théophile Gramme (who did his work in France) accidentally discovered that his generator would also work as a motor. A workman setting up Gramme's exhibit at an exhibition in Vienna mistakenly connected one generator to the wires from another already in operation. To everybody's surprise, the second machine began to spin. As with Bell's first transmitter, the inventor's genius lay in seeing the possibilities opened up by an accident that a less agile mind might have brushed aside.

The first steps in electric lighting were also taken in Europe. In the early nineteenth century, Sir Humphry Davy found out how to make a continuous electric arc in air. But, as with the electric motor, this device was not practical so long as it had to get its current from a battery. Therefore the arc light also had to await the steam-driven generator. When the latter arrived, in the 1860s, arc lights began to be used for such things as lighthouses and ships' masthead lights.

An engineer in the Russian Army, Paul Jablochkoff,[2] started west to attend the Centennial Exposition in Philadelphia but got only as far as Paris. There he took a job in the Breguet factory, which was making Gramme's generators. Here Jablochkoff developed the Jablochkoff candle, a device with two rods of carbon separated by insulation except at the tips. This candle had only limited use; it gave a brilliant light but lasted less than two hours. The Jablochkoff candle was superseded in the 1880s by the arc-lighting system developed by Charles F. Brush of Cleveland, Ohio.

Then why do we say that Edison invented the electric light? Because the harsh glare of the arc lights was much too bright for indoor use. If you reduce the voltage on which the arc light works, though, the light does not just dim; it goes out. A generation of inventors struggled with the problem of "subdivision of the electric light." By that, they meant making an electric lamp that should use only a fraction of the current of an arc light and turn out only a fraction of its illumination.

Edison was not merely a successful inventor of an electric light; he was a major architect of the electrical revolution. Although no scientist in the strict sense of the word, he was one of the most prolific inventors the world has ever seen. The story of the electrical revolution, at least in the United States, is as much Edison's story as it is that of any other man.

Thomas Alva Edison (1847–1931) was the son of a Canadian who settled in Milan, Ohio. Samuel Edison made shingles and prospered for a while. Although a good man, he did not understand his gifted son at all. When young Thomas ("Al" to his friends at the time) burned his father's barn for fun, his father gave him a public beating in the streets of Milan—perhaps not such a mistaken treatment after all.

When the boy was five or six, a swimming companion drowned. Edison went home without saying anything about it. This quality of detachment became more and more marked throughout Edison's life.

When a railroad was built along the south shore of Lake Erie, it bypassed Milan because the owners of stock in a local canal did not want it. As a result, the Edisons were impoverished and moved to Port Huron, at the eastern tip of Michigan. Sam Edison became a dealer in feed, grain, and lumber, but with indifferent success.

Thomas Edison left school after three months. He later explained that his mother had taken him out because the teacher complained that he was "addled"—meaning he asked too many questions. A likelier reason, however, is that his father was too poor to pay the school fees.

In any case Edison's mother, a former teacher, gave him an adequate elementary education at home. He acquired a passion for natural science from reading R. G. Parker's *School of Natural Philosophy*, though his enthusiasm for experiment took such ill-chosen directions as filling his father's chore boy with Seidlitz powders to make him fly. He distressed his mother by dripping sulfuric acid on the furniture until his chemicals were banished to the cellar. After an attack of scarlet fever impaired his hearing, he became progressively deafer.

At twelve, Edison went to work. He ran a news and vegetable stand in Port Huron and got a concession on the Grand Trunk Railway between Port Huron and Detroit. Then he became a railway telegrapher but got into trouble again and again for sleeping on the job after spending his off-duty hours on his experiments.

From 1863 to 1868, Edison worked as a wandering telegrapher. He was a notably fast operator who could "copy behind"—that is, write several sentences behind the message coming in without forgetting or getting mixed up. His last telegraphic job was with the Western Union in Boston, where he read through the entire works of Michael Faraday. He also started work on his first patented invention, an electric vote recorder for legislatures.

In the telegraph office in Boston, swarms of cockroaches climbed to the table on which the clerks kept their lunches. Edison made a trap of two strips of tinfoil fastened around the edge of the table and connected to the poles of the main battery. As the roaches climbed over the strips they were electrocuted until the floor was heaped with their corpses.

Then, with the backing of several local people, Edison left Western Union to become a free-lance inventor in Boston. One of his first steps was to take his vote recorder to Washington. Here a Congressman told him:

"Young man, that won't do at all! That is just what we do *not* want. Your invention would destroy the only hope the minority have of influencing legislation . . ." by parliamentary tactics of delay.[3]

During his free-lance period in Boston, Edison invented a duplex telegraph (on which two messages could be sent over the same wires at the same time) and worked on stock tickers. He employed several men and personally strung wires over people's roofs to the offices of his subscribers. Differences arose with his backers, who sold his patents to a telegraph company. As Edison at that time had had no business experience, he got almost nothing for his work.

So Edison went to New York to look for a more profitable connection. An engineer he knew, named Pope, let him sleep in the offices of the Laws' Gold Indicator Company on Wall Street while he lived on five-cent meals of apple dumplings and coffee.

One day, while Edison waited for a job interview with the officers of the Gold Indicator Company, the system broke down. Three hundred office boys rushed in yelling from the brokers' offices. While Laws and the superintendent dithered, Edison found a broken contact spring in the master ticker. He thought, he said, that he could repair the damage.

"Fix it! Fix it! Be quick for God's sake!" screamed Laws.[4]

Edison did and got the job. When Pope resigned to become a consulting engineer, Edison was promoted to take his place. After a series of mergers, Edison's company was absorbed by Western Union. Not wishing to work for Western Union again, Edison quit to become a free-lance inventor once more, taking Pope as his partner.

General Marshall Lefferts, the president of Western Union,

retained Edison on a free-lance basis, but without any definite contract. Edison continued to improve stock tickers until Lefferts called him in and asked him how much he thought the company should pay him for the rights to his inventions.

Edison had no notion of how much. He thought of asking for $5000 and letting himself be chaffered down to $3000. In desperation he said:

"Well, General, suppose you make me an offer."

"How would forty thousand dollars strike you?"[5]

Edison came "as near to fainting as I ever got," but managed to say yes. Three days later he signed the contract and was given the first check he had ever handled. At the bank, the teller told him to endorse it. The deaf Edison failed to understand, thought that he must have been given a worthless paper, and returned to General Lefferts.

Lefferts explained and sent Edison back to the bank with a clerk to identify him. The teller thought it would be a good joke to give Edison his forty thousand in small bills. Edison sat up all night guarding his vast wad, until next day Lefferts showed him how to open a bank account.

With this money, Edison opened a shop of a new kind in Newark. This was a commercial laboratory whose product was inventions. As he knew nothing about bookkeeping, he ran his shop in what seemed to others an eccentric manner. Friction soon arose with his partners, whom he bought out.

In Newark he developed new kinds of telegraph for sending two messages on the same wire in the same direction, and for sending two messages in opposite directions, and for sending two messages in each direction. He also developed an automatic telegraph.

Edison became involved in a war between Western Union, controlled by Commodore Vanderbilt, and the Atlantic and Pacific Telegraph Company, controlled by Jay Gould. Of all the American robber barons of the time, Gould—avarice incarnate—was the most rascally.

Edison furnished inventions to each of the rival companies in turn. He was nearly broke when Gould saved his house by paying $10,000 for a telegraphic relay of a new type. Then Gould, after persuading Edison to drop Western Union and to sell his quadruplex telegraph to Atlantic and Pacific, swindled him out of the promised price. When Gould got control of both systems, Edison quit telegraphy.

During his Newark period, Edison, amazingly fertile, also invented waxed wrapping paper, the electric pen (a device for cutting stencils in longhand), and the mimeograph. He took out, on the average, a patent a month. But his head was so full of plans that he became very absent-minded.

Once, on the last day allowed, he went to the city hall in Newark to pay his taxes. When he got to the window and was asked his name, he had forgotten it. By the time he had gone through the line again it was too late. He had to go back the next day and pay the tax plus a 12½ per cent penalty.

An even odder lapse of memory occurred on the Christmas Day that Edison married Mary G. Stilwell, a plump young woman who worked in his shop. Right after the wedding, something went wrong at the works. Edison rushed off to fix it and, forgetting his bride, stayed there working far into the night.

During this period, Edison also made sparks by high-frequency induction, which later became part of the basis of radio. He erroneously announced that he had found a new "etheric force." This announcement brought severe criticism from scientists, who did not care to be lectured on their own specialties by a mere tinkerer.

This era saw some foolish hostility between scientists, who sneered at mere inventors, and inventors, who sneered back at mere theoretical scientists. Edison sneered with the rest. He continued all his life to make slighting remarks about physical and mathematical theoreticians, although he was on friendly terms with many of them and hired some to work for him.

Being an inventor and a manufacturer at the same time was too much of a strain, even to a man of Edison's amazing energy. In 1876, still under thirty, he bought an estate at Menlo Park, New Jersey, a local stop on the Pennsylvania between Elizabeth and Metuchen. Here he remained for twelve years. His Menlo Park period is associated with the carbon telephone transmitter, the phonograph, and the electric light.

In his thirties, Edison was a solidly built man of good height, clean-shaven amid a forest of beards, with a large pale nondescript face. By forty his thick dark hair had grizzled. He usually appeared in a rumpled dark suit, shabby from burns and stains, although in later years his second wife could turn him out neatly on occasion. His manner was cheerful, unassuming, detached, and deliberate.

He kept fantastic hours, sleeping two or three hours out of the twenty-four and expecting his men to do likewise. Although he drove them like one of Pharaoh's overseers, many found his "winning ways and manners"[6] incentive enough to make them keep on at this pace.

Those who liked him said he was usually kind, friendly, and considerate, but often irascible when things went badly and utterly intolerant of stupidity. Yet the dominant impression of his personality is one of detachment—of a man with no time for ordinary human emotions.

A conference between Edison and his aides sounded like a riot as Edison paced up and down, speaking in his loud flat voice, while the aides trotted beside him and shouted into his ears. He refused to use a hearing aid because, he said, his deafness relieved him from the noises that distracted most people, and besides "my wife would want to talk to me all the time."

However, his deafness sometimes embarrassed him. In 1902 Sir William Thomson, now the patriarchal, white-bearded Baron Kelvin, came over for a farewell visit. Edison was on the reception committee along with Pupin, Westinghouse, Tesla, and Elihu Thomson. They arranged a banquet for the grand old man of physical science at the Waldorf-Astoria.

As Edison was at the height of his fame, speaker after speaker, after eulogizing Lord Kelvin, worked in a few compliments to Edison. The latter, not hearing, applauded until his wife shouted into his ear:

"You mustn't clap so, Tom. They are talking about you!"[7]

Naturally, everybody else heard her, too. Poor Edison turned crimson and tried to sink out of sight. But Kelvin and the rest arose and applauded until he had to take a bow.

Edison not only admitted but also bragged of the fact that he was no theoretical scientist but a trial-and-error inventor. However, he was not at all erratic or unsystematic in his inventive procedures. He was methodical as well as fertile, energetic, self-confident, single-minded, and persistent. He used a shotgun method of attacking problems: first read everything, then try everything.

With time and experience, Edison became quite shrewd and competent in money matters. He was not greedy for money for its own sake. Most of his profits he plowed back into more inventions. On the other hand, he was not always scrupulous when promoting his products or when complacently accepting credit for inventions in which he had played little or no part.

When people were not yet used to the idea of collective or corporate invention, they muttered about Edison's "stealing the brains" of his assistants. In fact, however, Edison's fault lay in the other direction. He tended, especially as he got older, to stick rigidly to his own program and to brush aside his engineers' suggestions. Edison's terrific, one-way drive enabled him to triumph over inventive obstacles that would have daunted most men. But it also led, when Edison got pointed in the wrong direction, to some resounding failures.

He had a large but spotty fund of self-taught culture, an earthy humor, and a fondness for practical jokes. His children found him a difficult parent. He either ignored them completely or played crude japes on them. He kept the speech and to some degree the manners of his uncurried youth. When in 1903 a new assistant asked about laboratory rules, Edison spat on the floor and yelled:

"Hell! There ain't no rules around here! We are tryin' to accomplish somep'n!"[8]

Although he liked to picture himself as a modest, retiring man, Edison actually had a keen sense of publicity and enjoyed Barnumesque ballyhoo. In later years he was lured into publicly expressing himself on many subjects outside his field, on the American journalistic theory that, if a man is an authority on weevils, his opinions on the Burmese situation or the rediscount rate must also carry weight. Edison's replies were sometimes shrewd and sometimes merely uninformed. On the whole, he made less of a fool of himself in this way than did his friend Ford.

At the time of his move to Menlo Park, Edison undertook some new work for Western Union on the telephone problem. His main contribution to this inventive race was the carbon microphone already discussed in the chapter on Bell. Edison might have accomplished more in telephony had he not been so severely handicapped in this field by his deafness.

He was still working in telephony in 1877 when he noticed that a telegraphic repeater, with which he had also been experimenting, gave forth curious speechlike sounds when its disks revolved rapidly. This gave him the idea that speech sounds, as well as the clicks and buzzes of telegraphic signals, could be permanently recorded on a moving surface and played back.

Edison next experimented with a strip of waxed paper, drawn under a diaphragm to whose center a pin was attached, while he shouted at it. This device was similar in principle to Bell's phonautograph.

After several months of quiet experiments with these devices, Edison handed a sketch to John Kreusi, his Swiss assistant. The apparatus, he said, ought not to cost more than eighteen dollars.

Kreusi was incredulous when Edison told him what it was for. Carman, the foreman of the machine shop, bet Edison a box of cigars that it would not work.[9]

When completed, the machine looked like a little hand lathe. It had a shaft with a handle at one end, a flywheel at the other, and a tinfoil-wrapped cylinder between. A guide carried a device with a diaphragm and a needle. As the handle was turned, the gadget moved slowly along the guide and the needle scratched a helical groove in the cylinder.

When the contraption was ready, Edison turned the handle and shouted at the gadget: *"Mary had a little lamb, Its fleece was white as snow!"*

He put it back in the starting position and turned the crank again. The machine squeaked:

> "Mary had a little lamb,
> Its fleece was white as snow."

Carman paid his cigars. A few days later, on December 7, 1877, Edison appeared at the offices of the *Scientific American* with the device wrapped in paper. He set the parcel on the desk of F. C. Beach, one of the editors, who asked what it was.

"Just a minute," said Edison, unwrapping. "Here we are." Beach cranked. The machine said:

"Good morning! What do you think of the phonograph?"[10]

While Beach goggled, the other employees gathered around begging for more demonstrations until Beach, fearing the floor would collapse, asked Edison to stop.

Edison obtained his patent almost without argument. The Patent Office examiner had found not a single anticipating patent, a rare situation indeed in this inventive age.

Although Edison got a lot of publicity from his phonograph, he soon became so busy with the electric light that he shelved the phonograph for almost a decade. He resumed work on it in 1887 and by 1893 had more than sixty-five patents in the field.

Others, too, improved the instrument. The biggest advance was Emile Berliner's record in the shape of a disk instead of cylinder, with a groove that wiggled from side to side instead of up and down. Edison's waxen cylinders survive in the Dictaphone.

Compared to the phonograph, the story of the electric light is a more typical modern invention tale. It is the story of a multitude of minds forging arduously towards the same objective, and of the triumph of one who reached the goal a little ahead of the rest.

Besides the development of the arc light by Davy, Jablochkoff, and Brush, a German-American watchmaker and optician named Goebel made battery-operated incandescent lamps about 1850. Subsequently, Lodyguine[11] in Russia, Swan and Lane-Fox in Britain, Hiram Stevens Maxim and Moses Farmer in the United States, and others experimented with glowing carbon rods in their efforts to subdivide the electric light.

In 1878, Edison took a trip out West to see an eclipse of the sun and to try out an instrument he had invented for measuring small changes in temperature. One of the party, a Professor Barker, urged Edison to tackle the problem of the electric light.

Later that year, Edison visited William Wallace's dynamo factory in Connecticut, where Wallace's partner Moses G. Farmer was working on electric lights. Edison rushed about the laboratory filling sheets with calculations. Having ordered a Wallace dynamo and a set of arc lights to illuminate his own laboratory, he told Wallace:

"I believe I can beat you making the electric light. I do not think you are working in the right direction."[12]

He and Wallace shook hands on it, and at dinner Edison signed his name and the date with a diamond-pointed stylus on one of Wallace's wine glasses.

Edison began experimenting with metallic filaments, including platinum, platino-iridium, nickel, boron, chromium, molybdenum, and osmium. He also studied the system of centralized distribution used by the gas companies with a view to adapting it to the sale of electricity.

For a while, Edison thought that he had solved his problem with a platinum filament. His patent attorney, Grosvenor Lowery, urged him to issue an optimistic statement in order to loosen the purse strings of the robber barons. So Edison announced success, boasting:

"I have obtained it through an entirely different process than that from which scientific men have sought to secure it. They have all been working in the same groove . . ."[13]

Edison was already so well known that this statement caused the price of gas stock to fall 12 per cent in a few days in London. Edison was severely criticized for his bragging, especially when he soon gave up his platinum filament.

The boast, however, had its intended effect. Lowrey organized a syndicate of capitalists to back Edison. These included a Morgan partner, the president of Western Union, and Vanderbilt. American capitalists were readier than before to speculate on inventions.

But the platinum filament did not prove practical. Platinum becomes incandescent at a temperature only a few degrees below its melting point. Therefore a slight overload melts the wire and causes the lamp to fail.

After a gloomy visit of the financiers to the laboratory for a demonstration in 1879, Edison resolved to give up fooling with platinum. During this time, when Edison was working hard and silently, in contrast to his earlier publicity, he was denounced as a charlatan and a story was printed that he was dying.

Edison also employed a team of engineers to design a constant-voltage electrical generator of low internal resistance. Engineers then mistakenly thought that the internal resistance of a generator must equal the external resistance of the circuit. This delusion hampered the development of electric light and power until Edison decided that there was no sensible reason for this rule and that he would ignore it.

Calculations convinced Edison that the only material that would serve his purpose was a thin thread of carbon.[14] In coming to this conclusion, Edison had really attacked the electric-light problem by "an entirely different process." His predecessors had all used comparatively thick metal wires or carbon rods, of low electrical resistance. To make these lamps glow, an electric current of high amperage was required. Hence a power-and-light system using such low-resistance lamps would require immense amounts of costly copper.

Edison, on the other hand, saw that to use a very thin filament would make a lamp of high electrical resistance. As a given voltage would send much less current through such a lamp, he would have to use a much higher voltage to get the same illumination. (Voltage is the measure of electrical *pressure*; amperage, of the quantity of electric *current*. With direct current, power is the product of the voltage and the amperage.) However, by using higher voltage and lower amperage, the power wires could be made much thinner and more economical.

But how to find a threadlike substance, containing a lot of carbon, that should keep its shape and strength when white-hot?

First, Edison bent a cotton thread into a loop, laid it in a mold of nickel, and put the mold in a furnace to bake for five hours. Then he tried to take the mold out of the furnace and the thread out of the mold without breaking it. The thread, almost completely carbonized, was so fragile that a breath would shatter it. After three weeks of trying thread after thread, Edison and his men got a light bulb that shone for forty hours before it burned out.

Still, a lamp whose filament breaks at the slightest jar is not practical. Therefore Edison tried all sorts of carbonaceous substances: bagging, baywood, boxwood, cedar shavings, celluloid, coconut fiber, cork, fishline, flax, graphite, hickory, lampwick, maple shavings, punk, tissue paper, twine, and some hairs from the beard of his old friend Mackenzie, who had taught him telegraphy when he was a boy.

The most successful substance found by these trials was Bristol cardboard, which gave a duration up to 170 hours. Some of Edison's first electric-light installations used Bristol-board lamps.

Early in 1880, Edison idly picked up a palm-leaf fan and pulled a splinter from one of its bamboo ribs. Bamboo fiber proved an even better material for lamp filaments. Edison adopted this material, contracted with a Japanese landowner to furnish him with bamboo, and sent a man to scour the tropics to find the species of this giant grass best suited to the purpose.[15]

Bamboo remained the standard material for filaments for nine years, until the General Electric Company developed a superior cellulose filament. This was followed by a filament of tantalum, which in turn gave way to the modern filament of tungsten.

Tungsten has the second highest known melting point, which makes it suitable for an incandescent lamp. On the other hand, it is an extremely hard, brittle metal, refractory to work with. The tungsten filament was made practical by William D. Coolidge's development of "ductile" tungsten—actually, tungsten powder molded into filaments under heat and pressure.

Edison put his perfected lamp on the market at forty cents a bulb, although at first they cost $1.25 apiece to make. In five years he had reduced the cost to twenty-two cents, but the price remained the same while sales rose into millions. While selling his lamps for individual installation, as on steamships, he also built a central generating station at Pearl Street, New York, and another in London.

During these years Edison seemed to be everywhere at once, prowling the trenches radiating from his Pearl Street station to inspect his mains and developing his improved direct-current armature with a laminated-iron core, and a subdivided commutator insulated by sheets of mica. All these features were new.

As with Fulton's first steamboat, schoolbook history makes Edison's electric light look bigger in the story of invention than it really is, while omitting the act for which the inventor deserves the most credit. In Edison's case, this was the colossal task of designing and developing a whole generating and distributing system to furnish the electricity to light the light.

Edison devised the main-and-feeder system and the three-wire system of distribution, to keep the current flowing evenly to all his customers despite sudden changes in the load or the input.[16] He also invented the first recording electric meter, to enable him to charge his customers in proportion to the electricity they consumed.

Edison's generating station in London opened on January 12, 1882. The next September the plant on Pearl Street started up with six "Jumbo" generators. On a preliminary test, a leak in the power mains set the horses on Fulton Street to dancing as the current made their hoofs tingle.

When the plant started in earnest, Edison had trouble with the governors of his steam engines. As he described the event, "Of all the circuses since Adam was born we had the worst then. One engine would stop and the other would run up to about a thousand revolutions, and then they would see-saw . . . When the circus commenced the men who were standing around ran out precipitately, and some of them kept running for a block or two. I grabbed the throttle of one engine and E. H. Johnson [one of Edison's engineers], who was the only one present to keep his wits, caught hold of the other and we shut them off."[17]

Edison's basic electric light patent, No. 223,898, was issued in 1880. Its claims read:

1. An electric lamp for giving light by incandescence, consisting of a filament of carbon of high resistance, made as described, and secured to metallic wires, as set forth.

2. The combination of carbon filaments with a receiver made entirely of glass and conductors passing through the glass, and from which receiver air is exhausted, for the purposes set forth.

3. A carbon filament or strip coiled and connected to electric conductors so that only a portion of the surface of such carbon conductors shall be exposed for radiating light, as set forth.

4. The method herein described of securing the platina contact wires to the carbon filament and carbonizing of the whole in a closed chamber, substantially as set forth.

Soon Edison had trouble with infringers. From 1885 to 1901 the Edison Electric Light Company spent over two million dollars prosecuting more than two hundred infringement suits. Not until 1892, when control of the patent had passed out of Edison's hands, was it finally sustained.

Some of the defendants cited Goebel's lamp as anticipating Edison's invention and therefore as invalidating his patent. In 1850, Goebel had a telescope mounted on a wagon, which he exhibited in New York City, charging so much a look. He made a number of battery-operated lamps consisting of evacuated glass tubes with thin carbon filaments. These lamps were placed upon the wagon to attract attention to the telescope.

Later, Goebel kept a jewelry store and used the lamps in the window. These lamps undoubtedly displayed the ideas that Edison used later. But, as Goebel's lamps were crudely made, they were neither bright nor durable enough for a practical means of illumination. They were used only as advertising novelties. Hence the courts held in each case that, as Goebel had neither applied for a patent nor built a practical lamp for domestic illumination, his work was an unfinished experiment.

Other defendants cited the previous patents to Sawyer and Man, Lane-Fox, and Edison himself, showing incandescent lamps using platinum wires or carbon rods as the incandescent elements. Was it patentable invention to substitute superior for inferior material?

The courts had long before decided that such substitution was not patentable invention unless it involved a new mode of construction, developed new properties or a new use, resulted in a new function, or otherwise brought about a revolutionary result. If the improvement was merely the sort of thing that any competent engineer could have foreseen, the change was the exercise of ordinary judgment and skill, not of the inventive faculty.

In the case of Edison Electric Light Co. v. U. S. Electric Lighting Co., however, the Circuit Court of Appeals of the Second Circuit held that the substitution of carbon for platinum in the lamp filament was patentable invention. Although lengthening the life of the lamp would not usually, by itself, be considered a good reason for granting a patent, the court explained:

It is true that carbon burners still break down, that the improvements neither of Edison nor of other inventors have made them absolutely stable, and in a sense it may be said that Edison only made them more stable than they were before; that it is a mere matter of degree. But the degree of difference between carbons that lasted one hour and carbons lasting hundreds of hours seems to have been precisely the difference between failure and success, and the combination which first achieved the result "long desired, sometimes sought and never before attained," is a patentable invention.

There remained the question of the anticipation of Edison's filament by the carbon pencils of Sawyer and Man. Ordinarily a change in size or proportions is not patentable, with exceptions like those that apply to substitution of materials. However:

> The carbon filament which constitutes the new part of the combination of the second claim of that patent, differs from the earlier carbon burners of Sawyer and Man, only in having a diameter of one sixty-fourth of an inch or less, whereas the burners of Sawyer and Man had a diameter of one thirty-second of an inch or more. But that reduction of one-half in diameter increased the resistance of the burner four-fold, and reduced its radiating surface two-fold, and thus increased eight-fold, its ratio of resistance, to radiating surface. That eight-fold increase of proportion, enabled the resistance of the conductor of electricity from the generator to the burner, to be increased eight-fold, without any increase of percentage of loss of energy in that conductor, or decrease of percentage of development of heat in the burner; and thus enabled the area of the cross section of that conductor to be reduced eight-fold, thus to be made with one-eighth of the amount of copper or other metal. . . . And that great reduction in the size and cost of conductors, involved also a great difference in the composition of the electric energy employed in the system; that difference consisting in generating the necessary amount of electrical energy with comparatively high electro-motive force [or voltage], and comparatively low current, instead of contrariwise. For this reason, the use of carbon filaments, one sixty-fourth of an inch in diameter or less, instead of carbon burners one thirty-second of an inch in diameter or more, not only worked an enormous economy in con-

ductors, but also necessitated a great change in generators, and did both according to a philosophy, which Edison was the first to know . . .[18]

Despite this victory, Edison always claimed that the patent cost him more in litigation than it was worth. Moreover, having perfected his electrical distributing system, he found nobody to manufacture its components for him. Therefore, although he had sworn off manufacturing when he moved to Menlo Park, he had to build his own factory. Since his directors would not advance the money for this, Edison built it out of his own resources.

The late seventies and early eighties saw the peak of Edison's titanic inventive efforts. Not only was he working on his electric light and power distribution system and beginning the development of the phonograph, but also inventing in the field of electric traction and starting work on his magnetic ore separator.

The electric-traction project was undertaken at the behest of Henry Villard, president of the Northern Pacific and one of Edison's backers. Inventors had experimented with battery-driven electric locomotives several decades earlier, and just before Edison entered the field the Siemens brothers demonstrated a primitive electric locomotive in Berlin.

Edison built a little electric locomotive with just enough room for the operator, a battery, and a motor driving the wheels by a friction pulley, Another small car carried seats for passengers. When he tried it out in 1880, the friction drive broke, so that the twenty-two riders—including an opulence of magnates—had to get out and push the train back home.

A month later Edison demonstrated another locomotive. This one had a pilot and an enclosed cab, so that it looked at least faintly like a real locomotive. Edison's assistant John Kreusi, driving, hit a sharp curve at twenty miles an hour. The engine jumped the track, tossing Kreusi and another man off into the dirt.

Somewhat shaken by his experience, the president of the Pennsylvania declared that railroad electrification had no future. Villard lost most of his influence when his railroad was thrown into receivership. Edison had too many irons in the fire to pursue the project anyway, so that active development of the electric train was taken over by a rival inventor, Stephen D. Field. An Edison-Field locomotive aroused much interest at the Railway Exposition in Chicago in 1883, but Edison had nothing more to do with this development.

In 1884, Edison's assistants Frank Julian Sprague and Edward H. Johnson (the engineer who shut off the steam when the Pearl Street engines ran away) set up their own company, the Sprague Electric Railway and Motor Company. This company pioneered in the field of electric street railways to replace horse-drawn streetcars, which had been running ever since the Irish-American John Stephenson opened the first such line in New York in 1832.

Sprague had been at outs with Edison, because Sprague thought that Edison was becoming mentally hidebound, while Edison regarded Sprague's insistence upon his own radical ideas as disruptive to the organization. On his own, Sprague developed the modern system of mounting a streetcar's motors on the axles. He also developed multiple-unit control, by which a single motorman in the leading car of an electric train governs the motors of all the cars by a single switch. This system is now used in all subway and electric suburban trains. A Belgian-American inventor, Charles J. Van Depoele, contributed the overhead trolley wire and the trolley pole with its little copper wheel as well as the graphite "brushes" of the modern electric motor.

Edison subsequently bought out Sprague's first company and marketed its products—streetcar motors and other parts—under his own name. This practice gave the false impression that Edison had also invented the electric trolley car.

From these inventions by Sprague and Van Depoele grew a vast reticulation of trolley-car lines, which in the early twentieth century covered eastern and central North America and western Europe like a fishnet, and which later withered away under the competition of the more flexible gasoline omnibus and the disruptive private automobile.

Edison's first wife died of typhoid fever in 1884. Although human ties and emotions meant less to Edison than to most people, and although Mary had been an ungifted little woman who ate candy until she became very fat, the inventor was much stricken.

Two years later, Edison married Mina Miller, the daughter of an Ohio capitalist. Mina was a rather sophisticated young woman with a mind of her own, who labored all her life to make a gentleman out of Edison.

The next year, Edison bought an ornate mansion in South Orange, New Jersey, and built a large modern research laboratory, with all the latest equipment for testing inventive ideas. The very size of the establishment, however, kept Edison from doing as much brilliant inventive work as before, because he had to give more time to administration. The Bell, Thomson, and Westinghouse companies imitated Edison in setting up their own research laboratories.

The late 1880s saw Edison involved in a furious controversy over the relative merits of direct and alternating current. Each has its advantages. Direct-current machinery is more flexible in speed and load. Alternating current, on the other hand, can be sent long distances at a lower cost.

Edison early committed himself to direct current, although this decision meant that he could not profitably send electric current farther than three miles from each of his generating stations. With alternating current, it was possible to have the generating stations fewer, larger, and more efficient.

When alternating-current systems began competing with his, Edison became fanatically devoted to his system. He brushed aside Frank Sprague's suggestion that he take up alternating current also. He refused to buy a European transformer system, the Z.B.D. system, when the rights to it were offered to him.

Edison attacked his alternating-current rivals by every means in his power. In the Battle of the Currents, he published a blood-red booklet, *A Warning from the Edison Electric Light Company*, asserting:

"It is clear that high pressure, particularly if accompanied by rapid alternations, is not destined to assume any permanent position. It would be legislated out of existence in a very brief period even if it did not previously die a natural death."[19]

In 1888, New York State adopted a law providing for the execution of criminals by electrocution. The first apparatus designed for this purpose was an electric chair at Auburn prison, powered by a steam-driven 2000-volt alternating-current generator.

The first victim was a murderer named William Kemmler.

As is usual in notorious murder cases, the defense attracted many sentimental sympathizers who thought this a cruel and unusual punishment. The Edison Company supported the defense until the case had been fought out in the newspapers, the sentence upheld by state and Federal courts, and Kemmler duly electrocuted on August 6, 1890. Then the Edison Company stopped its horror propaganda about the agony of electrocution and tried to frighten users of alternating current by stressing the instant death to which it exposed them.

Actually, there is no significant difference between the risks of a.c. and d.c. Like other machinery, both are reasonably safe if correctly installed and prudently used.

After the Battle of the Currents had raged for years, J. P. Morgan engineered a merger between the Edison Electric Light Company and its leading rival, the Thomson-Houston Company. The new company was the Edison General Electric Company, with Villard as its first president. This was one of the first companies to set up (in 1900) an independent research department.

Edison was a director of this company. But the company soon dropped "Edison" from the name and froze Edison out of one of his jobs, as manager of the subsidiary Edison Lamp Company. Edison lost interest and started out on his own again. While improving his phonograph, he also went into moving pictures and ore-handling machinery.

The Battle of the Currents petered out in a gradual victory for alternating current. Many years later, Edison admitted that the biggest blunder of his life had been his rejection of alternating current.

By 1890, the time of Edison's great smashing successes was over, although Edison continued to invent for decades more. His iron-mining venture, in fact, cost him most of the fortune that he had gained from earlier successes.

He developed a magnetic ore separator and ponderous crushing machinery to process the low-grade ore of northern New Jersey, and spent several years working at his iron mine with all his old drive. The machinery worked well enough once the bugs had been taken out of it.

But in 1892 the Mesabi Range—an enormous deposit of high-grade ore, waiting to be scooped out of the flat Minnesotan prairie—was opened up. This competition made New Jersey ore unprofitable, even when mined by Edisonian machinery. Edison finally cut his losses, sold his machinery to the Portland Cement Company, and went back to South Orange.

Here he set his men, at the request of Michael Pupin, to testing 8000 chemicals to find the one best suited to use on a fluorescent X-ray screen. About 1895, they found calcium tungstate to be the best. Edison himself went into the field of motion pictures.

European inventors like Muybridge, Friese-Greene, and Le Prince had already pioneered in cinematography. In 1889, Edison, in Paris for an exposition, saw the motion-picture camera developed by Étienne Marey. Back home he thought about this embryonic camera. He learned that George Eastman (1854–1932) of Rochester, New York, had developed a flexible photographic negative film that could be made in long strips.

At thirty-six, Eastman was the nation's leading inventor and maker of photographic equipment. He was a slender, well-built, coldly reserved man with an inventive drive as strong in its field as Edison's own. The photographic camera was already half a century old when Eastman took it up in the late 1870s. By countless inventions and small improvements, made by Eastman, his subordinates, and others from whom he bought the rights, Eastman made photography into the popular hobby that it is today. He had no woman in his life but his mother, gave away his vast fortune in philanthropies in his old age, and killed himself at last to escape the sufferings of disease.

With a twenty-five-dollar Eastman camera and strips of Eastman film, Edison set to work with a British assistant, William L. K. Dickson, to make a practical motion-picture camera. They created one much in advance of Marey's.[20]

They also experimented with the projection of pictures on a screen, but without much success. So Edison turned his back on projection, claiming that it would soon saturate the demand by showing motion pictures to too many people at once.

Instead, he developed a peep-show device called the Kinetoscope. To provide film strips for the Kinetoscope, he built the world's first motion-picture studio in South Orange. This was a sinister-looking structure covered with black tar paper, called the "Black Maria." The Black Maria was pivoted at one end while the other ran on a rail so that it could turn to catch the sun. In it performers danced, boxed, fenced, and guided a trained bear to make fifty-foot films.

Others took up the idea of projection on a screen, notably Marey, Méliès, and the Lumière brothers in France. For years Europe led America in the development of the motion-picture drama until World War I gave Americans a lasting lead.

When he saw that people were determined to see movies projected on a screen, Edison shifted his ground. In 1908 he built up a trust, the Motion Picture Patents Company, to monopolize the industry.

Edison had learned a lot about ruthless business tactics from his long association with the robber barons. He bought all the motion-picture patents he could get, including one for a practical projector invented by Thomas Armat. This projector, like Sprague's streetcar equipment, was marketed under Edison's name. Thus arose another legend, that Edison had invented the whole motion picture and its accessories.

However, if Edison contributed nothing inventively to the motion-picture projector, he did perform a pioneer experiment with sound motion pictures. He made a little film with a phonographic accompaniment. The picture had two familiar Edisonian themes: practical joking and deafness. A youth and a maiden are introduced by friends, who tell each that the other is deaf and must be shouted at.

The sound movie, however, did not prove practical in the days when the phonograph's only power was the mechanical jiggling of the needle. The sound so produced was too weak to fill a theater. Moreover, it proved very difficult to keep the sound and the pictures synchronized. Sound motion pictures became effective only with the development of electrical amplification in the 1920s.

In 1917, the United States Supreme Court ordered the Motion Picture Patents Company dissolved under a consent decree, on the ground that it violated the anti-trust laws. This did not much bother Edison, as the trust had already repaid his debts and made him a millionaire again. Besides, he had gone on to other projects.

One such scheme was poured concrete houses—a sound idea

that failed to win acceptance because it was too far ahead of its time. Another, somewhat more successful, was his alkaline storage battery.

The storage battery was invented in 1859 in France. Twenty years later, another Frenchman invented a storage battery of the modern type, using lead and sulfuric acid.

Edison nourished the idea that, if a radical improvement in storage batteries could be effected, the electric automobile would supplant the gasoline automobile, which was just becoming popular. Edison had patented an electric automobile in 1893 and sold these cars, the Edison Electrics, for years, in competition with several other makers of electrics. Looking like glass showcases on wheels, these vehicles were liked by old ladies for their quietness and ease of control.

So, in 1900 Edison launched his men on a search for better battery materials. He finally settled on a battery using a combination of iron and nickel with potassium hydroxide.

The alkaline storage battery was launched in 1904 with extravagant publicity. Soon it proved unsatisfactory. Edison took back all the defective batteries, shut down production, and spent five years in running down the causes of the defects.

The project cost a million of Edison's own money before he finally put a perfected battery on the market. The alkaline battery proved useful in many installations, especially in railway and marine uses. But it never did work very well in automobiles, let alone enable the electric automobile to compete with the gasoline buggy. While not a failure, the alkaline battery was far from the triumph that Edison had aimed at.

In 1915, when the United States seemed likely to become involved in the First World War, Edison urged that scientists be organized in preparation for war, as the Union had done with its National Academy of Sciences in the Civil War. When the United States did indeed enter the war, Edison was made chairman of the Naval Consulting Board, set up to process inventions submitted to the Navy. His fellow-members included Millikan, Compton, Sprague, Hudson Maxim, de Forest, and several other leading inventors and scientists.

Edison was now so deaf that he had to keep track of what was said by notes or telegraphic tapping. He made a number of proposals, mainly for anti-submarine warfare. Some were practical and some were not. Afterwards he grumped:

"I made about forty-five inventions during the war, all perfectly good ones, but they pigeonholed every one of them. The naval officer resents any interference by civilians . . ."21

However, that is a common fate for war-born inventions. Although money flows freely in wartime, materials and labor become scarce, so that a worthy invention may not become practical until after the shooting is over.

At Edison's insistence, the Naval Research Laboratory was set up after the war, although the government did not follow Edison's advice that it be made an entirely civilian affair. He had a poor opinion of naval officers as scientists and inventors, believing that most of them were terrified that something new on which they were working might go wrong and harm their careers.

In later years, Edison took life more easily, making automobile tours with his friends Ford, Firestone, and Burroughs; sailing out from his house in Florida to fish; and, when he could escape his wife's accusing eye, enjoying a quiet chew of tobacco. He cheerfully shocked the godly by professing religious unbelief.

His later inventions were all minor, such as a method of making rubber from goldenrod. Automobile tires made of this goldenrod rubber proved far more expensive than those of imported rubber.

Even in his comparatively unproductive old age, though, Edison could always produce something new and newsworthy. In the early 1920s, he began giving an information test to candidates for jobs as executives in his companies. He asked such questions as: Who was Bessemer and what did he do? What countries bound France? Who invented logarithms? What kind of wood is the heaviest? How is celluloid made?

Several publications like the *Literary Digest* made fun of this method of choosing applicants. Edison retorted that, while a good memory might not make an executive, an executive had to have a good memory. So he was testing the men's memories.

Now, of course, aptitude testing is commonplace. Some of the tests now given applicants for jobs are probably no better for picking the ablest candidate than the crude general-information quiz that Edison employed.

Even if he did not do all the things that some of his admirers credited him with, Edison's real accomplishments were astonishing enough. With 1093 patents to his name,[22] he was the most productive inventor in the history of the United States, and possibly the most productive in the history of the human race.

XII

THOMSON

AND ALTERNATING-CURRENT

POWER

The electrical revolution did not really flower until the dynamo or generator had been perfected. The electric generator works on the following principle: If one moves a conductor, such as a copper wire, through a magnetic field, so that the wire cuts the magnetic lines of force, a voltage appears in the wire. If the ends of the wire are connected outside the field, forming a closed circuit, an electric current flows in this circuit.

The inventors of the generator found that, while the principle is simple, the machine has one unyielding complication. As the north poles of the armature (the rotating part) pass the poles of the field magnets (the stationary part), the terminals receive an electromotive force, or voltage, in one direction. Then, as the north poles of the armature pass the south poles of the field magnets, the terminals receive an electromotive force in the opposite direction—and, of course, conversely with the south poles of the armature.

As there is no such thing as a magnet with only one pole, the generator makers either had to accept a current that flows first one way and then the other—that is, an *alternating* current —or they had to provide the machine with a rotating switch that automatically reversed the connections as the poles of the armature passed between one pair of field-magnet poles and the next. With such a switch, the electromotive force is in one direction only.

Hippolyte Pixii in Paris devised such a switch, called a *commutator* ("direction reverser") as early as 1832. But the inventors had exchanged one complication for another. Commutators sparked with such fury that the generator sometimes had to be stopped. As the sparks melted little pits in the copper surfaces of the commutator, the sparking got worse each time.

There were two ways around this difficulty. One was to improve the contact between the commutator and its sliding contacts, called "brushes" because at first they were literal brushes of copper wire. Charles J. Van Depoele solved this problem by substituting a thick plug of graphite, curved to fit the cylindrical surface of the commutator, in place of the copper brush. Although copper conducts electricity several hundred times as well as graphite, the thickness of the graphite overcame this difficulty.

The alternative was to accept alternating current and design machinery to use it. Some electrical apparatus such as the incandescent light works as well on alternating as on direct current. Other devices like storage batteries work on direct current only. In the 1880s, the man who did as much as any one man to solve the problems of alternating-current power was Elihu Thomson.

Born in England, Thomson was brought to Philadelphia as a boy. He went so quick in school that his teacher insisted that he take a two-year vacation to let the others catch up with him. Besides, he wanted to enter Central High School, which would not accept him until he was thirteen.

During his enforced vacation, he investigated a local foundry and tried to copy its methods. The result was a stream of molten iron trickling about the floor of his mother's kitchen.

Next he tackled electrostatics. He made an electrostat out of a wine bottle, a crank, a leather pad, a piece of silk, and a Leyden jar. His father scoffed at the slight shock the apparatus gave. So Thomson made a half-dozen jars of his own design, connected them up on a cold winter's night, cranked the electric bottle, and innocently asked his father to complete the circuit. The shock threw the elder Thomson on his back, where he lay cursing helplessly until his wife ran to pick him up. He stared hard at his son while rubbing his arms, then said:

"Sonny, I was wrong. I'll never laugh at you again."[1]

Central High School was the equivalent of a college, with stiff, highly competitive courses. Thomson graduated in 1870 and, after a couple of routine industrial jobs, became a teacher there. An older teacher, Edwin J. Houston,[2] attached himself to Thomson as a partner. For nine years, until Thomson shook him off, he shared equally in the earnings from Thomson's inventions, although he contributed little if anything towards them.

For the next few years, Thomson worked along several lines. He proved that the effects of nitrous oxide are those of partial suffocation rather than those of poisoning. He dabbled in optics and made his own microscope. He worked on a telephone like that later made by Bell but gave up before he reached success. He disproved Edison's theory that the creation of sparks by induction was due to a new "etheric force." He experimented with signaling by induction—the predecessor of wireless telegraphy.

His first really effective invention occurred by accident. As often happens, Thomson's genius lay in seizing upon the accident, understanding it, and putting it to use.

In the winter of 1876–77 he was lecturing on electricity at the Franklin Institute. In his last lecture, he meant to demonstrate heavy low-voltage current from a Leyden jar. When this current surged through two copper wires in loose contact, it made a bright green flash as the copper vaporized at the point of contact.

The first time, Thomson got his flash. The next time, nothing happened. Thomson looked and saw that the wires were welded together. Thus was arc welding discovered. Thomson cannily put the apparatus aside and went on with his lecture. Eight years later, when alternating-current generators were available, he revived the invention.

He also worked on the problem of subdividing the electric light. He originated the system of mounting lights in parallel instead of in series so that, if one light went out, the whole set would not be extinguished at the same time.

In the winter of 1879–80 he visited Edison at Menlo Park. Edison showed him around the plant and gave him a light bulb to test. Thomson did so and announced that he thought that Edison was on the wrong track. This time Edison was right and Thomson wrong.

This was but one of a long series of technical disagreements between the two. Later their respective companies became involved in furious litigation, suing each other for infringement and other torts. But through it all, Thomson and Edison remained good personal friends, as far as their terrific work schedules allowed time for friendship.

Thomson also invented a centrifugal cream separator, which he sold to the company of the Swedish engineer, Gustaf de Laval. De Laval marketed the separator under his own name, so that it is still called a de Laval separator. Needing a small, fast engine to turn the separator, de Laval invented the first practical steam turbine.

Thomson's electrical work carried him farther and farther into the expanding field of alternating current. For instance, he invented the shell transformer.

The transformer, on which the transmission of alternating current depends, was invented by Gaulard and Gibbs in Europe. It is a unique machine in that it never wears out, because it has no moving parts. It consists of two coils of wire wound around the same iron core, which usually has the form of a closed loop. The coils are insulated from the core and from each other. If an alternating current is sent through one coil, an alternating-current potential will come out of the other coil. This potential can be used to energize a circuit, as if the coils were connected.

The reason for this behavior is that, as the current in the first coil (the *primary*) increases, decreases back to nothing, and increases in the other direction, the magnetic field set up around the primary coil expands and contracts through the other coil (the *secondary*). Thus it gives rise to a voltage in the secondary coil as if the coil were moved through a stationary magnetic field. In the generator, the conductor is moved through a magnetic field; in the transformer, the magnetic field is moved through the conductor. The effect is the same in each case.

However, the transformer works on alternating current only,

as direct current sets up a constant, static magnetic field. The current from the secondary coil has the same frequency, in cycles per second, as the current sent into the primary.

Now, there is a simple relationship between the kind of current one gets from the secondary coil and the number of turns of wire comprising the two coils. If the number of turns be the same, the voltage (electrical pressure) and amperage (the current; that is, the rate at which electrons flow through the circuit) are the same.

But, if the number of turns in the secondary be greater, the voltage in the secondary is proportionately greater, while the amperage is proportionately less. If the primary has ten turns and the secondary a hundred, the voltage of the secondary circuit is ten times and the amperage one-tenth those of the primary. Conversely, if the number of turns in the secondary be less, the voltage is less and the amperage greater.

So one can, by means of a transformer, change an alternating current from one of high amperage and low voltage into one of low amperage and high voltage and *vice versa*. But why change the current?

Electricity does not flow through conductors for the asking. It must be pushed against resistance, just as water has to be pushed through pipes. Resistance means a loss of energy in the form of heat.

However, the heat loss varies directly as the voltage and also directly as the *square* of the current. If the amperage be increased tenfold, the heat loss increases a hundredfold. Therefore, it is worth while to raise the voltage if one can at the same time reduce the amperage.

Charles Siemens and William Thomson in England, and Elihu Thomson in America, saw that by "stepping up" alternating current (changing it to high-voltage, low-amperage current) at the generating station and then "stepping it down" for safety's sake at the other end, they could profitably transmit power over much longer distance than with direct current.

George Westinghouse, having entered the electrical field, bought the American rights to the transformer of Gaulard and Gibbs. Thomson invented a transformer of his own. Whereas the original transformer belonged to the core type—that is, the wire was wrapped around the iron core—Thomson invented the transformer of the shell type, with the coils inside and the iron outside.

A group of capitalists offered to set up a laboratory for Thomson in New Britain, Connecticut. The company was called the Thomson-Houston Company, although Houston had little part in it. Thomson built the company into a large and flourishing business, developing alternating-current power and light systems much as Edison was doing with direct current.

In New Britain, Thomson invented the horn-gap lightning arrester. When lightning flashes across the spark gap, a magnetic field forces the arc up the horns until the arc breaks. Thomson applied the same principle to a magnetic switch, which has been used on streetcars ever since.

He also made incandescent lamps of the Edison type, although he had earlier been skeptical of them. At this time the courts were showing a hypercritical attitude towards patents. Many manufacturers, including the Thomson-Houston Company, thought they could therefore infringe Edison's electric-light patent with impunity. Edison let the infringers alone for a while, then went after them. The courts fooled the infringers by holding Edison's patent valid.

When control of Thomson's company passed into the hands of a group of shoe manufacturers of Lynn, Massachusetts, Thomson moved his shop to Lynn. He delayed marketing his alternating-current power and light system until he found a way to protect houses from the high voltage in the primary coil of the step-down transformer, in the rare event that a break in the insulation should direct the high voltage into the house circuit.

This precaution is the grounding of the secondary coil. If you look in your fuse box, you will see a wire coming out of the transformer casing and clamped to a water pipe. This is Thomson's invention.

Thomson also patented arc welding. As this invention did not come within the scope of his contracts, he started his own company to exploit it, with notable success.

He invented the wattmeter, which measures the power being used on an electric line. Power, as I have told you, is the product of volts and amperes.[3] Thomson's elegant solution was to connect the armature (the moving part) of the instrument in series with the main line, so that it recorded the amperage, while the field coil was connected in parallel with the customer's branch and so recorded voltage. The deflection of the pointer is proportional to the *product* of these two electromagnetic forces, and hence proportional to the wattage.

When the Thomson-Houston Company was merged with the Edison Electric Light Company to form the Edison General Electric Company, Thomson refused to become a director of the new company, although he continued to work for it. He disliked administrative work and said he was not cut out for it. Now having plenty of money of his own, he preferred to put more of his time on pure science.

One of his projects was to investigate the strange burns from which early workers with X rays suffered before the dangers of penetrating radiations were realized. Thomson experimented on two of his own fingers. Although he was left with two stiff, scarred fingers, he established that lead foil stops the rays but that aluminum does not. His experiments with high-frequency currents led to diathermy and the electric knife.

At the Columbian Exposition of 1893, Thomson amused himself by baiting quacks and sellers of cure-alls. A salesgirl was demonstrating an electrical "body invigorator." Thomson badgered her with questions until she burst out:

"What do you know about electricity anyhow?"

As Thomson walked off laughing, he heard a man say: "Goodness sakes! Don't you know who that was? That was Professor Thomson. He *invented* electricity!"[4]

As with Edison, Thomson's later discoveries were minor compared to those of his youth. Although Edison was the most prolific inventor in the history of the republic, Thomson was perhaps the second most productive, with 692 patents. If Edison was ahead of Thomson as a pure inventor, Thomson was the more admirable all-around man. Besides a fertile inventor he was a profound research scientist, an expert patent attorney, and a keen businessman.

It is no detraction from Edison's well-earned honors to say that Thomson ought to be better known. In his contributions to the electrical revolution, he was but little behind Edison; yet for every American who knows about Thomson, thousands have heard of Edison.

In his later years, Thomson spent much time pursuing his

hobbies of photography and astronomy. He argued with his friend Percival Lowell, the astronomer, over the so-called canals of Mars. Lowell was sure that these faint streaks on the surface of the red planet were real canals, built by intelligent beings. Thomson thought they were the tracks of herds of migrating animals, which, by trampling and fertilizing the desert, gave it a color different from that of its surroundings. Scientists have not yet settled the true nature of the *canali*.

Although Thomson's last project failed, it was an honorable failure from which much was learned. In the 1920s the astronomer George Ellery Hale, forced out of active research by a nervous disorder, devoted himself as an organizer and administrator to promoting the cause of astronomy.

Hale decided that it was time to build a reflecting telescope even larger than the 100-inch Hooker reflector on Mount Wilson, to see farther into space and settle some of the many questions about distant galaxies. With money from the Rockefeller General Education Board, a group of scientists from California Institute of Technology formed an Observatory Council to build a reflector 200 inches in diameter.

The Council pondered various materials of which to make the mirror. These included a number of metals: steel, stainless steel, speculum, Invar, and Stellite. They included glass, either in one piece or built up. They included a composite structure of glass on metal. And they included quartz.

The Council decided to try quartz first, because it offered the greatest rewards if it could be done but also posed the most difficulties. Quartz (silicon dioxide, silica, crystal) is one of the substances least affected by heat. On the other hand, it melts at a higher temperature than glass—about 2600°F compared to 2000°—and is hard to handle in masses. Then, if quartz failed, they would try Pyrex glass, which has a thermal coefficient of expansion almost as low as that of quartz. If Pyrex failed, they would essay the other alternatives in turn.

The General Electric Company took the quartz contract and assigned the task to Thomson. As an astronomer once observed, the "coefficient of difficulty" of making any gadget goes up as a power of the size. Therefore Thomson did not undertake a 200-inch disk at the start, but worked on a series of pilot disks of increasing size, so that troubles could be met and conquered one by one.

In large pieces, quartz is even more liable to air bubbles than glass. Thomson tried casting a slab of opaque quartz and welding on small pieces of clear quartz that could take the necessary polish. This did not work because, as the disk was made larger, it became harder to attach the clear slabs evenly.

The next scheme was to spray a rain of molten quartz on the opaque disk so that it would form a glaze. This gave good results on eight-inch and twelve-inch disks but required an oxyhydrogen flame from a nozzle revolving slowly, like that of a rotary lawn sprinkler, inside the casting chamber. A special building had to be built for this apparatus, as the flame roared like a space rocket. The whole installation cost $75,000.

They poured the 60-inch disk, but a careless member of the staff opened the door of the oven a few hours before the deadline. The disk cracked.

They poured a second disk. During pouring, a brick fell from the roof of the furnace and contaminated the melt.

Thomson's assistant Ellis began mending the cracked disk with a special blowtorch. He was doing fine when the power failed. A switch had blown in the main power house. When the disk cooled rapidly, the crack sprang open again with a thud, larger than ever.

Ellis went to see the Observatory Council to plead for more time and money, but they turned him down. Thomson might succeed, but again he might spend their entire fund without overcoming his difficulties. Who could tell? It was a hard judgment to make, but the Council decided to drop quartz for Pyrex glass. Nobody will ever know whether Thomson would have succeeded in the long run.

The Council therefore ended its contract with General Electric and made one with the Corning Glass Works in upstate New York. The Corning Glass Works managed to overcome extraordinary difficulties, including an earthquake and a couple of floods, which came near to washing the disk away. The entire project, to the time when the telescope was put into use on Mount Palomar in 1948, took twenty years.

Just after the General Electric contract had been canceled, two Corning engineers went to Lynn to buy some of the furnace equipment that had been used on the quartz disks.

Feeling uncomfortable, they were shown into Thomson's office and found the old man writing. After a minute he looked up and said evenly:

"Gentlemen, I am humbly sorry to have kept you waiting. Please tell me what I can do to help you make the 200-inch Pyrex disk a success."[5]

That was a real scientist.

Of the many engineers and inventors who created the electrical revolution, one of the most important, after Edison, Siemens, Gramme, Sir William Thomson, and Elihu Thomson, was a tall, thin, Mephistophelean-looking man named Nikola Tesla (1856–1943), the inventor of the induction motor.

Now, the Mad Scientist has been a stock character in fiction ever since Aristophanes portrayed Socrates as one in *The Clouds*. (In real life, Socrates was an anti-scientific philosopher; but that mattered not to the playwright, who was firing a blast at all eggheads and other disturbers of ancient tradition.) In the science fiction of twenty years ago, the scientist's madness took such forms as turning the heroine into a wart hog or blowing up the universe.

Truth to tell, the lives of scientists give the impression that, if anything, they are saner than most people. One reason for this is that it takes such a long and rigorous training to become a scientist that those with mental weaknesses tend to be weeded out. It is like the argument used by Lord Dunsany's Arab guide to prove what a healthy place the desert is. "The Arabs in the desert," said Smail ben Ibrahim, "are never ill. If an Arab is ill he dies."[6]

When scientists do become psychotic, their mental ailments show much the same variety as those of common men. One aberration that appears in science, as it does elsewhere, is the paranoid personality. This is the person whose ego is so inflated and so pathologically sensitive as to make him intolerably self-conceited, suspicious, truculent, vindictive, obsessed with imaginary wrongs and insults, unable to brook any denial or admit any error.

When the paranoid reaches the point of delusions of grandeur and persecution, we lock him up. In the meantime, he makes life interesting for everybody he comes in contact with. Tesla, for all his genius, is a case in point.

Tesla was born in Smiljan, Croatia. As a boy he displayed a prodigious memory. When his summons to military service in the Austro-Hungarian Army came, he hid out in the mountains while his father pulled wires to have his draft-dodging overlooked.

Tesla studied electrical engineering at the Polytechnic Institute of Graz, Austria. A professor, Poeschl, explained that motors sparked because there was no way to stop the commutator from sparking. Tesla proposed replacing the commutator with a slip-ring and using alternating current. Poeschl spent an hour showing the class why Tesla's idea would not work. (Of course, it did work, as Elihu Thomson and others would presently prove.)

Tesla graduated from the University of Prague and got a job in the Central Telegraph Office of the Hungarian government, which had just added telephones to its equipment. He worked night and day on these telephones until he brought on a breakdown.

In 1882, while watching a sunset in Budapest, Tesla thought of some lines from Goethe's *Faust*. These led him to his greatest idea: the induction motor.

The ordinary electric motor works by means of two sets of magnets. One set forms a turning wheel-shaped part called the rotor or armature. The other forms a fixed part surrounding the armature, called the stator or field.

There are two kinds of magnets: the so-called permanent magnet, which is a mass of magnetized iron; and the electromagnet, which is a coil of wire, carrying an electric current and usually wrapped around an iron core. One can make a motor with permanent magnets in the armature and electromagnets in the field, or *vice versa*. Most large motors, however, have electromagnets in both field and armature. The current is delivered to the whirling armature by ring-shaped contacts (the commutators and slip-rings that Tesla argued about with his professor) mounted on the armature shaft.

In the induction motor, there is no electrical connection between the rotor and the rest of the motor. Nor are there any permanent magnets. The field has a set of electromagnets, excited in turn by a three-phase alternating current, so that the stator's magnetic field spins round and round.

Ordinary alternating house current is single-phase, surging

back and forth through a single circuit and making sixty complete cycles every second. In a three-phase system, there are three conductors instead of two, joined at the far end of the circuit. The current in all three wires alternates, but in succession, so that when the maximum current is flowing away from the generator through one conductor, it is coming back to the generator through the other two. And when a maximum current is flowing into the generator through one conductor, it is flowing out through the other two.

The rotor of an induction motor is a drum-shaped structure of copper bars welded together, often called a "squirrel cage." As the magnetic field of the stator rotates, it creates electric currents in the rotor by electromagnetic induction, as it would if the stator's magnetic field stood still and the rotor were turned. These currents create a set of electromagnetic poles in the rotor, which act much as do those of an ordinary armature.

As a result, the rotor is dragged around after the whirling stator field. If there is no load, the rotor turns almost as fast as the stator field. When a load is applied to the shaft, the rotor slows down but continues to turn.

Although there is something almost magical about it, the induction motor is so simple and flexible that it is one of the commonest types employed to drive pumps, blowers, cranes, hoists, and other factory machines, wherever three-phase alternating current is available.[7]

Presently Tesla lost his job in Budapest and went to Paris. There he got a position with the Continental Edison Company.

Tesla, however, was an extreme individualist who spent much of his life haughtily walking out on jobs because he thought himself wronged or insulted. Soon he got into an argument with his employers over an expense account and quit again. Charles Batchelor, Thomas Edison's old associate and now an executive of the Continental Edison Company, gave Tesla an introduction to Edison and told him to try his luck in America.

On the ship, Tesla succeeded in losing his wallet and all his spare clothes, so that he reached the United States with four cents in his pocket. Edison took him on with misgivings. For one thing, Tesla had a phobia against writing notes or reports or making drawings. He insisted on doing all his calculations in his head before telling anybody what he was up to. For another, Tesla was devoted to alternating current, while Edison, having committed himself to direct current, had become bigoted on the subject.

Still, Tesla made himself useful by devising improvements in Edison's electrical machinery in his spare time. He offered to improve Edison's generators. Edison said:

"There's fifty thousand dollars in it for you if you can do it."

Tesla did and asked for his money. Edison brushed him off by saying: "Tesla, you don't understand our American humor."[8]

Furious, Tesla quit again. For a time in 1887 he was reduced to working as a day laborer. Then he got backing for a small company of his own. The Tesla Electric Company made induction motors, on which Tesla had taken out a number of patents.

Edison's rival, George Westinghouse, heard of Tesla. He came to see the magical motor and offered Tesla a million dollars plus royalty for the exclusive right to make it. Tesla accepted. For a while he worked for Westinghouse in Pittsburgh, but quit in his usual huff when Westinghouse's engineers questioned his extreme assertions.

Later, when the Westinghouse Company was caught in a panic and the bankers told Westinghouse to get Tesla to scale down his royalty, Tesla said: "Mr. Westinghouse, you have been my friend; you believed in me when others had no faith . . ."[9] and melodramatically tore up his contract. This grand gesture cost him millions.

For several years, Tesla was very productive, inventing generators, transformers, induction coils, condensers, and electric lamps. He experimented with high-frequency alternators that generated currents alternating 10,000 times a second and discovered the peculiar surface effects of such currents. He also worked with tuned circuits.

At this time he was a gaunt man, over six feet two and weighing less than 150 pounds, with black hair and eyebrows over gray eyes. A long satanic face tapered from wide Slavic cheekbones down to a narrow mouth and pointed chin. He dressed with quiet elegance, wearing an invariable derby. His manner was courtly, his English fluent if accented. Most of his ample income he spent on Lucullan banquets for the social élite.

Tesla received a hard blow when his laboratory, into which he had put most of his capital, burned in 1895. He had, characteristically, neglected to insure it.

For several years, Tesla was kept going by a number of eminent capitalists, from whom he collected money to build another laboratory. His backers included J. Pierpont Morgan, John Jacob Astor, John Hays Hammond, and Thomas Fortune Ryan. Knowing of his real achievements, these investors expected him to go on making great inventions, especially as his claims and prophecies grew more grandiose every year.

What happened was quite different. The creative side of his nature dried up, so that he had but few patents issued after 1905. At the same time, the paranoid side, which had always been in evidence, took over more and more.

For decades, Tesla experimented with oscillators, machines for making high-voltage sparks, and other gadgets. But, although he staged impressive demonstrations, nothing useful ever came out of these tests.

A boyhood conviction that lightning caused rain led him to spend years trying to bring rain to the arid West by shooting artificial lightning-bolts from a mountaintop in Colorado. In 1900–02 he built a 145-foot wooden tower on Long Island, with a copper doughnut 100 feet in diameter on top. By means of this tower, Tesla was going to broadcast all over the world.

However, this was only expensive fooling around. Tesla had become the world's most eminent crank. He was now a paranoid egotist who, when he went to the Allis-Chalmers Company to demonstrate an impractical steam turbine that he had designed, insisted that Allis-Chalmers fire certain workmen whose looks he did not like.

When in 1912 the Nobel Prize was offered jointly to Tesla and Edison, Tesla refused it. It was wrong, said he, that he, the great scientific discoverer, should be bracketed with a mere tinkerer like Edison. He had never forgiven Edison for the latter's mean little trick with the fifty-thousand-dollar offer. The startled Nobel Committee gave the prize in physics to a Swede instead.

Tesla ran his affairs in a way that makes such unworldly incompetents as John Fitch and Charles Goodyear look like prudent and thrifty businessmen. When he had money, he spent it on lavish entertaining. He would not bother to collect the royalties due on his older inventions, saying with lordly disdain:

"That is all small-time stuff. I cannot be bothered with it."[10]

As his experiments failed to produce results and his backers lost faith or died off, Tesla found himself retired willy-nilly from active engineering. He could not hold an ordinary salaried job because of his inability to work with others.

During the First World War, his wonderful tower on Long Island was demolished for fear that Tesla—an Austro-Hungarian by birth—might use it to send information to the Central Powers. After this war, most of Tesla's remaining life was spent quietly at the Hotel New Yorker, during his last seven years on a pension from the Yugoslav government.

Here he indulged his many quirks and phobias. For instance, such was his horror of germs that, if a fly alighted on his dinner table, the table had to be cleared and the meal started over. He practiced curious diets like milk and whiskey, boasting that by such means he would live to be 125. Much of his time he spent feeding pigeons. A bachelor, he had a weird platonic love affair with a female pigeon.

Every birthday, Tesla held a news conference at which he announced a great forthcoming invention. One year it was wireless transmission of power; then interplanetary communication; then a death ray; then a scheme for lighting the whole night side of the earth by artificial aurora. Although many were taken in by Tesla's pretensions, nothing ever came of these plans.

Tesla also presented "proof" that Einstein was wrong and often declared that "atomic power is an illusion."

He died quietly in 1943. But the useful, creative part of him had died many years before.

XIII

SELDEN

AND THE AUTOMOBILE

First, let us admit frankly that, although there is a popular legend that Henry Ford invented the automobile, the automobile is not really an American invention at all. For one thing, it was not invented by any one man, but by a host of inventors. For another, most of these inventors were Europeans.

Nevertheless, the automobile does come into the story of American invention. Some American pioneers contributed to the art. One of the nation's most famous patent cases involved an automobile patent. And the invention itself became the basis of one of the nation's greatest industries.

The modern automobile is a combination of many inventions. The general idea of an engine-propelled road vehicle followed quickly on the heels of Watt's steam engine. The first man to make such a vehicle run was a captain of engineers in the French Army, Nicolas Joseph Cugnot.

About 1770, Cugnot built a three-wheeled steam carriage to tow artillery. To get traction on the single front wheel, Cugnot hung his boiler out in front of the wheel. The engine, with a pawl-and-ratchet drive, was mounted over the wheel itself. Although this arrangement gave plenty of traction, it made the vehicle almost impossible to steer.

On demonstration, the machine groaned and puffed along the streets of Paris at two and a half miles an hour, stopping every hundred feet to get up steam. It marched . . . But then Cugnot found himself headed for a wall, and all his frantic straining at the windlass would not turn it in time. Crash! Cugnot was tossed into the Bastille to teach him not to damage the property of King Louis' subjects. His second steam car fared no better, nor did one that the Dutch Army tried as an artillery carriage a few years later. But Cugnot, happily for him, invented a gun, which was such a success that he ended his days on a pension from Napoleon.

Beginning in 1801, Richard Trevithick, the locomotive pioneer, also built several steam road carriages. One of these had main wheels ten feet in diameter, a single cylinder mounted between these wheels, and a coach body perched high up over the mass of machinery. One of Trevithick's road engines made all of eight miles an hour and went as far as six miles without breaking down.

Other inventors in Europe and America built steam carriages during the following decades. Several of them ran as omnibuses on regular schedules in England during the 1830s. Walter Hancock, one of the most active of the British steam coach builders, made a small one for his own use. This was probably the world's first private automobile.

Then this development was choked off in Great Britain by hostile legislation. For one thing, the stagecoach companies, the horse breeders, and other interested parties lobbied against this new competition. Moreover, these vehicles, weighing over three tons and running on huge iron-tired wheels, punched great holes in the dirt roads.

As a result, Parliament passed laws restricting the operation of steam coaches and raised their toll charges to prohibitive heights. The most drastic of these laws, in force from 1865 to 1896, required a man with a red flag to walk in front of the vehicle.

Even without these laws, it is not likely that the steam coaches would have succeeded. They did not take hold elsewhere, being too full of engine and too feeble and fragile for the roads of the time. Moreover, they could not compete with the more efficient and comfortable railroad.

To make powered free-wheel cars practical, an engine much lighter for its power than the steam engine was needed. This meant, practically speaking, an engine without boiler or furnace; in other words, an internal-combustion engine. In such an engine, the heat and pressure resulting from the burning of fuel act directly upon the propelling machinery instead of boiling water to push a piston or twirl a turbine.

The internal-combustion engine was suggested by the gun, which is, in a way, a kind of internal-combustion engine. Engines driven by explosions of gunpowder were tried but did not work. The first internal-combustion engine that ran at all was Cecil's hydrogen engine of 1820. This was really a vacuum engine like that of Thomas Newcomen, the vacuum being made by the explosion of a mixture of hydrogen and air to form water.

The first internal-combustion engine that operated at all well was that which Étienne Lenoir made in 1860. The Lenoir engine, popular for several years, worked on a principle like that of Ericsson's hot-air engine. Liquid fuel was burned outside the cylinder, and the hot gas from this combustion entered the cylinder by a slide-valve mechanism like that of a steam engine.

The Lenoir engine ran smoothly. In the 1860s and 70s a number of patents were issued to various inventors for vehicles powered by Lenoir engines, and some of these naphtha carriages were built and run.

However, the Lenoir engine was a perfect hog for fuel. Therefore it gave way, in the 1880s, to engines in which the fuel and air are put into the cylinder, compressed by the piston, and exploded. One of the most successful of these was that made by Julius Hock, an Austrian railroad engineer.

Another was devised by Nikolaus August Otto in 1876. Otto's engine is called a four-stroke-cycle engine because, for every explosion in a cylinder, there are four strokes of the piston, two up and two down. On one downstroke, the piston draws into the cylinder a mixture of air and gasoline vapor. On the following upstroke, the piston compresses the mixture. Then an electric spark explodes the mixture, driving the piston down. The fourth stroke of the piston pushes the burned gases out the exhaust valve. The Otto engine proved at least twice as efficient, in economy of fuel, as the Lenoir engine.

Other engineers tried to get more power out of an engine of a given size by running it on the two-stroke-cycle principle. That is, every downstroke of the piston is a power stroke. But the exhaustion of the burned gases, the sucking in of a new charge of fuel and air, and the compression of the inflammable mixture all take place during a single upstroke.

Thus the two-stroke-cycle engine delivers twice as many power strokes as the Otto engine for a given number of revolutions of the crankshaft. On the other hand, there is always some mixing between the burned gas, about to be exhausted from the cylinder, and the incoming charge of vaporized fuel and air. Hence either some of the burned gas stays in the cylinder during the power stroke, or some of the fresh charge is blown out the exhaust port with the burned gas, or both.

As a result, the two-stroke-cycle engine is less thrifty of fuel than the Otto engine. Therefore two-stroke-cycle engines are used nowadays in such applications as lawn mowers and outboard motorboats, where light weight is more important than strict economy of fuel.

Another of the many inventions that went into the practical automobile was the pneumatic tire. This in turn depended upon the discovery of vulcanized rubber.

The Indians of Central America used rubber centuries before Columbus. They made rubber balls with which they played an elaborate game. The eighteenth-century French explorer Charles la Condamine brought the stuff to Europe's attention. At first it was used merely for erasing, whence its name.

In the 1820s, rubber was tried for overshoes and raincoats. It proved satisfactory at the right temperature but became brittle in cold weather and melted with a fearful stench in hot.

The Roxbury India Rubber Company, among others, got stuck with a lot of rubber goods returned in a decomposing state. This company's owners confided their troubles to a young man named Goodyear, who had wandered into their shop.

Charles Goodyear (1800–60) was a dreamy drifter who had failed in the hardware business and now, in 1834, was trying to keep out of debtor's prison. Goodyear conceived a passion for making rubber practical. For years thereafter he sought financial backing, borrowed from his relatives, and lived on next to nothing while experimenting with rubber. Some of his time he spent in debtor's prison. His family were impressed into the work.

In the late 1830s he thought that he had succeeded by mixing sulfur with rubber and took a contract for mail bags from the government. But the bags failed. Somebody described him thus: "If you meet a man who has on an India rubber cap, stock, coat, vest, and shoes, with an India rubber money purse, without a cent of money in it, that is he."[1]

While visiting a factory in Massachusetts whose owner sometimes made rubber articles for him, Goodyear tried the effects of heat on articles of sulfur-impregnated rubber, including one of the ill-fated mail bags. He found that, if pressed against a hot stove, the articles were charred like leather instead of melting like pure rubber. Further trials showed that, if a piece of sulfur-bearing rubber were scorched, the part adjacent to the scorched place turned into cured, stable rubber.[2]

Goodyear began another series of experiments to find the right proportions and temperatures to perfect this vulcanizing process, as he called it. For several years he continued his experiments by such desperate expedients as selling his children's schoolbooks.

When Goodyear got his patent, in 1844, and people began to realize that he really had something, he became embroiled in litigation with infringers. He won a decisive victory in 1852 with Daniel Webster as his lawyer, before the United States Circuit Court in New Jersey. This was Webster's last important case; he was in rare rhetorical form:

> . . . is Charles Goodyear the discoverer of this invention of vulcanized rubber? Is he the first man upon whose mind the idea ever flashed, or to whose intelligence the fact was ever disclosed, that by carrying heat to a certain height it would cease to render plastic the India Rubber and begin to harden and metallize it? Is there a man in the world who found out that fact before Charles Goodyear? Who is he? Where is he? On what continent does he live? Who has heard of him? What books treat of him? What man among all the men on earth has seen him, known him, or named him?
>
> And who is that somebody? . . . If Charles Goodyear did not make this discovery, who did make it? Who did make it? . . . We want to know the name, and the habitation of the man upon the face of the globe, who invented vulcanized rubber, if it be not he, who now sits before us.[3]

The court decided for Goodyear. Now Goodyear began to experience the first faint dawning of success. At least, enough money came in so that he and his family ate regularly.

But not even his legal victory could give Goodyear financial sense. He spent borrowed money lavishly on promotion, was imprisoned once more for debt in Paris, and died owing $200,000.

The great use of rubber in the automotive industry is of course in tires. The pneumatic tire was invented in Europe in the 1840s but was invented ahead of its time, so that the inventors failed to profit from it. It was almost forgotten when a Scottish veterinarian named John Boyd Dunlop reinvented it in 1888. Now there was a flourishing bicycle business to use the tires, so that Dunlop made millions from his tire despite the weakness of his patent.

Many of the pioneers in the automotive and airplane fields started out with bicycles. The bicycle was invented in Europe, going through several stages before becoming practical.

First there was Drais von Sauerbronn's "Draisine" without pedals, propelled by striking the feet against the ground. It appeared in 1799 and under the nickname of "dandy-horse" reached its vogue in the 1820s. Then it died out as people found it too strenuous a steed for pleasure.

Next came the "velocipede" of Lallement and Michaux, with two equal wheels and pedal cranks on the first. Its riding qualities are indicated by its common name of "boneshaker."

Then appeared the appalling "ordinary" of the seventies, with a front wheel four or five feet in diameter. Once one got the thing rolling it was less tiring than its predecessors because it applied the rider's foot-power more efficiently. But a fall from one was as serious as from a horse.

In 1876–77, Lawson in England and Pope in the United States combined Rousseau's chain-and-sprocket drive with other improvements to launch the "safety," the modern bicycle. By the nineties the safety had driven the ordinary out of business, and swarms of American bicyclists were demanding that the United States fix up its terrible roads so that they could use them in comfort. The good-roads movement in turn encouraged the spread of the automobile.

In 1879, when interest in the new internal-combustion engines was rising, George Baldwin Selden (1846–1922) of Rochester, New York, applied for a patent on a "road locomotive" driven by "an engine of the compression type." Selden was a patent attorney—George Eastman's patent attorney, in fact. He was also an inventor of some ability, having already taken out several patents on machinery for making barrel hoops.

Instead of building an automobile, Selden built and tested a three-cylinder motor. This motor was an improved version of that invented by George B. Brayton of Boston in 1873. It is sometimes classed as the first two-stroke-cycle engine, although its principle differed from that of modern two-stroke-cycle engines. The fuel-air mixture was compressed in a separate cylinder before being admitted to the power cylinder.

Selden knew about the Otto engine but seems to have fallen out with the company that exploited the Otto patents in the United States. A note in Selden's diary referred to the Otto engine as "another of those damned Dutch engines."

While tinkering with his engine, Selden set out to raise capital to build an automobile. Meanwhile he craftily delayed the issuance of his patent, as he knew that his monopoly would run for only seventeen years from the date of issue, and there was no point in starting it before there was any automobile industry for it to dominate.

In his efforts to raise money, however, Selden persistently failed. Part of his failure may have been due simply to bad luck. One man who promised to back him died suddenly; another went bankrupt; and so on.

Part of it, however, was probably due to his own personality. A shrewd patent attorney, an able inventor, and a competent mechanic, Selden was no salesman. Impatient and irascible, he approached his prospects in a forceful, dogmatic way that usually put their backs up. One Rochester man was on the point of investing $5000 when Selden exclaimed:

"Jim, you and I will live to see more carriages on Main Street run by motors than are now drawn by horses."

The prospect stared and said: "George, you are crazy, and I won't have anything to do with your scheme."

Twenty-five years later, Selden met the same man, who said: "Well, George, you were right years ago when you said there would be more automobiles on Main Street than horses."

"Yes," snarled Selden, ignoring the outstretched hand, "and I wasn't so damned crazy as you and the other fools said I was!"[4] He walked off and never spoke to that man again.

For sixteen years, Selden continued to tinker with his engine, juggle his patent application, and seek capital. In 1895 his patent, No. 549,160 for a Road-engine, issued. George Eastman signed the drawing as a witness. The second claim reads:

> 2. The combination with a road-locomotive, provided with suitable running gear including a propelling wheel and steering mechanism, of a liquid hydrocarbon gas-engine of the compression type, comprising one or more power cylinders, a suitable liquid-fuel receptacle, a power shaft connected with and arranged to run faster than the propelling wheel, an intermediate clutch or disconnecting device, and a suitable carriage body located above the engine, substantially as described.

Of the six claims, the fourth claimed as part of the combination simply "a hydrocarbon engine"; all the others claimed a "hydrocarbon gas-engine of the compression type." The fourth claim contained other limitations.

Note that a device either infringes an entire claim of a patent or it does not infringe that claim at all. A claim dominates only such devices or processes as contain every element set forth in the claim, whether or not they contain additional elements as well. If the device lacks any element mentioned in the claim, the claim does not dominate the device. On the other hand, an invention can be dominated by some claims of a patent but not by others.

In the drawing and specification, Selden showed and described a Brayton engine and said nothing about the Otto engine, although he did say: "Any form of liquid-hydrocarbon engine of the compression type may be employed in my improved road-locomotive."

By the time Selden received his patent, many companies were making horseless carriages. Gottlieb Daimler in Germany, who had been employed in the Otto Engine Works, built a light, fast gasoline engine, developed from the designs of Otto and Hock. In 1885 he installed this engine in a bicycle and startled the people of Mannheim by chugging over their ancient cobblestones in the world's first motorcycle. A motor tricycle followed and then a four-wheeled automobile with the engine under the rear seat. Daimler had trouble because, without a differential gear, one rear wheel or the other had to skid in order to turn a corner.

Around 1885, Daimler's younger rival, Karl Benz, also began building and running three- and four-wheeled automobiles in Mannheim.

Interest also rose in France. Emil Levassor, of the Parisian carriage firm of Panhard & Levassor, went to Germany to buy a set of motorboat engine plans from Daimler. When he saw how Daimler had installed his engine in a boat, up forward with a propeller shaft extending aft to the stern, he thought that this arrangement would solve the automobile problem. Back in Paris he set another German mechanic, Nikolaus Krebs, to building a front-engined automobile.

Presently Benz went to work for Panhard & Levassor also. The result of their efforts was an automobile, completed in 1894, with most of the modern features: a V-engine in front under a hood, a water-cooling system, a sliding-gear transmission and differential, hub brakes, elliptical springs, and so forth.

Meanwhile Daimler worked up his automobile business, calling his company the Mercedes Company after his daughter. Benz, too, formed his own company, which eventually merged with that of Daimler to form the firm of Mercedes-Benz.

At the same time, other inventors in England, France, Germany, Austria, and the United States built a swarm of vehicles, powered by gasoline, stream, electricity, or clockwork that had to be wound up every three miles. At this time, "every machine needed about five hours of tinkering for every hour of running."[5]

Elwood Haynes and Charles E. Duryea pioneered in car-building in the United States, though their automobiles had but little effect on the evolution of the machine.

In the late 1890s, the fashionable rich began importing French automobiles and using them as sporting vehicles. Then rural physicians began to buy them, as they found that with an automobile they could make as many calls in a day as they could with a buggy in a week.

The American petroleum industry, which had already waxed great on the basis of the chemical discoveries of the wreath-bearded Benjamin Silliman, Jr., welcomed the new machines as an outlet for their gasoline. Gasoline had up to then been a

useless and dangerous by-product of the refining of kerosene
for lamps.

The idea of a cheap automobile for everybody was conceived
by Ransom E. Olds. The son of a Lansing machinist, Olds in
1899 launched his Oldsmobile from a factory in Detroit, which
thus became the automotive capital of the United States. After
losing money on a high-priced horseless carriage in his first year,
he produced a 700-pound, $650 "runabout," which dominated
the American market for several years.

Olds fell out with his backer and quit to form another company, Reo. But his great idea was taken up by a gaunt, thin-
lipped tinkerer named Henry Ford. Ford had been fumbling for
several years at the door of automotive success, changing his
backers, and experimenting with cars of different kinds.

Ford, born on a farm in Michigan, hated all farm work save
such as could be done by machinery. As a youth he worked as a
machinist and as an engineer for the Edison Illuminating Company of Detroit. In 1897 he met Edison at an Edison Company
banquet in New York. Ford described his automotive dreams to
the older man, who smote the table and said:

"Young man, that's it! You have it—the self-contained unit
carrying its own fuel with it. Keep at it."[6]

Edison also urged Ford to strive for low unit cost and large
production. So in 1906 Ford brought out his Model T: a black
boxlike vehicle, not pretty but light, cheap, and rugged, well
adapted to back-country conditions. With minor changes this
machine dominated the American market for twenty years. Fifteen million were made.

Ford and his executives developed to a high degree the arts
of mass production with interchangeable parts, line assembly,
and finally conveyor assembly. Later Ford claimed to have
invented the entire art of mass production. This was untrue.
Leblanc, Whitney, Colt, and many others had prepared the way
for him. But then Ford, while a man of undoubted genius, was
also a man of ludicrous ignorance outside of his field of making
automobiles.

Ford had a long and picturesque career. He was a man of
strong political convictions and violent prejudices. He paid his
workers unprecedentedly high wages but worked them up to
the last ounce of their endurance.

In 1899, George Baldwin Selden sold control of his patent to the Columbia Motor Car Company, under a contract by which he received a percentage of their profits from the exploitation of the patent.

In 1900 this company sued the Winton Motor Carriage Company (afterwards the Winton Engine Corporation, a General Motors subsidiary) for infringement. The suit ran until 1903.

In order to demonstrate to the court that Selden had really conceived a functioning invention, the plaintiffs paid the Pope Manufacturing Company, whose main business was bicycles, to build an automobile according to the plans contained in the original Selden patent application of 1879. The automobile had the name "Selden" and the date of conception, 1877, painted on its side. This obsolete contraption drove to distraction the engineer in charge of the project, but he finally got it to run after a fashion.

At this point the ten companies licensed to build cars under the Selden patent formed the Association of Licensed Automobile Manufacturers, in order to collect and pay over the royalties of 1¼% of the retail price of all automobiles sold, due Selden and the Columbia Motor Car Company. Later in 1903 the Columbia Company (which shortly became the Electric Vehicle Company) and Selden filed an infringement suit against the Ford Motor Company and seven other defendants who had refused to pay royalties. In 1909, after the suit was decided in favor of the plaintiffs, most of Ford's co-defendants entered the Association.

Ford, however, never conceded others' patent rights unless compelled to do so. Swearing that he would fight to the last ditch, he appealed. In 1911 the Circuit Court of Appeals for the Second Circuit reversed the District Court's decree. This did not make too much difference to the owners of the Selden patent, which had less than a year left to run anyway. The Association had received about two million dollars, of which Selden got one-tenth.

The decision (Columbia Motor Car Company v. C. A. Duerr & Company) is full of subtle legal reasoning. One can still argue the pros and cons of its rightness and justice. It held, in effect, that vehicles with the Brayton engine and the Otto engine were two distinct species of the same genus, which genus also included vehicles powered with the Lenoir engine. The Otto and Brayton engine combinations could be considered as belonging to the same species only if the engines in question were equivalents. The court decided that "the two engines do not perform the same functions in substantially the same way" and hence were not equivalent.

Now, two species may be claimed in one patent only when the patent contains a claim on a genus that includes both species. In this case it was manifestly impossible to have such a genus claim, because one species of the genus—the Lenoir-engined vehicle—had been old when the patent was applied for. Therefore, if the patent claimed both Otto-engined and Brayton-engined vehicles, it must needs be invalid. In 1879 Selden could probably have taken out one patent on an Otto-engined vehicle and one on a Brayton-engined vehicle, but this he had not done.

Whether the patent was invalid depended upon the meaning given the words "of the compression type," which appeared in the claims. In ordinary engineering parlance, there is no question but that both Brayton and Otto engines are "of the compression type." But the patent, as stated, showed and described the Brayton engine only.

So, to save the patent from invalidity, the court stretched a point and interpreted "compression" as referring to engines of that type alone. As all automobiles were then using Otto engines, the claims did not dominate them. Hence the patent was held valid but not infringed. The decision said:

> But, like many another inventor, while he had a conception of the object to be accomplished, he went in the wrong direction. The Brayton engine was the leading engine of the time, and his attention was naturally drawn to its supposed advantages. He chose that type. In the light of events we can see that had he appreciated the superiority of the Otto engine and adapted that type for his combination his patent would cover the modern automobile. He did not do so.[7]

As a result of this decision, the Association of Licensed Manufacturers was dissolved and no more royalties were paid to the owners of the Selden patent. Using his share of this money,

Selden had meanwhile, in 1906, set up his own automobile company, the Selden Motor Vehicle Company. Alas! Selden did not prove successful as a manufacturer and soon lost most of the gains from the exploitation of his patent.

At the same time, the manufacture of automobiles advanced in high gear: 3700 in 1899, 11,000 in 1903, 44,000 in 1907, and 485,000 in 1913. The number of manufacturers also swelled until there were 183 manufacturers in the United States and Canada in 1917. (Compare the present list of American manufacturers, hovering around the half-dozen mark!)

With so many competing companies, all employing engineers and inventors to advance the product, the patent situation soon became hopelessly tangled. Nobody knew what sort of automobile he might legally make. To bring order out of this chaos, the automobile manufacturers in 1915 formed the Automobile Manufacturers Association, which set up a patent pool.

A patent pool is an agreement among a number of companies, making the same product, that any of them may make, use, and sell the invention dominated by a patent owned by any member of the pool *ad libitum*. It is like a cross-licensing agreement between two manufacturers, but on an industry-wide scale.

This agreement was originally for ten years and was renewed at five-year intervals thereafter, until it was allowed to expire as no longer needed after the Second World War. Such patent pools often benefit the industry by saving the cost of patent litigation and allowing the wider use of new inventions. They may also benefit the consumer by lowering the price of the product.

On the other hand, patent pools are more or less to the disadvantage of independent inventors. No company belonging to a patent pool will pay much for a patent offered by such an outsider, because all its competitors could use the invention as well. As an example of how such agreements work out in practice, an automobile executive estimated some years ago that his company bought rights to about eight of the 8000 inventions submitted to them annually; that is, one-tenth of one per cent.

In this way, independent invention in the automobile industry was early reduced to negligible importance, and the heroic age of invention, in that field, was ended almost before it had begun.

XIV

LANGLEY, THE WRIGHTS,
AND FLYING

Men talked for centuries of what fun it would be to fly. They created wistful legends of flight: of Daedalus and his waxen wings, of the Persian king Kai Kaus and his eagle-powered aerial throne, of Prince Ahmad and his flying carpet. Some flying enthusiasts, in the seventeenth century, made wings and jumped off roofs with them, breaking legs or necks.

Man's first actual flights were made in balloons, invented in 1782 by the brothers Montgolfier in France. Balloons came into use during the nineteenth century for circus attractions, means of exploring the upper air, and military observation posts. During the American Civil War, a young German army officer, Ferdinand, Count von Zeppelin, eagerly watched the operation of the Union's observation balloons as a neutral observer.

During the last half of the century, several European inventors, mostly French, combined the balloon with a power drive. In these machines, a car hung from a sausage-shaped bag. Projecting from the car were airscrews turned by steam, electricity, gasoline, or muscle power. Powered balloons of this type were called "dirigible" (that is, steerable) balloons or simply "dirigibles."

Count Zeppelin went home to Baden from the Civil War, rose to general, retired in 1891, and went back to his first love, ballooning. Seizing upon the new Hall-Héroult process for making aluminum in quantity, he invented the rigid dirigible airship. In this craft, a skeleton of light aluminum girders maintained a cigar-shaped outer envelope while a row of fifteen or more balloonettes inside this structure contained the lifting gas. Gondolas below the main envelope housed the power plants and the control cabin.

During World War I, the Germans built a number of Zeppelins, as rigid airships came to be known, for bombing and naval scouting. They proved very vulnerable, however, because bombs and tracer bullets easily fired the hydrogen gas with which they were inflated.

After this war, the Americans, British, and Germans built several enormous rigid airships for naval and commercial use. But one by one they were destroyed in storms and accidents. Even using the denser but noninflammable helium gas instead of hydrogen did not save them. By the time of World War II, the airplane had evolved so far that there was no more excuse for huge, costly, and fragile airships, wafting through the sky like the ghosts of whales.

The airplane presented a harder problem than the airship. Without a gas bag to hold it up, it could not stop in mid-air if something went wrong. To build a workable airplane, one had to know already how to fly, and how could one learn to fly when no airplane existed? Moreover, air proved the most treacherous road that men had ever tried to travel—as wayward as water, as slippery as ice, and as evanescent as thought.

In the early nineteenth century, Sir George Cayley worked out many of the laws of air. Like Borelli in 1680, he asserted that men might as well forget muscle-powered wings, because men have no muscles so strong in proportion to their total weight as the flying muscles of birds.

In 1848, Cayley's fellow-Briton John Stringfellow built a model flying machine, a birdlike affair with a ten-foot wingspread and a pair of airscrews driven by a small steam engine. It flew for forty yards. In the eighties and nineties, Clément Adair in France and Hiram Stevens Maxim in England built full-sized steam-driven flying machines. On trials these rose a few inches, soared for a few yards, and crashed.

Simon Newcomb, the American astronomer, was not wrong

when he said that the solution of the flying-machine problem awaited "the discovery of some new principle." Half the problem was how to get much more power from an engine of a given weight. The internal-combustion engine furnished the answer to this question.

The other half of the problem was how to control the craft in the air, to keep it from going into an unwanted dive or spin. In the last quarter of the nineteenth century, glider enthusiasts partly solved this problem. The leaders of this enterprise were Lilienthal in Germany, Pilcher in England, and Montgomery and Chanute in the United States. The first three of these all perished in pursuit of their hobby, but Chanute survived to hand on his hard-won wisdom to the Wrights.

Before the Wrights' success, however, came the work of Langley. Although Langley did not quite succeed in flying, the aeronautical principles that he worked out were used by all later builders of heavier-than-air flying machines.

One day in the nineties, a visitor to Alexander Graham Bell's estate on Cape Breton Island found an astonishing sight. Three men were engaged in solemn scientific research. All were large, imposing men of distinguished achievement, solid reputation, full-bearded presence, and Jovian dignity. They were:

Alexander Graham Bell, inventor of the telephone and now, in prosperous maturity, a patron of young scientists and scientific societies;

Simon Newcomb, astronomer, mathematician, and economist, professor of mathematics in the United States Navy with the rank of rear admiral, professor of mathematics and astronomy at Johns Hopkins University, and editor of the *Nautical Almanac;* and Samuel Pierpont Langley (1834–1906), architect, engineer, mathematician, physicist, astronomer, and secretary of the Smithsonian Institution.

They were trying to find out why a cat lands on its feet. To this end they were dropping a cat upside down from the porch of Bell's house to the terrace below. Over and over, one dropped the cat while the others watched it paddling the air with its paws. Not wishing to hurt pussy, they had placed a pillow on the terrace for it to fall on.

As secretary of the Smithsonian, Langley occupied the highest administrative post in American science. He was born in suburban Boston, the son of a successful wholesale merchant. When, as a boy, Langley showed an interest in astronomy, his father gave him a telescope.

After receiving a high-school education in Boston, Langley went straight into architecture and civil engineering in Chicago. At this time it was still possible, at least in the United States, to rise high in the technical professions without college training.

At thirty, Langley forsook engineering for pure science. After a year's scientific pilgrimage to Europe, he got an assistantship at the Harvard Observatory in 1865. The following year he taught mathematics at the United States Naval Academy. In 1867, he became director of the Allegheny Observatory and professor of physics and astronomy at the Western University of Pennsylvania, which later became the University of Pittsburgh.

Here Langley worked for twenty years. He was a scientist of the kind whose whole life lay in his work. Not for him the simian follies that enliven so many biographies; he lacked the time. He was a large florid man; shy, withdrawn, witty, and irascible. He worked hard, never married, and protected his tender ego by a shell of cold dignity. He was the last person, one would think, to get himself into the position of a national laughingstock.

To obtain a regular income for the observatory, Langley devised a method of automatically sending telegraphic time signals to all the stations of a railroad, so that their clocks could be kept synchronized. Moreover, he persuaded the Pennsylvania Railroad to enter into a contract with the observatory to receive these signals twice a day at its various stations.

During his stay at Pittsburgh, Langley made some lasting contributions to science. Astronomy at this time was in transition. Theretofore, astronomers' main concern had been with the positions and movements of the heavenly bodies. Newcomb had spent decades in calculating tables of planetary motion more accurate than any known before. Now, however, astronomers were beginning to study the heavenly bodies by means of new instruments like the spectroscope, to find out what they were made of and what conditions were like upon and inside them.

Langley was an astronomer of the new school. His specialty was sunspots, long a subject of controversy. When Galileo had first called attention to sunspots, some protested that nothing so divinely pure as the sun could have spots. Later it was wondered whether they were clouds of smoke or other opaque matter.

Langley surmised that sunspots were funnel-shaped eddies like tornadoes in the sun's atmosphere. Nineteen years later, George Ellery Hale proved by means of his spectroheliograph that this was indeed the case.

In 1878, Langley invented the bolometer. This delicate instrument measures radiant energy by the electric current that is made to flow in a blackened thread of platinum when light falls upon it. The bolometer detects radiation as slight as that from the body of a cow a quarter-mile away.

With his bolometer, Langley began measurements of the distribution of radiation in the spectrum of the sun, the transparency of the atmosphere to solar rays, and the amount of energy radiated to the earth by the sun. Research into these matters is still going on eighty years later, by means of high-altitude balloons and earth-satellite vehicles.

In 1881, Langley organized an expedition to Mount Whitney, California, to measure solar radiation at high altitudes. Although his measurements were accurate, an error in his equations gave him a figure of three calories per square centimeter per second, instead of the currently accepted figure of 1.938. He also advanced the still-disputed theory that changes in the earth's weather, including ice ages, are caused by variations in the brightness of the sun.

In 1887, Langley was called to the Smithsonian Institution as assistant secretary under Spencer Baird, the zoölogist and conservationist. Within that same year, Baird died and Langley succeeded him.

Langley had already begun investigations in the almost virgin science of aeronautics, and he vigorously pressed these researches during the rest of his life. While some others like Lord Rayleigh were also investigating the field, Langley did more than any other man to put aeronautics on a scientific basis.

He built a whirling table with two thirty-foot arms, rotated by an engine. He mounted shapes of brass on the ends of their arms to measure their lift, drag, and other aerodynamic qualities. He found that, contrary to expectations, curved airfoils developed more lift than flat ones. He also discovered that the faster they went the more lift they exerted.

From his turntable, Langley went on to powered models. First they were driven by rubber bands, then by light little steam engines of Langley's own design. He called his models "aerodromes," from the Greek *aēr*, "air," + *dromeus*, "runner." The wings that supported them he called "aeroplanes."

Langley's *Aerodrome No. 6* made several impressive flights. It was fourteen feet long, with two pairs of wings in tandem and a pair of airscrews just aft of the forward wings. On November 28, 1896, it buzzed over the Potomac for more than half a mile, like a monstrous dragonfly from the Age of Coal. When it ran out of fuel, it settled gently on the water, floating by the buoyancy of its empty fuel tank.

Despite his experiments with the cat, and despite the pleas of his brilliant assistant Charles Matthews Manly to put wheels on his machines, Langley refused to give them any alighting gear. They simply came down on their lower guy posts. Such a machine could alight on water only with some risk and not on land at all.

Langley was now ready to drop the project. He had proved what he set out to prove. He had material for fine fat reports and did not intend to send his own ponderous sixty-two-year-old body aloft.

But his enthusiastic friend Bell, a regent of the Smithsonian, thought that more should be done with the idea. So did the Bureau of Ordnance of the War Department. So did President McKinley. Who, in Langley's position, could resist such flattering persuasion? Therefore, with $50,000 from the War Department and $20,000 in Smithsonian money, Langley set out to build a man-carrying aerodrome.

He worked at it from 1898 to 1903. The knottiest problem was the engine. Langley knew that, as his machines grew larger, they had to become more efficient if they were to fly at all.

This followed from the square-cube law. If you double the dimensions of a flying machine, you increase the wing area, and hence the lifting power, by four. But you also increase the mass by eight. For this reason, living fliers like the condor have never exceeded twenty-five or thirty pounds, and Sindbad's fabulous roc, which bore off elephants to feed its young, would be quite impossible.

Hence Langley switched from steam engines to gasoline engines in order to get more power per pound. When he could not persuade any commercial factory to make him an engine weighing less than ten pounds per horsepower, his assistant Manly designed the world's first radial engine. This was a 52-horsepower, five-cylinder, water-cooled engine weighing less than three pounds per horsepower.

Langley and Manly built two aerodromes: a quarter-sized model, weighing 58 pounds, and a full-scale machine 55 feet long and 48 feet across the wings, weighing 730 pounds.

The model flew well, for about a thousand feet. Then Langley and his men hauled the parts of the large aerodrome to the roof of a houseboat on the Potomac, which Langley used as a launching platform. Here they bolted the machine together.

Several newspaper editors thought that, if the secretary of the Smithsonian ran such an experiment, there must be something to it, even if most people considered all flying-machine inventors crackpots. So they sent reporters to the scene. A military guard shooed the journalists away from the houseboat. They camped on the Virginia shore, where they suffered from heat, rain, mosquitoes, and boredom. As time passed, they washed their quinine down with whiskey and worked up a grudge against Langley.

On October 17, 1903, Manly donned a life preserver and climbed into the aerodrome. The propellers whirred and the catapult whanged. But, alas, the forward lower guy post caught in the launching mechanism. Splash! The machine dove into the muddy Potomac. Manly was fished out unhurt, and the aerodrome but little damaged.

Langley determined on one last effort before his money ran out. On December 8, he tried again, despite bad weather. Again, something in the launcher fouled the aerodrome. The rudder and after wings collapsed; the machine nosed up steeply and crashed. While Langley was making sure that the dripping Manly was unhurt, a tugboat crew reduced the machine to a total wreck in raising it out of the water.

The papers gave a shriek of derision. Even the New York *Times,* trying to be kind, joined the cackling chorus:

> We hope that Professor Langley will not put his substantial greatness as a scientist in further peril by continuing to waste his time, and the money involved, in further airship experiments. Life is short, and he is capable of services to humanity incomparably greater than can be expected to result from trying to fly.[1]

Congress put a clause into next year's appropriation act for the Army, forbidding the use of governmental money on flying machines. So Langley gave up the project. Although Langley's tandem-wing design was longitudinally unstable, Langley had come close to success.

Nine days after Langley's last attempt, Orville Wright made the first successful flight, at Kitty Hawk, in the machine that he and his brother Wilbur had built. Langley was pleased when he heard of the Wrights' success. During his few remaining years his relations with them, if not close, were friendly. A little more than two years after his second bid to launch a piloted airplane, Langley died of a stroke.

Langley failed where the Wrights, with far less resources, succeeded, largely for the following reason: The Wrights first learned to fly in gliders and then put an engine into a glider they already knew how to fly. Langley, on the other hand, first built a powered flying machine in the hope that the pilot could learn to fly it after it was airborne. In other words, he had gone about his task the wrong way round; but that is the wisdom of hindsight.

As for the ridicule so unfairly heaped upon Langley, this formed part of a common nineteenth-century American attitude: a lusty pioneering scorn of the thinker, the scientist, the high-brow, the man who would rather learn something new than pursue such normal, healthy goals as wealth, power, and vigorous physical activity, like killing animals or Indians. This attitude persisted through the first half of the twentieth century and did not really begin to abate until rivalry between the United States and the Soviet Union somewhat elevated mental achievement in the eyes of the masses. But much of the older attitude lingers on even yet.

In 1895, the brothers Wilbur and Orville Wright, who ran a bicycle repair-and-retail shop in Dayton, Ohio, read in a newspaper about the glider flights of Otto Lilienthal near Berlin. Next year, they learned that Lilienthal had skidded down the steep slope of air to his death. Although this hardly seems like the sort of news to encourage anybody to take up gliding as a sport, it did just that for the Wrights.

The Wrights were the sons of a bishop of a minor Christian sect. When they were boys, their father once brought home a flying toy. This was a little model of cork and bamboo, with paper airscrews whirled by rubber bands. A French invalid named Pénaud had invented the device, which he called a *hélicoptère*. The Wright boys' interest in flight was at once aroused when the bishop set the toy to flitting batlike about the house.

Although the Wrights' two older brothers and their sister Katherine all went through college, the two younger Wrights decided not to go. Instead, they quit high school before finishing and went to work, first at printing and then in their bicycle shop. Wilbur (1867–1912) was the dominant one of the pair. He looked like an inventive genius: tall, gaunt, thin-lipped, hawk-nosed, and gimlet-eyed. Orville (1871–1948) was smaller, mus-tached, and comfortably ordinary-looking. He was a shy, retiring man, but stubborn in matters of principle.

Their lack of formal education and the fact that they took up aviation as a sport may give the false impression that they were slapdash amateurish tinkerers. Instead, their invention of the airplane is an outstanding example of intelligent and systematic application of the scientific method. If self-educated, they were, in their chosen field, exceedingly well-educated. Moreover, when it was too late, they regretted their decision not to go to college. It would, Orville conceded, have saved them much fumbling.

The Wrights began by reading Octave Chanute's *Progress in Flying Machines*. Chanute, a French-born civil engineer, had taken up gliding as a hobby at sixty. His first glider had five pairs of wings, one above the other. Where Lilienthal had controlled his gliders by swinging his body about beneath the glider, Chanute, being a little old for such acrobatics, equipped his gliders with movable control surfaces.

The Wrights also read Langley's *Experiments in Aerodynamics,* a paper by Lilienthal, and anything else they could get on the subject of flying. The deaths of Lilienthal and other glider pilots, they decided, had been due to lack of lateral control. Previous flying machines had been equipped with rudders to steer them right and left and elevators to make them go up and down. But there was no control to keep a machine from tipping over to one side or the other in flight.

Orville proposed the first solution: namely, to mount the outer sections of the wings on pivoted shafts, so that they could be rotated about the lateral axis. When one wingtip was turned up and the other down, the first would give more lift than the second.

Second thoughts, however, convinced them that this scheme would not work because it entailed too much structural weakness and mechanical complication. But, a few weeks later, Wilbur had another idea. Why not, he said, make the wings flexible and twist them by control cables? Thus, said he (twisting a cut-open cardboard box between his hands to demonstrate) the wings on one side should meet the air at an angle different from those on the other.

In 1899 they built a biplane kite, like a model glider with five-foot wingspread. They tried out their wing-warping system by means of cords manipulated from the ground and found that it worked. (Two years before, Professor Edson Gallaudet of Yale had experimented with a similar wing-warping kite, but stopped his experiments and quit his job when told that his fooling with "flying gimcracks" had led to his "making an ass of himself and a laughingstock of the faculty.")

The Wrights lay on their backs watching birds, although they found this less helpful than they had expected. As Orville explained later: "Learning the secret of flight from a bird was a good deal like learning the secret of magic from a magician. After you once know the trick and what to look for, you see things that you did not notice when you did not know exactly what to look for."[2]

Learning from the Weather Bureau that Kitty Hawk, a sparsely settled place on the coast of North Carolina, had strong steady winds, they went there with a larger glider. In September 1900, when the bicycle business slacked off for the winter, they flew this glider, also, as a kite. Although the wing-warping worked fine, the lift was not what they had expected.

In 1901 they came back with a bigger structure, which they flew both as a kite and as a glider. They attacked their problem cautiously, keeping the glider close to the ground while they learned the tricky art of managing it. Chanute, with whom they had corresponded, visited their camp and marveled at their progress. He bucked them up when Wilbur, in a discouraged moment, declared that not in a thousand years would men ever fly. He also paid the railroad fare of a young man with medical training to come and board with them in case they needed some broken bones set.

Back in Dayton, they built their own wind tunnel and calculated their own tables of lift and drag, as they found all those of their predecessors, even Langley's, too inaccurate to be useful.

In the autumn of 1902 they returned to Kitty Hawk with a new glider. Whereas Chanute and Langley had used cross-shaped control surfaces, combining rudder and elevator, the Wrights used separate control surfaces in front and a fixed vertical tail fin behind.

With this machine they made more than a thousand flights. However, they now met a new hazard. Every so often, the machine would tilt to one side and come down with a corkscrew motion, whirling round and round on one wingtip, despite all the pilot could do.

After much thought, Orville hit upon the reason for this perilous action, later known as the tail spin. If the craft tilted sidewise and if the pilot did not quickly correct the tilt, the machine would slide sidewise in the air. The sidewise component of the air stream, striking the tail fin, tended to turn the craft in the direction that it was sliding. The remedy, said Orville, was to make the tail fin movable.

Their next step was to obtain an engine. Like Langley, they found nobody who could or would make one light enough, so they had to design their own. They brought the weight down to seven pounds per horsepower. They mounted this engine in an improved version of their 1902 glider, with a movable rudder.

In the fall of 1903 they were back again at Kitty Hawk. Mishaps and bad weather lengthened their preparations, so that not until December 14 were they ready to fly. Wilbur won the toss as to who should pilot the craft. The airplane, which had skids like sled runners instead of wheels, was launched from a little car that ran along a track. Because of the lack of wind, it was decided to launch it down the side of Kill Devil Hill, where the slope would give extra take-off speed.

However, the start proved abortive. The airplane climbed too steeply, stalled, and came down hard, breaking several parts.

On December 17 they were ready to try again. They had invited the local people to come and look. But on that cold, windy morning only five showed up: three men from a nearby lifesaving station, one other man, and a boy.

It was Orville's turn to pilot. He set up his camera pointing at the place where he thought he would take off and asked one of the witnesses to press the button. Then he boarded the *Flier* and lay prone.

The engine whirled a pair of propellers behind the wings by a drive of bicycle chains. With Wilbur running alongside to steady it by holding the wingtip, the *Flier* rolled down the track into the wind for forty feet, lifted, rose ten feet above the ground, wobbled into the teeth of the gale at a ground speed of ten miles an hour (an airspeed of 30 mph) and flew for 120 feet. Then it settled down upon the sand.

They made three flights that day, each longer than the last. Then a gust upset the airplane on the ground and damaged it too much for further flights that season.

Orville wired his father the news of their success. Another brother, Lorin Wright, gave out careful, accurate statements to the newspapers.

However, the telegraph operator at Norfolk, disregarding a request from the Wrights, tipped off Moore, a local reporter for the Norfolk *Virginia-Pilot*. Moore, failing to obtain any accurate information on the flight, made up a story full of fantastic statements that the airplane had flown three miles and that it had a propeller behind to push it and another beneath to raise it.

Since Langley's failure, most newspapers had become allergic to flying-machine stories. Only three papers bore accounts. These were short and wildly inaccurate, as they were based upon Moore's nonsense as published in the *Virginia-Pilot* and sent out by the Associated Press.

During the next few years, occasional small stories about the Wrights appeared here and there in the press. The stories were often accompanied by editorials stating that the whole thing must be a hoax. In its issue of October 1905, the *Scientific American* averred that all this talk about the Wrights' flights must be false because, if any such thing had happened, energetic American journalists would surely have told the world about it.

In the spring of 1904, the Wrights began flying another airplane from a field near Dayton. A couple of times they invited reporters. But, with the perversity of inanimate objects, the engine refused to work. So the journalists went away more convinced than ever that flight was impossible.

When nobody was around, the machine flew beautifully. By the end of 1905, the Wrights were making flights of half an hour. The field was bordered by two busy roads and a streetcar line, but the flights lengthened so gradually that the local people became used to them without knowing it. One day a visitor from out of town rode out on the car line with a local farmer when the airplane buzzed overhead.

"What's that?" yelled the astounded visitor.

"Just one of them crazy boys," explained the native. "Dern fools tryin' to make a machine that can fly. Both crazy and always was. You can't go agin nature."[3]

The Wrights had not tried to keep their accomplishment secret. Neither, after their previous experiences, did they court much publicity. They went ahead with their flying and let the world make what it would of it. Being frugal bachelors, they paid their own way out of the profits of their bicycle shop. As they did most of their mechanical work themselves, the cash outlay for their first airplane was less than $1000.

During 1906–07 they built several airplanes and took out their basic patent, No. 821,393 to O. & W. Wright, of May 22, 1906. This patent dealt essentially with the wing-warping system of lateral control. The third claim reads:

3. In a flying-machine, a normally flat aeroplane having lateral marginal portions capable of movement to different positions above or below the normal plane of the body of the aeroplane, such movement being about an axis transverse to the line of flight, whereby said lateral marginal portions may be moved to different angles relatively to the normal plane of the aeroplane, and also to different angles relatively to each other, so as to present to the atmosphere different angles of incidence, and means for simultaneously imparting such movement to said lateral marginal portions, substantially as described.

This claim will make better sense if you remember that by "aeroplane" the inventors meant what we today call a "wing." Note that the patent mentions "lateral marginal portions capable of movement to different positions . . ." but says nothing about whether this movement shall be effected by bending a wing or turning a hinged aileron. Orville Wright's original form of lateral control had, in fact, been much like the hinged aileron. The wording of the claim is in accordance with the principle of patent-claim writing, that the more a claim says the less it dominates.

The Wrights also wrote their Congressman, asking whether the government would be interested. Representative Robert M. Nevin of Ohio passed the inquiry on to the Army's Board of Ordnance and Fortification. The board wrote the Wrights that it could not "make allotment for the experimental development of devices for mechanical flight" since the Wrights' machine "has not yet been brought to the stage of practical operation." Further letters from the Wrights brought the reply that the Board would do nothing "until a machine is produced which by actual operation is shown to be able to produce horizontal flight and to carry an operator."[4]

These were usual letters of the kind that governmental departments use to brush off perpetual-motion cranks. Under the circumstances, they were asinine.

In 1908, Wilbur Wright took an airplane to France for exhibition flights. While he was abroad, President Theodore Roosevelt told William Howard Taft, his Secretary of War, to look into reports of the Wrights' success. Orville Wright, still is the States, flew several Army officers, who became enthusiastic. Orville offered the government an airplane for $25,000.

Then came tragedy. Orville Wright was flying Lieutenant Thomas E. Selfridge when a propeller blade split and fouled a guy wire. The airplane crashed, killing Selfridge and dealing Orville Wright injuries that took months to heal. Also, it transpired that the Federal government had no money to pay for such a purchase, and that Congress would balk at the suggestion.

Selfridge was one of the group of four young aviation enthusiasts whom Alexander Graham Bell had gathered in Nova Scotia. The others were civilians: Glenn H. Curtiss, a motorcycle maker of Hammondsport, New York, and two Canadians, J. A. D. McCurdy and Frederick W. Baldwin. Bell had organized them as the Aerial Experiment Association and paid the three civilans' salaries to develop airplanes.

Baldwin did most of the designing. By the summer of 1908, they were building machines that flew a few hundred feet before coming down, usually to crack up.

Their third machine, however, was a workable airplane. They painted its cloth-covered wings, which improved its performance by keeping the air from leaking through the fabric. The airplane also embodied Baldwin's invention of hinged ailerons, instead of the Wrights' wing-warping system. After Selfridge's death the group broke up, and Curtiss built airplanes in his motorcycle factory.

Meanwhile Wilbur Wright, in France, was being acclaimed for his flights in a way that was quite new to him. When he had made a series of flights from Hunaudières and Auvours, Orville Wright, still convalescing, and their sister Katherine joined him. They flew at Pau, near the Spanish border, to the edification of kings and prime ministers. They flew in Italy.

In June 1909, they arrived back in Dayton, Ohio, wondering why all the whistles were blowing and bells were ringing. Dayton had at last discovered its eminent sons.

The previous year, two of the army officers who had flown with the Wrights had gone to the White House. Theodore Roosevelt listened, then rasped:

"Twenty-five thousand dollars, is it? That's a lot of money." Then he jumped up. "Gentlemen! I do believe I've got it!" He rushed to a filing cabinet, pulled out a folder, grinned, and shouted: "Yes, it's still here! An even twenty-five thousand dollars!"[5]

This piggy bank was an emergency appropriation, which Congress had passed during the Spanish-American War, and which the President might spend at any time without giving Congress an accounting. Orville Wright finished his qualification tests in July 1909, delivered its first airplane to the Army, and left for Germany to make exhibition flights.

Capitalists now came forward with money to set up the Wright Company. The Wrights began building airplanes and suing a host of infringers of their patent. One of these was Glenn Curtiss. Another was Louis Blériot, builder of the first airplane of more or less modern type, with the engine and propeller in front and the rudder and elevators on the end of a long tail in the rear.

In 1912, in the midst of this litigation, Wilbur Wright died of a typhoid infection. Orville pressed the suits.

Curtiss' airplane had separate ailerons on Baldwin's plan, mounted between the upper and lower wings. He thought that this arrangement would circumvent the Wrights' patent, which showed their wing-warping system only. However, the court (Wright Co. v. Herring-Curtiss Co. *et al.*) held the Wright patent broad enough to dominate any method of presenting the movable parts of the right and left wing structures at different angles.[6]

Now, strictly speaking, Curtiss' ailerons were not "marginal portions" of the main planes (although ailerons of the modern type are). But the court felt that anybody who had solved a problem, at which so many others had failed, deserved the reward of a broad interpretation of his patent. So it applied the "doctrine of equivalents," according to which a patent dominates not only the invention claimed but all fair equivalents.

One cannot help thinking that if the same doctrine had been applied in the case of Selden's automobile patent, Selden, too, would have won his case. The court sympathized with the Wrights, who had gone ahead and built a number of flyable airplanes. But it took a more critical view of Selden, whose achievements, for whatever reason, had been mostly on paper.

In any case, Curtiss had to pay royalties. He continued to look for loopholes in the Wright patent, devising an airplane in which only one aileron moved at a time. He also borrowed the Langley aerodrome from the Smithsonian, where its battered remains had been repaired and reassembled. Curtiss took the machine to Hammondsport and rebuilt it. He changed the bracing, moved the wings, made many smaller changes, and fitted the craft with a pair of seaplane pontoons. (Curtiss was the inventor of the seaplane.)

With these improvements, in 1914, the aerodrome made several flights of a few seconds' duration from the waters of Lake Keuka. Thus Curtiss hoped to weaken the Wrights' patent position by showing that, with a little luck, the aerodrome could have flown and that the Wrights were therefore not the aerial pioneers that they claimed to be.

Orville Wright bought out his original backers and sold his company to another group for a comfortable fortune. He spent the rest of his life in Dayton, experimenting with aeronautical improvements like the automatic stabilizer and the split wing-flap air brake. A merger between his company and that of Curtiss, to form the Curtiss-Wright Company, ended further threatened lawsuits.

Orville Wright also carried on a long feud with the Smithsonian Institution, where Langley was succeeded as secretary by Charles D. Walcott, a paleontologist. Walcott, in an excess of partisan loyalty to his former chief, set himself to prove that Langley and not the Wrights deserved the credit for having made the first flyable flying machine.

First, he sent the Langley aerodrome to Curtiss' factory at Hammondsport, where Curtiss rebuilt and flew it. Then Walcott exhibited this flying machine in the National Museum with the label:

THE FIRST MAN-CARRYING AEROPLANE IN THE HISTORY OF
THE WORLD CAPABLE OF SUSTAINED FREE FLIGHT

This label outraged Orville Wright, as it gave the impression that the aerodrome could have flown before Curtiss' reconstruction and before the Wrights' own flight. Whether it could so have flown, without the launching-gear accidents, has never been settled.

Walcott would have been glad to get the original Wright airplane for the museum, but only if he could credit Langley with clear priority. After a lengthy dispute with Walcott, Orville Wright in 1928 sent the *Flier* of 1903 to England for loan to the Science Museum at South Kensington.

Walcott died in 1927. His successor was Charles Greely Abbott, a meteorologist who spent much of his life investigating Langley's hypothesis that earthly weather is controlled by variations in the sun's radiation. Abbott, urging Wright to give the 1903 airplane to the National Museum, changed the label on the aerodrome to the innocuous reading:

LANGLEY AERODROME. THE ORIGINAL SAMUEL P. LANGLEY
FLYING MACHINE OF 1903, RESTORED

Wright, however, insisted upon keeping his airplane in England until the Smithsonian acknowledged itself in the wrong. After an investigation, Abbot issued a formal apology to Wright in 1942 for "acts and assertions of former Smithsonian officials that may have been misleading or are held to be detrimental to the Wrights."[7]

Wright then agreed to bring his airplane back. This could not then be done because of the Second World War, which the *Flier* spent in a bombproof British cave. In 1948, just after Orville Wright's death, it arrived back in its native land and is now on view at the National Museum.

In judging the Wrights' great achievement, we must bear two things in mind. One factor in their success was the intelligent way in which they attacked their problem, first mastering all that was known of aeronautics in their time and then going on from there, step by logical step.

The other factor in their success was the fact that the age was ready for them. The technology existed that made their invention workable. Such essential elements as steel tubing, wire cable, gasoline, and practical designs for internal-combustion engines were available. A century earlier, when these things did not exist, they would not have been able to reduce their ideas to practice.

But, in admitting that the age must be ready for the inventor, let us not fall into the opposite fallacy. This is that, once the age is ready, the invention will somehow be produced by anonymous "social forces," and that the individual inventor therefore does not count for much. True, there have been many inventors who, like Fitch and Bushnell, failed because they were too far ahead of their time.

But there have also been ages that did not produce inventions technically within their reach, simply because no individuals came forward with these ideas. The Hellenistic age *could* have produced the windmill, the horse collar, the printing press, the wheeled clock, and the optical lens with its offspring the eyeglass, the microscope, and the telescope. But it did not. If it had, who knows to what stage the world might have progressed today?

FESSENDEN, DE FOREST,

AND RADIO

In 1899, a freighter ran down the East Goodwin lightship, whose duty it was to warn ships away from the treacherous Goodwin Sands off the southeast corner of England. The sinking ship sent out a call for help to the South Foreland Lighthouse by a new invention, wireless telegraphy; and lifeboats arrived in time to pick up the lightship's crew. The fame of this rescue led to a rush of orders for the magical new device, invented by a well-heeled young Italian named Guglielmo Marconi (1874–1937).

Thus began the last stage of the electrical revolution. Already, at the end of the nineteenth century, millions of men were reading by electric light, traveling by electric car and train, speaking by telephone, sending messages around the world by telegraph wire and cable, and being whisked to the tops of the first skyscrapers by elevators, lately electrified by the versatile Frank J. Sprague. There remained for the twentieth century only the electrical conquest of empty space.

The first suggestions of wireless communication appeared in the discovery of induction by Faraday and Henry in the 1830s. By mid-century it was plain that electric currents, sparks, and leakages from conductors affected other conductors at a distance.

During the last half of the century, the laws that governed these effects were worked out, mostly by Maxwell in Britain and by Helmholtz and Hertz in Germany. Heinrich Hertz not only discovered how to generate radio waves and pick them up again by simple detecting apparatus, but also learned to measure these waves. He found that radio waves, while they belonged to the same general class of electromagnetic vibrations in space as light waves, have properties quite different from those of light. The longer waves—a foot or a yard in length, for instance—penetrate many materials opaque to light.

Other scientists such as Sir William H. Preece, engineer-in-chief of the British Post Office, investigated along similar lines. Elihu Thomson in the 1870s experimented with a spark coil and a detector, feeling his way towards wireless messages, until he got side-tracked into generators and arc welding.

Edison, in 1885, patented a "grasshopper telegraph." It consisted of a plate covered by tinfoil on top of a railroad car, with a telegraphic apparatus connected to it. This gadget would pick up messages sent to the moving train along a neighboring telegraph wire. Unfortunately, it also picked up the messages in all the other wires at the same time, making a meaningless jumble.

In 1892 Sir William Crookes, inventor of the cathode-ray tube, wrote of the possibilities of wireless communication. He told what had yet to be done to make this possible. Marconi, a small slight youth with a large head and ears, set out to take these last steps.

Marconi combined several known elements. One was a detector called a "coherer," just invented by Edouard Branly in France, according to a design proposed by Oliver Lodge in Britain. This was a tube full of metal filings, which stuck together when a tiny induced current flowed through them. After the current had ceased, an automatic hammer tapped the tube to shake the filings loose.

Another element was a structure with one end grounded and the other reaching high into the air, invented by Popov in Russia as part of his apparatus for detecting lightning at a distance. The structure was named an "antenna" after the hornlike sensory organs of insects. Marconi improved the coherer, connected it with the antenna or aerial, and put a telegraph key into the circuit.

Helped in his experiments by his friend Preece, Marconi got the backing of some British capitalists to start Marconi's Wireless Telegraph Company, Ltd., with Marconi as chief engineer. The Italian Navy also took up the new invention.

Year by year, Marconi's sending radius rose. In 1897 he communicated between two Italian warships twelve miles apart. By 1899 he was communicating between two American battleships at a distance of thirty-six miles. On December 12, 1901, Marconi staged the first transatlantic wireless communication. In St. John's, Newfoundland, he heard the three dots, meaning the Morse letter *s*, from his sending station at Poldhu, England.

From then on, Marconi's story is more one of finance and litigation than of invention. He was able, retiring, unassuming, likable, and lucky. His rich father cheerfully paid for his early experiments and, by the time he was ready for his major work, the world was ready for his device. His earnings from his invention were respectable but far from fabulous.

With the example of the telephone before them, inventors could hardly wait to devise means of sending, not merely dots and dashes, but spoken words through empty space.

Like most great technical arts, radio broadcasting was not invented by any one man, even though several inventors—especially Edison, Fleming, Fessenden, de Forest, and Armstrong—have either claimed the honor or had it claimed for them by their admirers. Radio has no single "father." But if, by "the father of radio broadcasting," we mean the man who first broadcast voices and music, which hearers understood, this distinction must go to Reginald Aubrey Fessenden (1866–1932).

One day in the 1880s, Fessenden called at Edison's electric lamp factory at Harrison, New Jersey, to ask for a job. Fessenden was a big, burly, bearded, ruddy young Canadian, the son of an Anglican clergyman. After a few years of schoolmastering in Canada and Bermuda, he wanted to exploit the mathematical ability that he knew he had.

Fessenden sent in his card with an application form. Back came a note in Edison's dainty handwriting: *"Am very busy. What do you know about electricity?"*

Fessenden knew quite a lot of the little that was then known. Nevertheless, he modestly wrote: *"Do not know anything about electricity, but can learn pretty quick."*

Edison: *"Have enough men who do not know anything about electricity."*

Later, when Fessenden did get the job and showed the slips to Edison, the latter grinned and said: "Things must have been going pretty badly that day."[1]

Fessenden worked as a tester and inspector for Edison, repairing defective electric mains. He was compelled to do this without permits to avoid the graft and delays involved in getting street-opening permits from Tammany Hall. Fessenden used to dig up a street, replace a section of main, and get the street back into perfect condition before the next police patrol arrived.

While Fessenden was so engaged one day, J. Pierpont Morgan, whose house had been one of the first electrified, rushed out roaring to ask why his house current had been shut off. Fessenden explained. Morgan invited Fessenden into his house and asked him how to keep it from catching fire all the time from defects in the electric wiring. Fessenden suggested encasing the wire in galvanized-iron pipe, and this became standard practice.

Fessenden rose to the post of chief inspector for Edison, held a job with Westinghouse, then worked for an electrical manufacturing company in Massachusetts. He held professorships at Purdue and Pittsburgh Universities and did much of the engineering on Westinghouse's stopper lamps, designed to circumvent the Edison patent. He took out a number of patents of his own, including some on the use of microphotography for keeping records. For a time he worked for the United States Weather Bureau on a system of wireless communication for the Bureau's weather forecasts.

While working for the Weather Bureau in laboratories on Cobb Island and Roanoke Island, along the mid-Atlantic coast, Fessenden invented an improved detector of wireless waves. This device, the "liquid barretter," soon ousted Marconi's coherer.

After a quarrel with the chief of the Weather Bureau in 1902, Fessenden resigned his governmental post. Fessenden was not an easygoing person but a super-individualist: headstrong, impatient, quick to take offense, lavish with his associates' money, and a non-stop talker who paid no heed to whether his hearer understood him. Much of his career was spent in quarrels, controversies, and litigation.

On the other hand, Fessenden was one of the most productive inventors in American history, taking out more than five hundred patents. One of his early patents was for a parking garage, with ramps and hoists like those in modern parking garages of the most advanced design. But this patent expired long before automobiles became common enough for Fessenden to profit from his idea.

During his stint at the Weather Bureau, Fessenden was seized by the idea of transmitting human voices and music directly, without wires.

Now, the human ear detects sound waves with frequencies of, roughly, fifteen to 20,000 cycles per second. Wireless apparatus, on the other hand, is sensitive to electromagnetic vibrations or Hertzian waves with frequencies from 15,000 to 100,000,000,000 cycles per second. Hence we cannot do in radiotelephony what we do in the ordinary telephone: simply change each sound wave into a pulse of electric current and then change it back at the other end.

Well, thought Fessenden, why not send out an electromagnetic wave of constant frequency, but vary or modulate the amplitude or size of the individual waves in time with the much slower sound vibrations that we wish to convey? This diagram will show you what I mean:

Sound wave:

Radio wave:

Radio wave, modulated
  by sound wave:

Then, at the other end, install a detector that responds, not to the individual radio waves, but to the groups of them that correspond to individual sound waves.

Fessenden tried using a spark gap as the source for his high-frequency Hertzian waves. But these waves proved full of vibrations in the same range of frequencies as audible sound. Hence, although Fessenden thought he could hear faint vocal sounds in his receiver, the speech was drowned out by the roar of static.

His next step, therefore, was to find a source of electrical oscillations of so high a frequency that they should engender no audible noise.

After Fessenden quit governmental service, he persuaded two rich Pittsburghers, the banker Thomas H. Given and the soap maker Hay Walker, to back him in the development of radiotelephony. They formed the National Electric Signalling Company, and Fessenden set up three experimental stations on Chesapeake Bay.

Then Fessenden found himself in conflict with another fertile and aggressive inventor, Lee de Forest. While Fessenden was running tests for the United States Navy between the U.S.S. *Topeka* and Sandy Hook, the De Forest Wireless Company installed a wireless shack a few feet from the naval station and (according to Fessenden) told its operator to foul up the tests. This he did by opening a powerful wireless transmitter and putting a brick on the key to keep it sending static, until Fessenden's crew bribed him with food and liquor to take off the brick.

Then Walker and Given urged Fessenden, as a publicity stunt, to stage the first two-way transatlantic wireless broadcast. Fessenden accordingly raised two huge towers, one on the coast of Massachusetts and one on the west coast of Scotland. Two-way communication was achieved on January 11, 1906. It continued for nearly a year, until the Scottish tower blew down.

Meanwhile, Fessenden wrestled with the problem of generating a "carrier wave"—a high-frequency Hertzian wave whose variations should carry the shape of the sound waves of speech and music. In 1903 he appealed to General Electric, which gave the job to Charles P. Steinmetz, the hunchbacked German genius who discovered the laws of magnetic hysteresis (or lag) and other mathematical laws of electromagnetism. Steinmetz designed an alternator (that is, an alternating-current generator) which put out current at 10,000 cycles per second. But it was not good enough.

Fessenden's next order was assigned to Ernst F. W. Alexanderson, a brilliant young Swedish engineer who had come to America to work near Steinmetz. After some failures and arguments about the design (in which Fessenden was wrong but insisted upon learning the hard way) the company made a 50,000-cycle alternator. Fessenden set up his new generator at the station at Brant Rock, Massachusetts, and warned nearby ships with Fessenden wireless apparatus to stand by.

On Christmas Eve, 1906, Fessenden staged the first radiotelephonic broadcast. The owners of Fessenden receiving sets, which had been clicking and buzzing Morse as usual, were astonished to hear voices and music coming from their apparatus. Fessenden played Handel's *Largo* on the phonograph and Gounod's *O Holy Night* on his violin. There were singing, speeches, and the reading of a poem.

During the next year, Fessenden carried on his experimental broadcasts, raising his range to five hundred miles. He also invented the heterodyne receiving system, which uses the difference between two high-frequency oscillations, only a little apart in frequency, to make a low-frequency "beat note."

Then this promising enterprise was wrecked by a long and bitter quarrel between Fessenden and his backers. The dispute was over such things as the control of a proposed Canadian subsidiary and the size of Fessenden's stock holdings in the company. At one stage, the conflict took the form of a physical tussle between Fessenden's wife (a Bermudian girl whom he had married in 1890) and two detectives whom Given and Walker sent to Brant Rock to remove the company's files.

Fessenden quit the company, sued, and won a judgment for $406,175. Although this judgment was fought through the higher courts, it sent the company into bankruptcy.

Fessenden then withdrew from radio and went into submarine signaling. He invented the fathometer or sonic depth finder and other acoustic devices. During World War I he worked on submarine detectors.

Fessenden pursued his feud with the National Electric Signalling Company long after the original backers, who had put over a million dollars into the project without any return, had disappeared from the scene. The company's assets passed through several hands and came into possession of the Radio Corporation of America. Owen D. Young, the chairman of the board of RCA, agreed in 1928 to pay off Fessenden's claims at a price that even that contentious genius considered fair. Hence Fessenden's last years, when he was made inactive by high blood pressure and a weak heart, were passed in comfort.

Fessenden harbored strange ideas. For instance, he was against the conservation of natural resources. He opposed the National Research Council, which he viewed as a kind of collective octopus destroying the individualism of inventors.

He developed a peculiarly dizzy variety of the lost-Atlantis theory of the origin of civilization. He published a book arguing that Atlantis had been in the Caucasus Mountains. Although the book abounds in preposterous ideas of geology, mythology, anthropology, and linguistics, it was plausible enough for H. G. Wells to give it a favorable mention in his celebrated *Outline of History*.

Fessenden passed his last years on his estate in Bermuda. There he became close friends with another aging and difficult genius, Albert A. Michelson, who had achieved fame by measuring the speed of light. After a series of heart attacks, Fessenden died in the summer of 1932.

Today, Fessenden's name is hardly known except to specialists in the history of technology. Bad luck, and his own peppery personality, combined to rob him of much of the recognition due him.

Nevertheless, he should be remembered first as one of the greatest inventors that North America has produced, and secondly as the first man to stage a real radio broadcast. If a field like radio, to which so many men of many nations have contributed their genius, can rightly be said to have a "father," Fessenden has as good a claim to the title as anybody.

All the "fathers" of radio were brilliant; many were also intense, aggressive, self-assertive, contentious men of great force and drive. They had to be to accomplish what they did. With these qualities, however, competition among them was bound to be keen and ruthless. Hence the youth of the radio industry was enlivened by the uproar of feuds and the din of litigation.

Among the inventors of radio, the brightest single name is that of Lee de Forest. Born in Iowa in 1873, de Forest was taken south to live when his father, a Congregationalist minister, accepted the presidency of a Negro college in Alabama.

Here the family was long ostracized by the local whites, who viewed any effort to educate the lately freed Negroes as a plot to destroy the "Southern way of life." When de Forest's father, who had taken the job from a strict sense of Christian duty, said good-day to a local Southern colonel, the latter crossed to the other side of the road, snarling:

"I don't wish to be spoken to, suh, by a damned Yankee!"[2]

Since the elder De Forest[3] who had studied under Newcomb at Yale, was an enthusiastic astronomer, Lee de Forest early acquired a scientific bent. His father, although disappointed that his son did not wish to follow him into the ministry, agreed to de Forest's entering the Sheffield Scientific School at Yale.

At Yale, de Forest overworked, half starved himself, worked summers to earn his tuition and, like many young scientific students, soon lost the religious beliefs on which he had been brought up. He grew to be a man of over average size, with blunt features and odd-looking deep-set eyes. His class voted him "the Nerviest in the class, and also the Homeliest!"[4]

After graduation, de Forest wisely determined to continue his studies. As a graduate student he worked under J. Willard Gibbs, perhaps the greatest single intellect in American science. Gibbs virtually created the science of physical chemistry and hugely advanced that of thermodynamics by his great treatise, *On the Equilibrium of Heterogeneous Substances* (1876-78) and by three others with equally formidable titles.

These works, consisting mainly of hundreds of equations, are as forbidding as their names. But modern methods of industrial chemistry and metallurgy depend largely upon them. Gibbs' work was so abstract and recondite that it would take a whole chapter to try to explain his most signal discovery, the "phase rule." When James Clerk Maxwell,[5] the lively little Scot who stood foremost among the brilliant physicists of the century, died at forty-seven, a member of the Connecticut Academy remarked:

"Only one man ever lived who could understand Gibbs' papers. That was Maxwell, and now he is dead."[6]

Personally, Gibbs was a slight man with a long horse-face and a high querulous voice. He lived quietly in New Haven nearly all his life, never married, and did practically nothing but think.

De Forest conceived a great admiration for Gibbs, describing him in his diary as "a great man with whom I want to be, as much for his ways and thought as for lessons . . ."[7]

Many years later, de Forest wrote: "His mind seemed infinitely discerning, intimately dealing with imaginaries. Often he would remark in that quiet peculiar voice, almost lost in his beard of sandy gray, 'We shall pretend we know nothing about this solution from nature.' . . . With long acquaintance I found him a kindly, human soul. When I required an additional course for my Doctorate he volunteered to give me his special course in Orbits. There, very solemnly for one hour each week, we sat facing each other while he discoursed on the paths of comet and asteroid. In that course . . . I was his only pupil"[8]

The Spanish-American War interrupted de Forest's graduate career. He enlisted in the Army, spent four months drilling, but never got out of the country. In 1899 he obtained his Ph.D. and took a job with the Western Electric Company in Chicago. He was supposed to be working as a telephone engineer but spent all his spare time on a wireless detector, which he called a "responder."

After holding several small technical jobs, de Forest taught at night so that he could devote his days to his detector. He made wireless tests, using the auditorium of the Columbian World's Fair at Chicago and a yacht belonging to a friend as sending and receiving stations.

In 1902, a Wall Street gambler named Abraham White helped de Forest to organize the American De Forest Wireless Telegraph Company. De Forest built experimental stations, sold wireless equipment to the United States Navy and other customers, and reported Army maneuvers by wireless for the Signal Corps. When his company began to prosper, the American Marconi Company engaged it in long and costly litigation to compel it to stop. In the end, the judge held the threatening claims of the Marconi patent either invalid because they were anticipated by Lodge, Popov, and Branly, or not infringed.

Fessenden also sued him for infringement of his detector patent. After three years, Fessenden won his case, but by that time de Forest was using another detector, the audion or triode tube. As this was de Forest's most important invention, let us try to understand it.

When Edison was trying to make a workable incandescent light, he found that a hot filament in a vacuum gives off electricity. When another electrode was put into the bulb, the electricity would jump from the hot filament to the electrode —when, and only when, the electrode had a positive charge. (The fact that electricity is a cloud or current of loose electrons, having a "negative" charge, had not yet been discovered.)

The next step was taken by an Englishman, John Ambrose Fleming. In the early 1900s, Fleming, one of the great Victorian physicists, acted as adviser to the British Edison companies.

Fleming took Edison's light bulb with an extra electrode and turned it into a rectifier. A rectifier is a kind of electrical check-valve or turnstile that lets current flow one way but not the other. The result may be illustrated thus:

Alternating current:

Rectified alternating current:

Now, if you send a high-frequency alternating current into an ordinary telephone circuit, nothing happens. The diaphragm of the earphone is pushed and pulled in such quick succession that it has no time to respond to any one impulse. Moreover, each impulse is canceled by a following one in the opposite direction.

However, if you rectify the same current, then all the pushes are in one direction. And if the electric impulses vary in force, coming in clusters, then a cluster of pushes (between two periods of no push) acts as a single push. If the time between one such cluster and the next is in the same region as the frequency of an audible sound, the diaphragm will move and send out a sound wave. See:

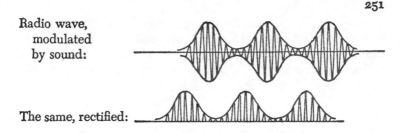

Radio wave, modulated by sound:

The same, rectified:

In 1905, Fleming described his device in a lecture to the Royal Society. De Forest read the lecture and at once began improving the device. His major change was to insert a little grid of iron wires between the hot filament in the Fleming valve and the electrode.[9]

Then, instead of trying to use the feeble currents picked up by the receiving antenna and rectified by the Fleming valve to shake the diaphragm of the earphone, de Forest connected the rectified current to the grid and impressed on the filament plate a much more powerful voltage.

When the grid had a negative charge, it stopped the flow of electrons from the filament to the electrode. When it had a positive charge it let the flow through. Thus it acted as a supersensitive valve.

In this way, a very small current could regulate a large one, and the variations in the latter would correspond to those in the former. If an engineer wanted still greater amplification, he could send his second current into the grid of another tube, to regulate the flow of a still larger current, and so on.

It was long before de Forest profited from his audion, however. The device had to be improved by laborious tests. De Forest, like his rival Fessenden, staged spectacular demonstrations with his experimental equipment, including one in which a broadcast from the Eiffel Tower was picked up five hundred miles away, and another in which Enrico Caruso sang.

At the same time, in 1907, de Forest became embroiled in difficulties with his promoters. When de Forest learned what highbinding was going on, he quit. He received his patents and a thousand dollars in cash and set up the De Forest Radio Telephone Company.

However, the infant wireless and radio industries seem to have had an irresistible attraction for swindlers and grafters. In

1911, the officers of the United Wireless Company were convicted of fraudulent stock sales; the next year there was a scandal in Britain over the profits made by some British officials out of Marconi stock. De Forest, no judge of men, attracted an inordinate share of such parasites.

In the case of the De Forest Radio Telephone Company, the president of the company went to jail. Although de Forest and others reorganized and kept their organization out of bankruptcy for several years, in 1912 he and several others were arrested for mail fraud.

While de Forest was out on bail, he offered the rights to his audion to the American Telephone & Telegraph Company, which said they would let him know but never did. Instead, they sent an agent named Meyers to approach de Forest.

Meyers said that he represented an anonymous group interested in the wire rights to the audion. He offered $50,000, assuring de Forest "on his word of honor as a gentleman" that he did *not* represent the telephone company. Being hard up, de Forest took the offer, although he would have charged A.T.&T.—and A.T.&T. would have paid—ten times as much.

The trial for mail fraud came up in 1913. The indictment charged the defendants with exploiting "a strange device like an electric lamp, which he called an Audion, and which device had proven to be worthless." In the end, the defaulting president and two of the directors were sent to jail. The jury acquitted de Forest.

De Forest recovered somewhat when the American Telephone & Telegraph Company came around to ask for the remaining rights to the audion. De Forest sold these rights in two packages. Knowing this time whom he was dealing with, he charged what the traffic would bear, a total of $340,000. This was a modest enough price, considering that the entire radio industry was built on this one invention, and that it also entered into all electrical amplification, including public-address systems, sound motion pictures, and electric phonographs. In fact, the audion was the only electrical amplifier in general use down to the invention of the transistor by Brattain, Bardeen, and Shockley in 1948.

In 1912, de Forest discovered that by overloading his audion he could make it act as an oscillator—that is, a generator of fluctuating current of any desired frequency. Also, by guiding some of the energy of the variations in the filament-plate circuit back to the antenna-grid circuit to reinforce the valve effect of the latter, the effectiveness of the audion could be increased many times over. This is known as the regenerative or feedback principle.

De Forest's patent application on the feedback circuit was thrown into interference with three other applications. These were by Irving Langmuir of the General Electric Company, by a German named Meissner, and by a young engineer just out of Columbia, Edwin Howard Armstrong (1890–1954). All had made the same discovery at about the same time, and Armstrong's patent was issued in 1914, before the interference began.

The resulting litigation dragged on for twenty years, using de Forest's time and energy long after he had sold all his rights to the patents involved and abandoned radio work. In 1919, de Forest left the radio field and entered that of sound motion pictures, in which he had already done pioneer work. He was one of the inventors of the photographic sound track and exhibited sound film in 1923 on Broadway. But the movie magnates turned him down, saying the public didn't want talking pictures. When sound motion pictures took hold at last in the late 1920s, others than de Forest profited.

Having been twice divorced, he married Marie Mosquini, Will Rogers' former leading lady. He entered the television field but was crushed by the Great Depression of 1932–33. He invented a diathermy apparatus and a system of cathode-ray scanning later used in radar. After World War II, a contract with the Bell Telephone Laboratory enabled him to run a well-equipped inventor's laboratory in California, and this he has continued to do down to the present day.

Edwin H. Armstrong was a pupil of Pupin at Columbia: a tall, bald, athletic man with a Newyorkese accent and a nervous tic. Armstrong's idea of fun was to perform gymnastic feats on top of a 400-foot radio tower.

In the four-party interference concerning the feedback circuit, the applications of Langmuir and Meissner were soon eliminated as too late. But the struggle between de Forest and Armstrong went on for years. They had met in 1913 at a session of the Institute of Radio Engineers and disliked each other on sight. During their long patent war they denounced each other in public and private.

When in 1920 de Forest read a paper on the audion at the Franklin Institute in Philadelphia, Armstrong stood up and interrupted to press his claim as the first inventor of the feedback circuit. "All de Forest invented was the audion! We'll concede that," cried Armstrong, until the chairman made him sit down.[10]

The interference was interrupted by World War I, in which Armstrong served as a major in the U. S. Army Signal Corps, doing radio research. At this time he invented the superheterodyne circuit as a means of detecting high-frequency German radio signals. On his return to the United States, Armstrong in 1920 sold the rights to his feedback and superheterodyne patents to the Westinghouse Electric Company.

The interference, still pending, was won by Armstrong but appealed by de Forest. Then Armstrong (with the backing of the Westinghouse Company) sued de Forest for infringement and won in the lower courts. De Forest appealed again.

The litigation, too complex to be followed in detail, became an outstanding battle in the history of the patent system. All through the 1920s it continued. When de Forest put out feelers for a compromise, Armstrong, as stubborn in controversy as Cyrus McCormick, rejected the suggestion; although, as both men had long since sold the patents in suit, the outcome was largely academic to them. But Armstrong was willing to fight all the rest of his life for what he considered his vindication.

The points at issue were extremely technical. Roughly speaking, de Forest had invented, in 1912, a telephone circuit that contained the elements of the feedback circuit. In 1913 Armstrong invented a feedback circuit specifically for radio.

De Forest claimed that he knew all along what his circuit was capable of and so was the first inventor. On the other hand, Armstrong asserted that de Forest had merely made an incomplete and accidental disclosure of the principle without realizing what it could be used for. Therefore he, Armstrong, was the true first inventor; de Forest had only begun to adapt his original circuit to radio amplification when he heard of Armstrong's accomplishments. These arguments were much like those used in the Edison-Berliner microphone case.

In the end, de Forest won the suits in the Federal Circuit Courts of Appeal. The court found him the first inventor of the feedback circuit, although many engineers thought that Armstrong had the better case. The Supreme Court upheld the verdict of the lower courts in 1928. Armstrong spent hundreds of thousands of dollars of his own money in trying to have the decision reversed but went down to final defeat in 1934.

Armstrong also invented the super-regenerative circuit, which attained wide use in police and aircraft radio. Then he plunged into the development of frequency modulation to defeat the plague of static. The idea of frequency modulation is old, but the other engineers who had worked on it all gave it up as impractical.

Ordinary amplitude modulation waves are very much like the electromagnetic waves sent out by such sources as lightning and sparking electric motors. Therefore the waves from the latter enter the AM set along with the broadcast waves and are almost impossible to screen out.

Armstrong's solution, first patented in 1933, was this. Instead of sending a carrier wave of uniform frequency but an amplitude that varied to correspond with sound vibrations, he sent a carrier wave of constant amplitude but whose frequency varied up and down within limits. The number of times the frequency of the carrier wave varied from its mean value corresponded to the frequency of the sound waves, and the extent to which each variation departed from the mean value corresponded to the amplitude of the sound waves. FM got rid of most of the static because such a system of waves is unlike anything in nature.

For several reasons, FM did not have quite the success that Armstrong hoped for. World War II (during which Armstrong worked on radar) interrupted its growth. When FM recovered after the war, it found itself faced with the competition of television—which, however, uses FM for its own sound.

Furthermore, Armstrong was bucking the vested interests of the radio chains, which had huge investments in AM apparatus. These investments they were loath to jeopardize.

Armstrong claimed that first the radio chains brushed his discovery off as of no importance. Then, when FM began to succeed on its own after the Second World War, the chains prevailed upon the Federal Communications Commission (by collusion and conspiracy, according to Armstrong) to cripple FM by arbitrarily changing the frequencies allotted to it and limiting the power of its stations. Finally, he said, the National Broadcasting Company and the Radio Corporation of America began infringing his FM patents and inducing others to do so.

So in 1948 Armstrong filed infringement suits against these two companies. For an individual to sue a large modern corporation is a little like a man's assaulting an elephant with his fists, even if the plaintiff be a millionaire as Armstrong now was. But such considerations never stopped Armstrong who, according to one's point of view, was either a gallant hero fighting for the right against hopeless odds or a fanatic with a mania for litigation. Perhaps he was a bit of both.

The suits, at enormous expense, ran for more than five years. Whole volumes of testimony were taken. Armstrong, who refused all offers of a compromise settlement, told his friends:

"They will stall this along until I am dead or broke."[11]

Armstrong jumped to his death from the terrace of his apartment in New York, without the cause being clear or apparent.

XVI

THE END

OF THE HEROIC AGE

On April 6, 1917, the United States of America declared war on the German Empire. Our nation, unready for war as it was, tried to mobilize its scientific talent as well as its manpower and materials against the Central Powers.

Of the war-born scientific organizations, the Naval Consulting Board had some success, under Edison's chairmanship. So did the National Advisory Committee on Aeronautics.

But many of the nation's technological efforts floundered. Attempting to improve on the designs of Allied guns and aircraft, the United States found, was such a lengthy process that American armies in the field were forced to depend almost entirely upon purchased French and British airplanes and artillery. The improved American models were not available until after the shooting had stopped.

The twenty months of American participation in World War I, in any case, speeded up certain changes in American invention. These changes had long been in the making, and they continued with ever-increasing force after the war was over.

One of these changes was the collectivization of invention. More and more, invention came to be practiced by organized groups instead of by lone individuals. Morse, managing his little group of telegraph inventors, foreshadowed this practice. Edison, organizing in Newark and Menlo Park a brand-new business —laboratories whose product was inventions—carried the process further. The General Electric Company, setting up its research laboratory as an independent department in 1900, showed the shape that things would finally take.

Today, while the occasional garret genius continues to ply his trade, an ever-larger proportion of invention is performed by engineers and technicians working for corporations. Today 61 per cent of the patents issued are assigned on issue to a company, compared to 12 per cent in 1885. Company inventors are usually organized into departments and sections; they are assigned definite projects to work on and problems to solve. Smaller numbers work in a similar way in governmental departments and university laboratories.

This system, like most human institutions, has advantages and disadvantages. Employees of corporations normally work under contracts that require them to assign all their patent rights to their employers. Their salaries are supposed to recompense them for these rights.

To make sure that an employee does not conceive a bright idea and then leave the company to develop it on his own, perhaps to the injury of the company's business, most such employment contracts contain a "trailing clause." By means of such a clause, the company can claim inventions made not only during employment but also for a period—a year, for instance—after employment has ended.

Hence such employees are not likely ever to make great fortunes from their inventions, as did Morse, Bell, and Pupin. On the other hand, neither are they likely to suffer lifelong poverty and misfortune, as did Fitch and Davenport. One cannot have it both ways.

Corporate invention gives the inventor a well-found laboratory, with excellent equipment paid for by the company. Technical help on knotty problems is ready to hand when he needs it. He need not worry about being scorned by society as a beggarly eccentric or becoming enmeshed in a tangle of law suits. He eats regularly, a consideration not to be sneered at.

On the other hand, work is often done under high pressure. The employee-inventor is expected to direct his efforts along lines in accord with the company's commercial policies and not to spend time fooling with any interesting idea that appeals to him. He is expected to produce results of definite commercial value and not to take too long about it.

If one of his inventions fails after the company has spent money to promote it, he will be blamed. But, if it succeeds, the sales and advertising departments will get most of the credit. In most companies, the chances of promotion to major executive positions are not so good for employees in a research or engineering department as they are in a department concerned with production or sales.

Moreover, many inventors are ornery individualists by nature, the very opposite of the "organization man." To such people, fitting themselves into a corporate mold and practicing teamwork and togetherness are apt to be particularly irksome.

Another change in American invention is the enormous increase in the size of the inventive effort that has taken place in the last half-century. Whereas practicing scientists and inventors could be counted in thousands near the turn of the century (9000 in 1880), the 1950 census showed about 200,000 persons describing themselves as "scientists" and 500,000 as "engineers."[1] Whereas the nation's annual research bill at the beginning of the century may have been a few million dollars a year, it now amounts to over six billion—an increase of something like a thousandfold.

Some of this money comes from the Federal government. Of the money spent by the government for scientific research, a large proportion goes into weapons engineering. Of the rest, spent by private companies, much goes into the devising of commercial products having only slight advantages, if any, over older goods.

Nevertheless, this tremendous mass of invention is bound to produce, and does produce, a widespread and continuing advance in a vast number of technological fields. The very bulk of modern technical activity, however, makes it impossible to write about it in anything like the detail with which I have treated the inventors of the heroic age. To bring my story up to date, telling as much about outstanding modern individuals, would require many volumes the size of this one.

In view of this extraordinary growth of inventive effort, it is certainly odd that, measured by the ratio of patent applications filed to the total population, American inventiveness seems to have been on a slow decline ever since its peak around 1920. In fact, by this measurement, it has already fallen below the point it occupied in 1880. European countries show a similar decline.

Some commentators blame this decline in inventive results on the Supreme Court's attitude towards the patent system. For several decades the courts have been declaring invalid a large majority—over four-fifths in some circuits—of the patents that come before them. Patents on minor improvements are treated with especial roughness. Some justices of the Supreme Court have been outspoken in their hostility to minor patents, declaring that only inventions embodying major scientific advances should be deemed worthy of the dignity of a patent.[2] This does not agree with the Constitution, which gives the purpose of the patent system as the promotion of "science and the useful arts," without preferring either over the other.

Many patent attorneys feel that the standard of invention for patentability has been raised, in court decisions, to an unrealistically high level. They think that improvements that make inventions in the prior art successful should be upheld instead of often being thrown out for "want of creative genius." Such a high standard of invention probably discourages some inventors from applying for patents at all.

In fact, the courts in recent decades found so many patents invalid on the ground that the inventor had solved his problem by trial and error instead of a flash of intuition that, when the patent law was revised in 1952, a sentence was inserted to the effect that "Patentability shall not be negatived by the manner in which the invention was made."[3] In other words, Congress has taken the sensible attitude that, in deciding which inventors to reward by patents, results should be what count most.

Others blame this apparent decline in inventiveness on other things, such as the Federal government's anti-trust policies, or the tendency of the better-educated to have fewer children than the ignorant, or progressive education, or the alleged conformism of modern American life, or the collectivization of invention in company-owned research laboratories. No doubt the actual causes are complex.

Part, at least, of this decline may be apparent rather than real. For one thing, today's patents, if fewer in proportion to the population, are individually longer and more technical. A larger percentage of them are worked than formerly. An increasing proportion of inventions are made by governmental employees, or are in the field of weapons, and in either case are unlikely to be patented. It has been estimated that half the inventions made today are in these categories.[4]

Even if national inventiveness remains the same, to make patentable inventions becomes harder as time goes on. Inventing, as a man once said about the art of fiction writing, is a craft that grows more difficult with practice.[5] The reason is essentially the same: once a story has been written, it cannot be written again; once an invention has been made, it cannot be made again—at least not for the first time. Although the number of possible inventions in any art may be astronomical, each invention made in that art leaves one less to be made. And the easiest ones, naturally, are likely to be made first and therefore to become unavailable to later inventors.

Any new art begins with a few great basic inventions. As time passes, the number of inventions in the field increases, but the inventions themselves become relatively smaller and less revolutionary, until most of them are minor refinements below the standard of patentability. No inventive art has ever attained the state where all the possible inventions in that field have been made. But many have reached a condition where improvements can be effected only by a steadily increasing effort, as if the inventors were climbing a slope that grows ever steeper.

In such an old art, as the Red Queen said: "It takes all the running you can do, to keep in the same place. If you want to get somewhere else, you must run at least twice as fast as that!"[6]

In the automobile field, for instance, the patent pool agreement among the motorcar makers, which had been in force from 1915 on, was recently (as I stated in Chapter XIII) allowed to lapse because it was no longer needed. The technical possibilities of the automobile field have been so thoroughly exploited that patentable inventions now play but a small part in the business.

Therefore we can speak of a third change in modern invention. This is a tendency for the proportion of basic inventions to shrink and the proportion of minor improvements to grow. In fact, an ever-increasing proportion of the technical changes that come about are not, legally, patentable inventions at all, but refinements of design based upon the careful choice of sizes, shapes, and materials. Such mere engineering refinements are not usually patentable in the United States, although German patent law allows a "petty patent"[7] in such cases.

Of course, an invention that seems today to be a minor improvement may open up a whole new art and in time come to be looked upon as a basic invention, as in the case of de Forest's audion. Therefore, when we look back over technological history, the older major inventions seem more significant than they probably will be considered in the long run, because they have had more time to affect our lives. But the general tendency is still towards smaller inventive steps and more of them.

Finally, as an art ages, it becomes more and more difficult to make significant inventions in that art without technical training. We cannot say that the day of the self-taught inventor, of the type of Edison, Westinghouse, or the Wrights, is over. Perhaps it never will be. In spite of all the disadvantages of lack of formal technical education, it has one compensating advantage. The newcomer in the field looks at the art with fresh eyes. He can therefore sometimes solve problems that have stumped the experts, because his mind is not too cluttered with objections.

Still, as time goes on, and more and more is learned about the nature of the universe, the pure flash of untrained inventive genius becomes less productive. With every passing year, the task of such an untrained inventor becomes harder and the competition that he must meet from trained scientific minds more severe.

So the heroic age of American invention has come to an end, as a natural outcome of the heroes' own acts.

The great inventors were trail blazers, and one does not blaze the same trail twice. Their position in history and folklore is like that of the great explorers and warriors. We may like to read of noble Hector's duel with fleet Achilles, or of the giant Harald Hardraade's leading his Northmen into battle, bellowing battle songs and whirling his two-handed sword. But nobody in his right mind would try to run a war that way today.

Their would-be successors must resign themselves to doing things differently. The modern warrior may find himself wielding a slide rule instead of a saber, and the modern explorer may end up counting soil bacteria or deciphering radio messages sent down by an artificial satellite, circling far out in starry space.

Likewise, the modern inventor may find himself one of a horde of highly organized technical employees, comfortably if not lavishly paid, grinding out minor commercial improvements to order.

But then, each age has its own tasks, and there is no turning back. If, to us, the inventors of the heroic age seem more glamorous than anything the present has to offer—well, to our descendants our own age, with its antibiotic medicines, its exploitation of nuclear power, and its beginnings of space flight, may seem equally glamorous. So let us thank the heroes who revolutionized human life in the last two centuries; and let us encourage their present-day successors, who in a thousand laboratories carry on the work of their forerunners of the heroic age.

NOTES

CHAPTER I

1. Also spelled Jenks, Jencks, or Jenckes.
2. Frontinus: *Strategematon*, III, introd.
3. Pliny: *Natural History*, XXXVI, cxcv (66); Petronius: *Satyricon*, li.
4. Howe, p. 73.
5. Franklin (1945) p. 720.
6. Van Doren, p. 159.
7. Stimson, p. 170; Jaffe (1944) p. 38f.
8. Kaempffert, I, p. 481.
9. U. S. Constitution, Article I, Sec. 6.
10. *The Story of the United States Patent Office*, p. 1.

CHAPTER II

1. Weiss & Ziegler, p. 195; Kaempffert, I, p. 489.
2. W. Wordsworth: *Rob Roy's Grave*.
3. Mirsky & Nevins, p. 148.
4. So defined by James Madison in *The Federalist*, No. 39. For a less favorable view of Whitney's contribution to the art of mass production, see Robert S. Woodbury: "The Legend of Eli Whitney and Interchangeable Parts," in *Technology and Culture*, I, 3 (summer 1960) p. 235.
5. Fuller (p. 11) denies that Bushnell left the country because of ridicule; the ridicule, he asserts, was aimed at the

British, and the true reasons for Bushnell's going abroad and changing his name are not known.

6. Sutcliffe, p. 203; Flexner, p. 322.

7. *The Story of the United States Patent Office*, p. 4. The long eloquent speech sometimes attributed to Thornton on this occasion is apocryphal.

8. Ibid., p. 5.

CHAPTER III

1. Turnbull, pp. 358ff.

2. A corruption of "working beam."

3. Darrow, p. 257.

4. About 88 pounds per square inch.

CHAPTER IV

1. Coulson, p. 64.

2. Ibid. p. 119.

3. A knot = a speed of one nautical mile (6080.2 feet) per hour. "Knots per hour" is incorrect, unless it refers, not to speed, but to acceleration.

4. Coulson, p. 126.

5. To family and intimates, Morse was "Finley," but on formal occasions he signed himself "Saml. F. B. Morse."

6. Coulson, p. 173.

7. Mabee, p. 149.

8. There were two Niepces: Joseph-Nicéphore Niepce, with whom Daguerre originally worked, and his son Isidore Niepce, who worked with Daguerre after his father died in 1833.

9. Mabee, p. 247.

10. Numbers xxiii, 23. It has been suggested (Rohan, p. 133) that the reason for using a Biblical quotation on this occasion was to disarm fanatical clergymen who suspected the telegraph of being a piece of Satanic black magic.

11. Mabee, p. 310f.

12. Ibid., p. 342.

13. Ibid., p. 316f. The speech was delivered 9 Oct., 1856, when Morse was in London with Field, promoting the Atlantic cable.

14. Dibner, p. 13.

15. Strictly speaking the *Niagara* was not a frigate but a heavy sloop, as she carried guns on one deck only, as against two for a frigate and three for a ship of the line.

16. Lewis, p. 80.

CHAPTER V

1. Rohan, p. 82.
2. Ibid., p. 165.
3. Mottelay, p. 26.
4. Johnson, p. 204.

CHAPTER VI

1. United States Code, Title 35, Sec. 101.

2. 5 Blatch 116, 1862; 2 Fisher 320; Berle & de Camp, p. 92.

3. 92 U.S. 347, 1875; Berle & de Camp, p. 90.

4. Pliny: *Natural History*, XVIII, lxxii (296); *Time*, 30 June 1958, p. 47.

5. Some descendents of Cyrus McCormick's brother Leander claim that all the credit for inventing the reaper should go to Robert and Leander; that Cyrus' only contributions were in organization, management, and selling. For this point of view, see Norbert Lyons: *The McCormick Reaper Legend* (N.Y.: 1955).

6. McCormick, p. 23.
7. Ibid., p. 55f.
8. Casson (1909) p. 128.
9. Ibid., p. 130.
10. Pratt (1953) p. 62f.
11. *Time*, Mar. 22, 1954, pp. 104-6.

CHAPTER VII

1. Church, p. 42. The Boothia Peninsula, at the northern extremity of Canada, is named for Felix Booth.

2. "Caloric" was one of the names given to an imaginary subtle, penetrating, weightless fluid, which physicists of the eighteenth and early nineteenth centuries supposed heat to be. The fluid was first called "phlogiston." Lavoisier discredited the original phlogiston theory but revived it in modified form as the caloric theory in 1789.

3. Pratt (1938–41) p. 239.

4. Ibid., p. 238.

5. Like the *Niagara*, the *Princeton* was technically not a frigate but a heavy sloop.

6. Church, pp. 142ff; Pratt, op. cit., p. 241.

7. Church, p. 249f; Pratt, op. cit., p. 267; White, p. 199f.

8. Church, p. 256; White, p. 212.

9. Pratt, op. cit., p. 269.

10. Ibid., p. 270.

11. Ibid., p. 329.

CHAPTER VIII

1. Casson (1907) p. 7.

2. Ibid., p. 9.

3. Also called "spiegel" (German for "mirror") or "spiegel iron."

CHAPTER IX

1. Kaempffert, I, p. 246.

2. Roby, p. 29.

3. Kaempffert, I, p. 272.

4. Ibid., p. 274.

CHAPTER X

1. Casson (1910) p. 30. Cf. also Mackenzie, p. 10; Coulson, p. 311; Burlingame (1940) p. 109; Dictionary of American Biography, *s.v.* "Bell, Alexander Graham."

2. Leonard W. Robinson: "Rediagnosis of History's Great Men," in *The New York Times Magazine*, Feb. 7, 1960, pp. 38–46.

3. Darrow, p. 283.

4. Ibid., p. 285.

5. Scott, p. 47.

6. He pronounced his given name to rhyme with *"my* Hugh."

7. Mackenzie, p. 158; Casson, op. cit., pp. 37ff; Coulson, p. 315; Woodbury (1944) p. 76. According to Bell's biographer Mackenzie, the well-known story that Dom Pedro cried: "My God, it talks!" when he put the receiver to his ear is apocryphal. Different accounts of this episode differ in detail, which is

not surprising in view of the fact that they were not written down until some time after it happened.

8. Casson, op. cit., p. 58.

9. 109 Federal Reporter 976–1056, 1901.

10. Casson, op. cit., p. 81

11. Ibid., p. 92; Darrow, p. 290.

12. Darrow, p. 291.

CHAPTER XI

1. Woodbury (1944) p. 213.

2. Or Pavel Yablotchkov, pronounced "YAH-blutch-koff."

3. G. P. Lothrop: "Talks with Edison," in *Harper's Magazine*, LXXX, 477 (Feb. 1909) p. 431. Some sources give the reason for Edison's leaving Western Union as adverse newspaper publicity about his cockroach trap, which caused him to be fired. Josephson, his most recent biographer, says (pp. 60–64) that he left voluntarily because telegraphy bored him.

4. Josephson, p. 74; Bryan, p. 55.

5. Darrow, pp. 265ff; Bryan, pp. 58ff.

6. Bryan, p. 116.

7. Woodbury, op. cit., p. 253.

8. Crowther, p. 312.

9. Bryan, p. 84. Accounts of this bet differ. Lothrop's article (*supra*) says that it was with Edison's partner Batchelor for a barrel of apples; Mrs. Fessenden, that it was for $25 in cash. Perhaps there was more than one bet.

10. Ibid., pp. 84ff; Darrow, pp. 275ff; Josephson, pp. 161ff.

11. Or Lodïgin, pronounced "luh-DIG-yeen."

12. Josephson, p. 178. See also Matthew Josephson: "The Invention of the Electric Light," in *Scientific American*, CCI, 5 (Nov. 1959) p. 98.

13. Interview published in the *New York Sun* during Oct. 1878; quoted in MacLaren, p. 75.

14. Josephson (p. 214) says that it is only a legend that Edison got the idea for using a carbonaceous thread by rolling a pinch of lampblack between his fingers, as stated by some earlier writers.

15. Josephson (p. 236) says that this expedition to the Amazon was a mere publicity stunt.

16. John Hopkinson invented the three-wire system simultaneously in England. Edison bought Hopkinson's patents and

hired Hopkinson to work for his British company until the latter's death in 1898.

17. Bryan, p. 165f.

18. 52 F.R. 300; Berle & de Camp, p. 106f.

19. Woodbury, op. cit., p. 170.

20. Dickson gave most of the credit for the camera to Edison, but Burlingame (1940, p. 327) thinks that most of it should go to Dickson.

21. Interview in *The World* for Feb. 13, 1923, quoted in Bryan, p. 241. According to Josephson (p. 451) the actual number of his submissions was thirty-nine.

22. Including 9 design patents and 22 patents in which Edison is named as co-inventor, but not including reissues. See the *Journal of the Patent Office Society*, March 1954, pp. 213-32, and April 1954, pp. 275-96.

CHAPTER XII

1. Woodbury (1944) p. 24.

2. Pronounced "HOUSE-ton."

3. In direct current, that is. In alternating current, watts = volts x amps x a quantity called the power factor, always less than 1.0.

4. Woodbury, op. cit., p. 212.

5. Woodbury (1948) p. 145.

6. Lord Dunsany: *Patches of Sunlight* (London, 1938) p. 207.

7. It is also possible to make a single-phase induction motor. But this brings in complications, as such a motor has no starting torque (that is, twisting force).

8. O'Neill, p. 63f.

9. Ibid., p. 82.

10. Ibid., p. 216.

CHAPTER XIII

1. Goodyear, I, p. 110.

2. Ibid., p. 118f. In an oft-heard version of this story, Goodyear accidentally dropped a blob of rubber latex mixed with sulfur on a stove, and the blob turned into vulcanized rubber. But that is not how Goodyear told it.

3. Fuller, p. 279f.

4. Barber, p. 67f.

5. H. P. Maxim (1937) p. 51.
6. Josephson, p. 405f.
7. 184 F.R. 893; Berle & de Camp, p. 378.

CHAPTER XIV

1. Mackenzie, p. 304.
2. Wright, p. 16.
3. Goldstrom, p. 49.
4. Wright, p. 66f; Kelly, pp. 150–55.
5. Brig. Gen. Frank P. Lahm (ret.): "How Teddy Saved the Air Force," in the *Philadelphia Sunday Bulletin Magazine,* Sept. 6, 1953, p. 14.
6. 204 F.R. 596.
7. Kelly, p. 332.

CHAPTER XV

1. H. M. Fessenden, p. 27.
2. De Forest, p. 22f.
3. The family spelled the name with a capital *D;* Lee de Forest adopted the lower-case *d.*
4. De Forest, p. 82.
5. The middle name was pronounced "Clark."
6. Rukeyser, p. 299.
7. Ibid., p. 307.
8. De Forest, p. 88.
9. De Forest claims (p. 210) that he invented a two-element tube of this type independently of Fleming. In most vacuum tubes, the plate and the grid form concentric cylinders surrounding the filament.
10. De Forest, p. 352.
11. Lessing, p. 291.

CHAPTER XVI

1. Some of these "engineers" are probably maintenance and operating employees, such as locomotive drivers and power-plant tenders, not scientific degree holders or practicing technical researchers. Also, many scientists and engineers are engaged in teaching and other routine, non-inventive work. But, even if these be excluded, the total number of active American scientists and engineers, attempting to advance human knowledge, is still probably a six-figure number.

2. Supplementary opinion of Justices Douglas and Black in Great Atlantic & Pacific Tea Co., v. Supermarket Equipment Corp., 87 U. S. Patent Quarterly 303. For details see Berle & de Camp, pp. 519f, 528–32

3. U. S. Code, Title 35, Sec. 103.

4. See S. C. Gilfillan: "An Attempt to Measure the Rise of American Inventing and the Decline of Patenting," in *Technology and Culture*, I, 3 (Summer, 1960) and the replies thereto by J. Schmookler and I. J. Kunik.

5. Charles S. Ingerman, editor of the *Ladies' Home Journal*, in a speech at the Philadelphia Regional Writers' Conference, 20 June 1951.

6. Lewis Carroll: *Through the Looking-Glass*, Chap. 2.

7. The German name for such a petty patent is *Gebrauchsmuster*.

BIBLIOGRAPHY

Robert Abels: *Early American Firearms*, Cleveland: World Pub. Co., 1950.

Carl W. Ackerman: *George Eastman*, Boston: Houghton Mifflin Co., 1930.

Gleason L. Archer: *History of Radio to 1926*, New York: American Historical Society, 1938.

H. L. Barber: *Story of the Automobile*, Chicago: A. J. Munson & Co., 1917.

Alf K. Berle & L. Sprague de Camp: *Inventions, Patents, and their Management*, Princeton: D. Van Nostrand Co., 1959.

John Newton Boucher: *William Kelly*, Greensburg, Penna.: 1924.

Thomas Boyd: *Poor John Fitch*, New York: G. P. Putnam's Sons, 1935.

Bernard Brodie: *Sea Power in the Machine Age*, Princeton: Princeton University Press, 1941.

C. L. M. Brown: *The Conquest of the Air*, London: Oxford University Press, 1927.

George S. Bryan: *Edison, the Man and his Work*, New York: Alfred A. Knopf, 1926.

Roger Burlingame: *Engines of Democracy*, New York: Charles Scribner's Sons, 1940.

_____ : *March of the Iron Men*, New York: Scribner's, 1938.

Herbert N. Casson: *Cyrus Hall McCormick*, Chicago: A. C. McClurg & Co., 1909.

_____ : *The History of the Telephone*, Chicago: McClurg, 1910.

_____ : *The Romance of Steel*, New York: A. S. Barnes, 1907.

William Conant Church: *The Life of John Ericsson*, New York: Scribner's, 1890.

David L. Cohn: *Combustion on Wheels: An Informal History of the Automobile Age*, Boston: Houghton Mifflin, 1944.

Helen Comstock: *The Concise Encyclopedia of American Antiques*, New York: Hawthorn Books, 2 vols.

Thomas Coulson: *Joseph Henry, his Life and Work*, Princeton: Princeton University Press, 1950.

John Houston Craige: *The Practical Book of American Guns*, Cleveland: World Pub. Co., 1950.

J. G. Crowther: *Famous American Men of Science*, New York: W. W. Norton & Co., 1937.

Edward S. Dana: *A Century of Science in America*, New Haven: Yale University Press, 1918.

Floyd L. Darrow: *Masters of Science and Invention*, New York: Harcourt, Brace & Co., 1923.

Lee de Forest: *Father of Radio*, Chicago: Wilcox & Follett Co., 1950.

Bern Dibner: *The Atlantic Cable*, Norwalk, Conn.: Burndy Library, 1959.

Herbert Dingle: *A Century of Science, 1851–1951*, London: Hutchinson, 1951.

F. L. Dyer, T. C. Martin, & W. H. Meadowcraft: *Edison, his Life and Inventions*, New York: Harper & Bros., 1979.

Thomas A. Edison: *The Diary and Sundry Observations of Thomas Alva Edison*, edited by Dagobert D. Runes, New York: Philosophical Library, 1948.

Helen M. Fessenden: *Fessenden, Builder of Tomorrows*, New York: Coward-McCann, 1940.

Reginald Aubrey Fessenden: *The Deluged Civilization of the Caucasus Isthmus*, Boston: T. J. Russell Print, 1923.

Donald Fleming: *John William Draper and the Religion of Science*, Philadelphia: University of Pennsylvania Press, 1950.

John Ambrose Fleming: *Fifty Years of Electricity*, London: Wireless Press, 1921.

James T. Flexner: *Steamboats Come True*, New York: Viking Press, 1944.

R. J. Forbes: *Studies in Ancient Technology*, Leyden: E. J. Brill, 1955–58, 6 vols.

Benjamin Franklin: *Benjamin Franklin's Autobiographical Writings*, edited by Carl Van Doren, New York: Viking Press, 1945.

———— : *Benjamin Franklin's Experiments*, edited by I. Bernard Cohen, Cambridge, Mass.: Harvard University Press, 1941.

———— : *The Ingenious Dr. Franklin*, edited by Nathan G. Goodman, Philadelphia: University of Pennsylvania Press, 1931.

Claude M. Fuess: *Daniel Webster*, Boston: Little, Brown & Co., 1930, 2 vols.

Edmund Fuller: *Tinkers and Genius: The Story of Yankee Inventors*, New York: Hastings House, 1955.

S. C. Gilfillan: *Inventing the Ship*, Chicago: Follett Pub. Co., 1935.

John Goldstrom: *A Narrative History of Aviation*, New York: Macmillan Co., 1930.

Charles Goodyear: *Gum Elastic and its Varieties*, New Haven: 1853–55, 2 vols.

John Winthrop Hammond: *Men and Volts*, Philadelphia: J. B. Lippincott Co., 1941.

Robert Held: *The Age of Firearms*, New York: Harper, 1957.

Henry Howe: *Memoirs of the Most Eminent American Mechanics*, New York: Harper, 1847.

Clarence J. Hylander: *American Scientists*, New York: Macmillan, 1939.

Bernard Jaffe: *Men of Science in America*, New York: Simon & Schuster, 1944–46.

———— : *Outposts of Science*, New York: Simon and Schuster, 1935.

Clifton Johnson: *The Rise of an American Inventor: Hudson Maxim's Life Story*, Garden City: Doubleday, Page & Co., 1924–27.

Matthew Josephson: *Edison*, New York: McGraw-Hill Book Co., 1959.

Waldemar Kaempffert: *A Popular History of American Invention*, New York: Scribner's, 1924, 2 vols.

Fred C. Kelly: *The Wright Brothers*, New York: Farrar, Strauss & Young, 1943–50.

Richard Shelton Kirby *et al: Engineering in History*, New York: McGraw-Hill Book Co., Inc., 1956.

Lawrence Lessing: *Man of High Fidelity: Edwin Howard Armstrong*, Philadelphia: Lippincott, 1956.

Charles Lee Lewis: *Matthew Fontaine Maury, the Pathfinder of the Seas*, Annapolis: U. S. Naval Institute, 1927.

Carleton Mabee: *The American Leonardo: A Life of Samuel F. B. Morse*, New York: Knopf, 1944.

Cyrus McCormick III: *The Century of the Reaper*, Boston: Houghton Mifflin, 1931.

Catherine Mackenzie: *Alexander Graham Bell*, Boston: Houghton Mifflin, 1928.

Malcolm MacLaren: *The Rise of the Electrical Industry During the Nineteenth Century*, Princeton: Princeton University Press, 1943.

Edwin T. Martin: *Thomas Jefferson: Scientist*, New York: Henry Schuman, 1952.

Hiram Percy Maxim: *A Genius in the Family*, New York: Harper, 1936.

———— : *Horseless-Carriage Days*, New York: Harper, 1937.

Hiram S. Maxim: *My Life*, New York: McBride, Nast & Co., 1915.

Ottmar Mergenthaler: *Autobiography of Ottmar Mergenthaler . . .* , 1898.

Jeanette Mirsky & Allan Nevins: *The World of Eli Whitney*, New York: Macmillan, 1952.

P. Fleury Mottelay: *The Life and Work of Sir Hiram Maxim*, London: John Lane-Bodley Head, 1920.

Albert Neuburger: *The Technical Arts and Sciences of the Ancients*, New York: Macmillan, 1930.

John J. O'Neill: *Prodigal Genius: The Life of Nikola Tesla*, New York: Ives Washburn, 1944.

Fletcher Pratt: *All About Famous Inventors and their Inventions*, New York: Random House, 1955.

———— : *The Navy*, New York: Doubleday, Doran & Co., 1938–41.

———— : *Stanton, Lincoln's Secretary of War*, New York: Norton, 1953.

Michael Pupin: *From Immigrant to Inventor*, New York: Scribner's, 1923.

Henry W. Roby: *Henry W. Roby's Story of the Invention of the Typewriter*, Menasha, Wis.: George Banta Pub. Co., 1925.

Jack Rohan: *Yankee Arms Maker: The Incredible Career of Samuel Colt,* New York: Harper, 1935.

Muriel Rukeyser: *Willard Gibbs,* Garden City: Doubleday, 1942–47.

William Berryman Scott: *Some Memories of a Paleontologist,* Princeton: Princeton University Press, 1939.

Charles Singer *et al.: A History of Technology,* Oxford: Clarendon Press, 1954–58, 5 vols.

Dorothy Stimson: *Scientists and Amateurs,* New York: Schuman, 1948.

The Story of the United States Patent Office, 1790–1956, Washington: U. S. Department of Commerce, 1956.

Alice Crary Sutcliffe: *Robert Fulton and the Clermont,* New York: 1948.

Keith Sward: *The Legend of Henry Ford,* New York: Rinehart & Co., 1948.

Hans Thirring: *Energy for Man,* Bloomington: Indiana University Press, 1958.

Holland Thompson: *The Age of Invention,* New Haven: Yale University Press, 1921.

Edwin Tunis: *Wheels,* Cleveland: World, 1954.

Archibald Douglas Turnbull: *John Stevens: An American Record,* New York: American Society of Mechanical Engineers, 1928.

Abbott Payson Usher: *A History of Mechanical Inventions,* Cambridge, Mass.: Harvard University Press, 1929–54.

Carl Van Doren: *Benjamin Franklin,* New York: Viking, 1938.

Ruth White: *Yankee from Sweden: The Dream and the Reality in the Days of John Ericsson,* New York: Henry Holt & Co., 1960.

Mitchell Wilson: *American Science and Invention,* New York: Simon and Schuster, 1954.

David O. Woodbury: *Beloved Scientist: Elihu Thomson,* New York: Whittlesey House, 1944.

———— : *The Glass Giant of Palomar,* New York: Dodd, Mead & Co., 1948.

Orville Wright: *How We Invented the Airplane,* New York: David McKay Co., 1953.

William Jay Youmans: *Pioneers of Science in America,* New York: D. Appleton & Co., 1896.

INDEX